NOT TO BE REMOVED
FROM THE LIBRARY

A Glossary
of Special Education

Open University Press
Children With Special Needs Series

Editors

PHILLIP WILLIAMS
Emeritus Professor of Education
University College of North Wales, Bangor.

PETER YOUNG
Formerly Tutor in the education of children with learning difficulties, Cambridge Institute of Education; educational writer, researcher and consultant.

This is a series of short and authoritative introductions for parents, teachers, professionals and anyone concerned with children with special needs. The series will cover the range of physical, sensory, mental, emotional and behavioural difficulties, and the changing needs from infancy to adult life in the family, at school and in society. The authors have been selected for their wide experience and close professional involvement in their particular fields. All have written penetrating and practical books readily accessible to non-specialists.

TITLES IN THE SERIES

Changing Special Education
Wilfred K. Brennan
Curriculum for Special Needs
Wilfred K. Brennan
The Early Years
Maurice Chazan and Alice Laing
Residential Special Education
Ted Cole
Working With Parents
Cliff Cunningham and Hilton Davis
Understanding Learning Difficulties
Kathleen Devereux
Special Education: The Way Ahead
John Fish

Deaf-Blind Infants and Children
J.M. McInnes and J.A. Treffry
Educating Hearing-Impaired Children
Michael Reed
Helping the Maladjusted Child
Dennis Stott
The Teacher is the Key
Kenneth Weber
How to Reach the Hard to Teach
Paul Widlake
Special Education in Minority Communities
Phillip Williams (ed.)
Dyslexia or Illiteracy?
Peter Young and Colin Tyre

In Preparation

Special Parents
Barbara Furneaux

Educating the Gifted Child
Joan Freeman

Beyond Childhood
Robin Jackson

A Glossary
of Special Education

Edited by
Phillip Williams

Open University Press

Milton keynes · Philadelphia

Open University Press
Open University Educational Enterprises Limited
12 Cofferidge Close
Stony Stratford
Milton Keynes MK11 1BY, England

and
242 Cherry Street
Philadelphia, PA 19106, USA

First published 1988

British Library Cataloguing in Publication Data
Williams
A Glossary of Special Education
1.   Special education — Great
Britain
Dictionaries
I.   Williams, Phillip
371.9′0941   LC 3986.G7

ISBN 0 335 15996 6
ISBN 0 335 15995 8 pbk

Project management: Clarke Williams

Printed in Great Britain
at the Alden Press, Oxford

Contents

Editor's Introduction   vi

Acknowledgements   vii

Introduction to the Glossary   ix

Glossary   1

Appendix A   *List of some useful Associations, etc.*   212

Appendix B   *List of some useful reference books*   221

List of Illustrations

ABA design and ABAB design (p. 1).
Audiogram (p. 18).
Communication using the Bliss Symbol System (p. 27).
The brain (p. 28).
Chromosomes (from a single male cell) (p. 37).
The ear (p. 66).
The eye (p. 76).
Finger spelling (p. 81).
Frequencies of Speech Sounds (p. 85).
Meningocele (p. 130).
Myelomeningocele (p. 137).
Normal curve, obtained from the heights of a group of 4-year-old children (p. 142).
Paget-Gorman signs (p. 149).
Peabody Language Development Kit (p. 152).
Sociogram for project work, two choices per pupil (p. 184).
A Thematic Appreciation Test card (p. 197).

Editor's Introduction

One man's technical term is another man's jargon. One man's shibboleth is another's stigma. Special educational literature may have little direct impact upon the pupils but it certainly smothers them in blankets of words. Standing at the crossroads between medicine and education, and between psychology and psychiatry, and often torn every whichway by isms and warring schools of theorists, it is not surprising that this should be the case. The general reader and the specialist from one specific discipline may well find themselves confronted by words with which they are unfamiliar or which appear to be used in some special, new or restricted sense. This Glossary has been conceived to help all who wish to fish in these troubled and ever-changing waters.

Phillip Williams explains how the Glossary came about and how it has been developed — its aetiology and ontology, as the Glossary has it. He also explains its rationale. Clearly, hard decisions have had to be made to determine what should be included and what left out. What has emerged is a work of great practical utility, consistency and conciseness. These are qualities which will commend it. It is, too, comprehensive, up-to-date and accessible.

I would like to think that every parent of a child with special needs would have a copy of this Glossary readily available. The Appendix of addresses of organisations and associations is a boon in itself. Members of the multidisciplinary teams, teachers, specialists, therapists, social workers and all in initial and in-service training will find the Glossary invaluable. Moreover, it will be a ready source book for translators and all who study special education in this country overseas.

But, above all, this Glossary will help all involved in the education of those with special needs to cut through the words, terms, tests, concepts, jargon and jabberwocky to see more clearly the children and their needs.

Peter Young

Acknowledgements

This glossary has been developed from material produced by a Community Programme Team based at the University College of North Wales and funded by the Manpower Services Commission. The support of the M.S.C. and the contributions of the team members, Keith Dawes, Myfanwy Allam, Derek Lester, Angela Pethig, Judy Morris, Ann Ormesher, Sue Egerton, Pat Griffiths and Dorothy Owen are gratefully acknowledged. Copyright in the original production, which was placed in libraries and special schools in Gwynedd, is held by the Crown: the readiness of H.M.S.O. to allow this glossary to be developed from it is also gratefully acknowledged.

Many people have helped this glossary to reach its present form. Useful criticisms of some very early ideas were made by David Boswell, Maurice Chazan, Robin Davis, Norman Davies, John Fish, Philip Graham, Seamus Hegarty, Jenny Jones, Richard Jones, Edward Lewis, Gordon Lowden, Tim Miles, Anne Oldhams, Mark Roberts, John Skelton and Peter Young.

I am grateful to the U.C.N.W. authorities and to my colleague Iolo Williams in particular for allowing a retired member of staff such generous use of facilities at the college and its School of Education. Specifically, Colin Baker helped over the computer programme and the library staff at U.C.N.W., in particular Carol Thomas and Winn Simpson, have been unfailingly tolerant of requests for their services.

Towards the end of the enterprise, the often anonymous secretaries of the associations, etc., listed in Appendix A generated a magnificently high response rate to a postal request to check details of their organisation, an operation master-minded by Glenys, my wife. At the same time, full drafts of the glossary were read by a multiprofessional team, consisting of Peter Barnes, Martin Bax, Bob Burden, Sam Forrester, Aled Griffiths, Gwyneth Roberts and Peter Young. I am truly grateful to them for the many amendments and improvements that they were able to suggest. Nevertheless full responsibility for what the glossary does (and does not) contain rests entirely with me.

viii

The author and publishers are very grateful to the following for permission to reproduce copyright material indicated:

Somerset Education Authority (1978), for the diagrams on pp. 27 and 85 and the photographs on pp. 149 and 152 (taken from *Ways and Means*, published by Globe Education, Houndsmill, Basingstoke, Hants).

Reed, M. (1984), *Educating Hearing-Impaired Children* (published by Open University Press) for the diagrams on pp. 18 and 81.

Young, P. and Tyre, C. (1983), *Dyslexia or Illiteracy? Realizing the right to read* (published by Open University Press) for the diagram on p. 28.

Potts, P. *et al.* (1982), Glossary for Course E241, *Special Needs in Education* (published by the Open University) for the diagrams on pp. 130 and 137.

Moore, B. *et al.* (1973), Data Collection, Block 3 of Course E341, *Methods of Educational Enquiry* (published by the Open University) for the photograph on p. 197.

Floyd, A. (1977), Methodology Handbook (revised edition), Course E201, *Personality and Learning* (published by the Open University) for diagrams on p. 142.

Introduction to the Glossary

Why this glossary was made

When the Warnock Report appeared in 1978 it recommended a host of changes in the way we educate children with special needs. The 1981 Education Act reflected many of these recommendations and two of the themes which were stressed, both by the Report and the Act, have led to this glossary. The first theme underlines the priority that should be given to educating handicapped children in ordinary schools. All teachers, not only those in special schools, are now involved in the education of children with special needs and psychological reports, clinical details, statements of educational needs, etc. are widely available and widely discussed.

The second theme underlines the importance of the parents. Parents now enjoy rights of access to information and rights of participation in educational decision-making which had not been established before 1983, when the Act came into force.

These twin principles of integration and participation have not been implemented easily. One particular problem has been communication, for integration and participation mean that in classroom and in conference, teachers and parents now read and hear the technical terms used by the specialists who work with handicapped children. In an ideal world, specialists explain their terms in words that the layman can understand, but the world is not ideal, specialists are busy and hardpressed and the shorthand of the technical term continues to be used.

So the purpose of this glossary is to produce reasonably simple explanations of terms used in special education for guidance of teachers and parents. There are others, too, who have hitherto stood at the margins of special education, for example administrators and Heads, who now find themselves much more closely involved. By the same token, it is hoped that this glossary will be of use to them. But it is not intended to offer detailed, technical explanations for the expert. For these, the various specialist reference books must be consulted.

How the Glossary was made

Between 1983 and 1985 the Manpower Services Commission's Community
Programme supported two teams of an editor/supervisor, teacher/writers
and a secretary, who worked under academic direction at the School of
Education, University College of North Wales. These teams collected terms
from various sources and produced a glossary, copies of which were
lodged in libraries and some schools in the area. Full details of the
procedure are given on p.xi, *Constructing the Glossary*.

During 1985–7, with the permission of the Manpower Services Commission and Her Majesty's Stationery Office, the work was heavily revised,
by re-writing, by removing about a third of the terms and by adding
others. This version is the result.

What the glossary contains

The principles which helped to decide which terms to include in the
glossary are outlined in the next section. But inevitably, the final decision
on inclusion or exclusion is a personal judgement. There are many Acts of
Parliament which have affected special education in different ways: the
glossary emphasizes the more recent ones but also includes a few pieces of
more important earlier legislation. Psychological and educational tests
feature heavily in reports on children — the issue is not whether to include
them, but where to draw the line. It is not possible to describe all those
tests in current use and so a selection has been made. Technical details
have not been given: the purpose here has been to offer a simple
explanation of what the test aims to do. Again a few older tests have been
included, usually those which were once widely used and are of some
historical interest. For tests and for some educational materials the names
of authors have usually been given, as have the names of the chairpersons
of relevant committees, whereas individuals, no matter how significant,
have not been included in their own right. But the bulk of the entries
consist of those terms that describe children's and young people's
characteristics and needs , the methods used for meeting them and the
educational and other facilities available. On the whole the boundaries of
special education have been fairly liberally drawn. For example, no attempt
has been made to restrict the contents to terms used in relation to children
of school age; some applying to pre-school children and to young people
beyond school age have been included. Nevertheless, these boundaries
constitute a territory which would have been differently demarcated by
others: the hope and intention is that the differences are not significant —
in any sense of the word — and that a reasonable balance has been struck
between a wider and a narrower coverage.

The question of balance applies to the detail of the definitions, too. It is
easy to complicate with an over-elaborate explanation. It is also easy to

simplify to such an extent that justice is not done to the meaning. The aim has been to steer a course between the encyclopaedia on the one hand and the dictionary on the other and to strike a reasonable balance between expansion and brevity.

Constructing the glossary

First, the terms indexed in books housed in the special education sections of the education library at the University College of North Wales were collected. This list of terms was expanded by including additional material from books from specialist libraries, in particular those at the Universities of Birmingham and Manchester, books from personal libraries, terms from articles in journals etc. The terms collected were collated by computer. This provided a print-out of the terms in alphabetical order. Against each term was a coded list of the sources in which it appeared and the number of times that it was referred to. The database constructed in this way comprised over fifteen thousand terms, some of which might have appeared only once in the literature, others appearing scores of times. The terms were then 'filtered'; irrelevant, obscure and unusual terms were filtered off, leaving a total of about two thousand or so terms from the original listing. These were then defined by teacher/writers, using the sources in which the terms appeared, together with support from the reference books listed at the end of this glossary and from many individuals who patiently provided information.

The resulting definitions were then edited, and monitored by the project director. At this stage a few more terms were filtered off and a few more added. A few definitions were sent out at an early stage to a group of helpful colleagues and in the light of their comments the level of difficulty and detail was modified. This process was repeated at a later stage of glossary development in order to try to make the material as useful and as accessible as possible. It resulted in the production of the terms which are explained within these pages. The procedure can be represented as follows:

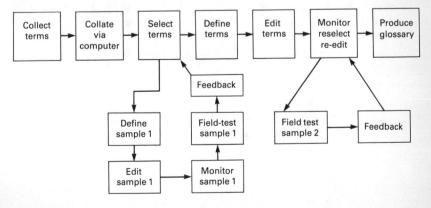

Several principles determined whether a term should be included or not: the number of times it featured in the database was one, but this was not a principle that could be rigidly followed. Some terms appeared several times but are better dealt with under a slightly different head: others appeared infrequently but are nevertheless included because of their considerable importance to a small number of people — some medical conditions are a good example of this, as are some of the legal terms relating to the minority of children and young people whose behaviour leads to conflict with the law.

'Current use' was the second principle which guided the choice of term. Nevertheless some examples of earlier teaching methods, older legislation, tests etc., have been retained because of their historical interest or influence on special education at the time.

The third principle was relevance. Some terms (which were indexed several times) were in current use, but were not relevant to special education although derived from the literature. Others were obscure and unusual, and these were excluded.

Finally, although the database was derived from British sources, libraries do hold books and periodicals which are published overseas, and much of the terminology in special education is, in any case, international currency. So while a British perspective is obvious in the selection of tests, legislation, facilities, etc., these constitute a small minority of terms and most of the glossary should be of use more widely.

How to use the glossary

All entries in the glossary are indexed in alphabetical order, apart from the list of Associations and useful reference books, which are separately indexed at the end of the glossary. Terms which appear in the explanations, but which are themselves indexed separately in the glossary are italicized. If the reader wishes to obtain more information, the italicized term can be looked up, though occasionally the cross referencing is there as much for the sake of accuracy as for the generation of more information. Sometimes, too, an entry suggests an additional term or terms which could be looked at for complementary information on the topic.

The use of the glossary should be very simple. Nevertheless if you, the user, come across particular difficulties, with reference to information which should be added, or general principles of usage which could be improved, I shall be glad to hear from you. Please write to:

Phillip Williams
Glossary of Special Education
School of Education
University College of North Wales
Lon Pobty
BANGOR
Gwynedd   LL57 1DZ

A

a- and dys- words, these prefixes are from the Greek. a- usually suggests 'loss of', as in apathy, loss of feeling, whereas dys- usually suggests 'difficulty with' or 'damage to', as in dyspepsia, difficulty with digestion (i.e. indigestion). The a- prefix suggests complete loss or total inability and hence a more profound or severe condition than the dys- prefix does. However, there are inconsistencies: e.g. *arrhythmia*, means disturbance of the heartbeat rhythm rather than total loss of rhythm which the a- prefix suggests. Moreover, meanings have changed: e.g. in older textbooks *alexia* meant usually a total lack of reading skills and *dyslexia* a partial lack, both a result of brain damage. In modern usage, however, *dyslexia* means difficulty in developing reading skills whilst *alexia* is the acquired disorder of the loss of reading skills by brain damage as a result of accident or disease. Inconsistency in the use of the a- and dys- prefixes has led some authorities to use them synonymously, referring to three symptoms of the *Gerstmann syndrome* as 'finger *agnosia, agraphia, acalculia*' or as 'finger *agnosia, dysgraphia, dyscalculia*'. Some authorities prefer one term to another whilst others will use the terms interchangeably.

ABA design, simple plan for research or enquiry into the effects of treatment on behaviour. The first A represents behaviour before treatment; B represents behaviour during treatment; and the second A behaviour after treatment has been withdrawn. The differences between the three conditions enable the effects of treatment to be assessed. This design is often used in *behaviour modification* with children with learning or behaviour difficulties.

ABAB design, extension of the ABA design to include a second period of treatment similar to the first. If the effect during treatment is repeated, the likelihood of the effect being due to chance factors, rather than the treatment is diminished. This helps to compensate for the absence of a *control group*.

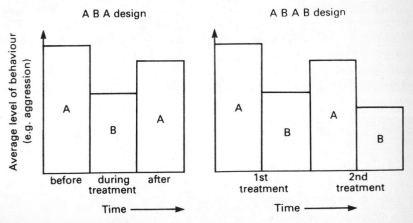

ABA design and ABAB design

abacus, frame with parallel wires or rods, along which coloured counters can be moved to help in counting and simple arithmetic; it is sometimes used as a teaching aid, particularly for children with *visual handicap* and for children with *learning difficulty (severe)*.

abduction, movement of a limb away from the centre of the body, as in raising an arm sideways; it is the opposite of *adduction*.

ability:
(1) general intelligence or all-round intellectual capability;
(2) a specific talent, e.g. perceptiveness, memory, imagination or reasoning;
(3) competence in a particular subject or activity, e.g. arithmetic or reading.

ability/attainment controversy, debate about the basis for identifying under-achievers. One body of opinion believes that any child whose attainment is significantly lower than his or her ability (usually as measured by an *intelligence test*) is an underachiever: the intelligence test is seen as a measure of potential. Others argue that since half the population have attainments that are higher than their intelligence scores suggest, the idea of intelligence test score as an index of potential achievement is logically flawed. Many hold that the difference between attainments and average performance of the age-group is a better basis for determining need for educational help. Yet others believe that both these alternatives are too simple as principles for determining whether and to what extent a child is underachieving.

ability grouping, method of assigning pupils to different classes or classroom groups according to their *ability*. It may be based on general ability (see *ability (1)*), when it is called *streaming*, or on ability in particular subjects (see *ability (3)*), when it is known as *setting*.

abreaction, release from repressed fears and emotionally charged memories by bringing the original (unconscious) experience to mind and reliving it in the imagination; the technique is used in *psychoanalysis* and *psychotherapy*. See *catharsis*.

absurdity test, reasoning problem in which the child is usually asked to point out what is absurd in a picture, story or statement; many intelligence tests include examples of these problems, e.g. 'the road to school is uphill all the way there and uphill all the way back.'

acalculia, loss or impairment of the ability to understand or handle numbers or mathematical symbols. It is used synonymously with *dyscalculia*. See *Gerstmann syndrome*.

acceleration, promoting a bright child to a higher class, usually a class of older children. This allows progress through the curriculum at a faster than average pace. It is one of the main ways of meeting the special needs of *gifted children*. See also *enrichment*.

A.C.E. Centre, see *Aids for Communication in Education Centre*.

achievement, often used in the restricted sense of attainment in a school subject, though the term is used more widely. Thus the *Hargreaves Report* describes four senses of achievement, achievement in written tests, in practical skills, in personal and social skills, and in motivation and commitment.

achievement age, see *attainment age*.

achievement quotient, originally, *attainment age* as a percentage of *mental age*. Thus a child with a *reading age* of eight years and a mental age of ten years would have an achievement quotient (for reading) of eighty (8/10 x 100). The achievement quotient was thus intended as an index of attainment in relation to potential. But it is now sometimes used in the sense of *attainment quotient*, i.e. attainment in relation to *chronological age*.

Achilles tendon, tendon that joins the muscles of the calf to the heel bone. The Achilles tendon reflex, which should result from a sharp tap at the back of the ankle, is used in assessing the state of the nervous system.

achondroplasia, or chrondrodystrophy, relatively common disorder resulting in reduced height and various problems with the bones; development, both physical and mental, is otherwise normal.

achromatic vision, total *colour blindness*, often associated with other defects of sight.

acoustic feedback, in a hearing aid, whistling noise which occurs when the earpiece is not in airtight contact with the ear and the volume control is set high.

acoustic impedance test, or impedance audiometry, method of measuring the way in which the *ear-drum* and the *middle ear* conduct and reflect sound waves. It can be used to diagnose *conductive deafness*, i.e. failure to transmit sound properly to the *inner ear*. See *ear* illustration (p. 66).

acquired defect, physical or mental disability which is not present at birth but develops as a result of injury or disease.

acrocephaly, Apert's syndrome or oxycephaly, form of *craniostenosis*, or *congenital* malformation of the skull. Skull growth ceasing too soon gives rise to a high, wide appearance, with the top pointed or conical in shape and eyes widely set. In the past, acrocephalic children have often been severely mentally retarded and educated in hospital. However, surgery within the first two years of birth minimizes deformities and reduces the likelihood of *mental retardation* and other disabilities by allowing the skull to remain open until brain growth is finished.

acting-out behaviour, attention-seeking, over-active or aggressive behaviour of a child in a situation, e.g. in a classroom, where more controlled behaviour is usually expected.

active listening, the use of facial expressions, gestures and statements, by which a listener conveys understanding of what a child is saying and encourages a child to use speech.

adapted physical education, physical education exercises and activities which have been adapted for *physically handicapped* pupils.

adaptive behaviour, U.S. term for an individual's ability to cope with the demands of independent living within the community in a socially appproved way; it draws upon the whole range of skills and abilities which are needed for this, ranging from the basic skills of washing and toileting to more advanced skills such as managing money. Those who have severe *learning difficulties* or are *physically handicapped* will usually have lower levels of adaptive behaviour than others, and a measure such as the *Adaptive Behaviour Scale* is a useful guide to a young person's potential for independent living.

Adaptive Behaviour Scale, measure of an individual's level of *adaptive behaviour*, produced by the American Association on Mental Deficiency. It can be used with children three years of age and upwards, and covers twenty-four behavioural characteristics or skills. This is one of a number of adaptive behaviour scales, e.g. *Vineland Social Maturity Scale*.

addiction, uncontrollable dependence on a habit-forming substance, in which stopping the habit causes *withdrawal symptoms* (e.g. hallucinations, convulsions, fever). See *drug addiction*.

adduction, movement of a limb towards the centre of the body, as in lowering an arm from an outstretched position; it is the opposite of *abduction*.

adenoids, tissue above and behind the soft palate, where the nose opens into the throat. Overgrown adenoids, which occur sometimes in children aged between about 5 and 12 years may give rise to difficulties in breathing through the nostrils (leading to breathing through the mouth) and in some severe cases to impaired hearing; speech may also be affected.

adolescence, the transitional period between childhood and adulthood, beginning with the onset of puberty and including the physical and psychological changes which lead to reproductive maturity and the completely developed adult. The term is often used as a convenient label for the period between the ages of roughly 12 to 20 years; however, young people vary considerably in their rates of physical and emotional growth and it is not possible to specify a precise age-range. Adolescence is a time of developmental challenges. Typically, these include those arising from loosening ties with parents and family, developing a sense of self-direction, working out values and beliefs, especially attitudes about sexual relations and preparing for finding employment or a career. The ordinary problems of adolescence can be complicated by *handicap* e.g. the realization that some social activities and entertainments may not be possible or full personal independence not attainable.

adoption, legal process in which parents give up their legal rights and duties in relation to their child (or children) to other persons. The main purpose of adoption is to provide a permanent, secure and loving home for the child. There has been in increase in the number of handicapped children successfully adopted in recent years. Compare with *foster child* and *foster parents*. See *custodianship*.

adrenocorticotrophic hormone (ACTH) or corticotropin, hormone secreted by the pituitary gland which regulates the activity of the adrenal cortex. It may be used as a drug in the treatment of juvenile rheumatoid arthritis (*Still's disease*) and in some severe conditions of *allergy* such as severe *asthma*.

Adult Literacy and Basic Skills Unit, organization which provides help for adults with literacy problems, including reading, numeracy and basic communication skills. It was established in 1980, replacing, with extended terms of reference, the Adult Literacy Resource Agency.

adult training centre (ATC), centre organized by the social services departments of local authorities for adults and school-leavers with severe *learning difficulty*. Its functions involve providing training in social skills, including the basic skills needed for employment. The *Warnock Report's* recommendations, based on those of the National Development Group for the Mentally Handicapped, included renaming ATCs 'social education centres', which would provide a programme of education and training for young people separate from arrangements for older people. Compare with *junior training centres* and *junior occupational centres*.

Advisory Committee on Handicapped Children, committee which advised government departments on the education of children with special needs. It was suspended when the Warnock Committee was set up in 1974. The *Warnock Report* recommended that a national advisory committee on children with special educational needs should be established; in 1983 a working party was formed to advise the *Department of Education and Science* on this matter. It, too, recommended that a National Advisory Committee should be established.

advisory service, advice and support service provided by *local education authorities* for practising teachers. Advisers for special education are concerned with the quality and scope of special education within the authority including both the ordinary and *special schools* and establishments, provision of in-service teacher training, professional advice to parents whose children require special education and policy advice to the authority. *The Warnock Report* made detailed recommendations about the work and organization of a full advisory and support service for special education, stressing that it should be closely integrated with a *local education authority's* other advisory services.

aetiology, study of the origin of something, e.g. a child's illness or *juvenile delinquency*.

affective disorder, disorder of mood or feeling which may lead to disturbances of thought and action, e.g. *depression*.

aftercare:
(1) services which may and in some circumstances must be offered to an adolescent over school-leaving age who has been *in care*. The general aim is to 'advise and befriend', but financial contributions can sometimes be made towards the cost of accommodation and maintenance, or in connection with education or training.
(2) services provided under the National Health Services Act, 1977 or the Mental Health Act, 1983 for the aftercare of the mentally disordered.
(3) supervision by a *probation officer* of certain offenders upon release from custody.

age equivalent, *chronological age* for which a particular score on a test is the *average*. See *age norms*.

age norms, average test scores of age groups, usually found in the test manual. Thus a test of reading ability may provide a table of average scores of children's ages, e.g. 8 years, 1 month; 8 years, 2 months, etc., which enables a test score to be converted into its *age equivalent* or *reading age*. If this is below the child's *chronological age*, it can be used as an indication of need for special help. See *norm-referenced test*.

agitographia, writing disability characterized by abnormally quick writing movements and the omission of letters and words.

agitophasia, see *cluttering*.

agitolalia, see *cluttering*.

agnosia, inability to recognize familiar images, sounds, etc. for example:
  (1) visual agnosia, in which the child can see adequately, but cannot recognize what is seen (even though able to recognize it through the other senses);
  (2) auditory (non-verbal) agnosia, in which a child is able to hear sounds but unable to interpret their meaning;
  (3) auditory (verbal) agnosia, in which the meaning of spoken words cannot be grasped although there is no difficulty in hearing them correctly;
  (4) tactile agnosia, in which familiar objects cannot be recognized by touch.

agoraphobia, abnormal dread of open spaces. See *phobia*.

agraphia, inability to express thoughts in writing. People suffering from agraphia seem unable to associate their 'mental pictures' of words with the movements of arm and hand needed for writing them. The term is sometimes used synonymously with *dysgraphia*.

AH4 test, *intelligence test* in occasional use with children over ten years old and with adults; devised by *Alice Heim*. One of a series of similarly labelled tests, AH1 to AH6, each said to assess aspects of reasoning and/or intelligence in groups of different ages and abilities.

aide, usually an unqualified person who helps professional workers, e.g. a teacher aide performs non-teaching duties in the classroom.

aids centre, permanent display of aids at a centre also providing information and demonstrations. There are several of these centres in the U.K., including some run by voluntary bodies such as the *Disabled Living Foundation* (see Appendix A).

Aids for Communication in Education Centre, A.C.E. Centre, (address in Appendix A) unit established in association with Microelectronic Educational Support Unit to provide information on the use of micro-electronics in educating children with communication difficulties. It also organizes workshops, evaluates equipment, co-ordinates research and provides some facilities. It is intended primarily to help teachers and schools; support for Health and Social Services staff is provided by the *Communication Aids Centres*.

air conduction, hearing via sound waves, i.e. vibrations in the air, travelling through the *outer ear*: they enter the *external auditory canal* striking the *eardrum* and making it vibrate. This is the first stage in the transmission of sound to the *auditory nerve*. See *ear* illustration (p. 66). Compare *bone conduction*.

akinesia, or akinesis, see *dyskinesia*.

alalia, see *speech difficulty*.

albinism, inherited deficiency of melanin, the dark-brown pigment in the skin, hair and eyes, giving rise to white or pale skin, white hair and pink irises of the eye. The associated *visual handicap* ranges from virtual blindness to virtually normal vision associated with extreme sensitivity to bright light.

albino, one who suffers from *albinism*.

alexia, sometimes called 'word blindness', loss of ability to read, i.e. to gain meaning from printed or written words. It can result from brain damage, either through accident or disease. See *a- and dys- prefixes*, *dyslexia*.

alignometer, apparatus for measuring and correcting body posture.

alingual, unable to speak at all.

allergen, substance which can cause an allergic reaction e.g. a common allergen is pollen, which in some people causes hayfever. See *allergy*.

allergy, unusually high sensitivity to something which, although intrinsically harmless, e.g. particular types of food, dust, flowers or pollen, produces an adverse reaction and physical upset in a person who is allergic to it, e.g. nettle rash, hay fever and eczema.

alpha-fetoprotein, one of the substances found in *amniotic fluid*. See *amniocentesis*.

alpha wave, one of four types of electrical waves which are recorded from the brain on an *electroencephalogram*. The alpha wave is most obvious when a person is mentally relaxed.

alphabetic method, or ABC method; out-moded method of teaching reading by first teaching the names and shapes of the letters of the alphabet. Constant repetition of the names of the letters, e.g. c – a – t, as in cat; b – a – t, as in bat; not only helps to learn the words but also helps children become familiar with the letter-clusters that are components of many different words. Contrast with *phonic method, whole-word* or *look-and-say method*.

alternating strabismus, see *squint*.

ambidexterity, ability to use both hands with equal skill and ease. Compare *handedness*.

amblyopia, poor *visual acuity* in one or both eyes after correcting with glasses or otherwise. Suppression amblyopia, commonly known as lazy eye syndrome, may arise when the child suppresses central vision in one eye to avoid *diplopia*, or double vision, which may be present in severe cases of *squint*.

American Sign Language, or Ameslan, a standard set of signs, used for communication by deaf people in North America in particular. It lacks some of the grammatical characteristics of English, but is nevertheless considered a true language, quite capable of conveying abstract ideas, etc.

Ameslan, see *American Sign Language*.

amnesic aphasia, inability to recall words and phrases.

amnesic apraxia, see *apraxia*.

amniocentesis, taking a specimen of *amniotic fluid* which is then analyzed to determine the presence or absence of a very limited number of *defects* and other malformations; for example, when there is a possibility of *anencephaly* the fluid contains higher levels of alpha-fetoprotein than would be found in a normal pregnancy. See also *genetic counselling*.

amniotic fluid, liquid surrounding the unborn baby in the womb. See *amniocentesis*.

amphetamines, series of synthetic drugs which stimulate the *nervous system*. Amphetamines have been used in the treatment of various conditions, e.g. *depression*, obesity and *hyperactivity* but with their potential for abuse and *dependency* and for other reasons they are now largely restricted in use.

Amsler grid, device for locating and recording defects in the field of vision, consisting of a grid of dark horizontal and vertical lines with one dark spot in the middle. The child looks at the grid with one eye closed; faults, distortions or blanks in the grid represent the existence and position of defects.

anal stage, phase in the *Freudian theory of psychosexual development* occurring between the ages of approximately one and three years when a child's interest is centred on anal activities. During this time the child is said to experience gratification, achievement or possible guilt in expelling or retaining faeces. Psychoanalysts believe that inappropriate handling at this stage — perhaps through an over-rigorous emphasis on toilet training — can lead to later personality problems.

analysis of variance, technique of analysing data to see whether differences between groups of scores are likely to be due to chance fluctuations. Thus a number of groups of children with reading difficulties might each be taught by a different remedial method. Analysis of variance could be used to indicate whether differences in progress could probably be ascribed to the teaching methods or could reasonably be explained as chance differences. See *F-ratio*.

anarthria, see *speech difficulty*.

analgesic, drug used to relieve pain without loss of consciousness.

anechoic chamber, or free-space room; sound laboratory, designed to eliminate internal sound reflections or exclude external noise, as in unobstructed free space. This enables *hearing acuity* to be measured precisely.

anencephaly, rare congenital condition in which part of the brain is absent; most anencephalics are stillborn or life expectancy is very short. It can be detected early in pregnancy, e.g. by *amniocentesis*.

angular gyrus, part of the cerebral cortex which coordinates the sound of spoken language with the sight of written language. See *brain* illustration (p. 28).

aniridia, congenital absence of the iris of the eye. Usually runs in families and is associated with severe *visual defect*. See *eye* illustration (p. 76).

ankylosis, stiffening or fixation of a joint, caused by disease or injury.

anomia, see *nominal aphasia*.

anorexia, lack or loss of appetite. Compare *anorexia nervosa*.

anorexia nervosa, prolonged refusal to eat, associated with emaciation, worry about body image and an abnormal fear of becoming fat. It occurs mainly but not exclusively in adolescent girls and is said to indicate underlying emotional stress or conflict, perhaps linked with the female role in current society. Treatment usually consists of measures to improve nourishment and *psychotherapy* to resolve any emotional disturbances.

anoxaemia, also anoxia or hypoxia, effect of deprivation or reduction in the normal supply of oxygen. It refers in particular to the short period before, during and immediately after birth when the oxygen supply to an infant's brain may be wholly or partially interrupted, which may lead to some disability.

anoxia, see *anoxaemia*.

anticonvulsant, drug used to control epileptic and other *fits* or *convulsions*, e.g. phenobarbitone and phenytoin. See *epileptic pupils*.

antimetropia, one eye is shortsighted (*myopia*) and the other farsighted (*hypermetropia*).

antisocial behaviour, behaviour which gives rise to social disapproval; e.g. vandalism and *delinquency*. It is a commonly used *classification* of children's behaviour, measured, for example, in the *Children's Behaviour Questionnaire* and is often contrasted with *neurotic behaviour*.

Apert's syndrome, see *acrocephaly*.

Apgar scoring system, system used to evaluate a baby's physical condition, usually one and five minutes after birth, in order to decide rapidly whether intensive care or specialized treatment is needed.

aphakia, absence of all or part of the lens of the eye. This is almost invariably the result of surgery to remove an opaque lens or *cataract*. See *eye* illustration (p. 76).

aphasia, loss of or impairment of the ability to understand or use language, caused by damage to the *cerebral cortex*. It is distinguished from other language problems caused, for example, by damage to the speech muscles or by hearing loss. The type of aphasia and its extent depends on the area of the cortex which is damaged. Thus *expressive aphasia* is associated with damage to the forward portion of *Broca's area*. Some aphasias can be successfully treated by intensive *speech therapy*; even when the power of expressive speech has been lost completely it is possible to teach aphasics to use a *sign language*. There are many different varieties of aphasia and different systems of classification. See *expressive aphasia, receptive aphasia*.

aphonia, See *speech difficulty*.

appeals procedure, established under the *Education Act, 1981*, when parents and the *Local Education Authority* are unable to agree over a child's *special educational needs*, after having followed the agreed consulation arrangements. Appeals can be made at two points. The first occurs when the authority, having assessed a child, decides that no *Statement* is necessary, i.e. a child's needs can be met without special arrangements. In this situation a parent who disagrees can appeal directly to the Secretary of State for Education and Science, who can direct the authority to reconsider its view but cannot require the authority to change it. The second opportunity arises when a parent and the authority are unable to agree on the content of a Statement. The parent then has the right of appeal to an Appeals Committee, established by the authority. Again, the Appeals Committee can ask the authority to reconsider its view but cannot insist that it be changed. If the parents are still dissatisfied they have a further right of appeal to the Secretary of State, who does in this instance have the power to direct the authority to alter the Statement.

apperception test, *projective technique* used in *child guidance clinics* and *school psychological services*, in which the child is shown pictures and encouraged to make up stories about each one. The stories the child tells are analyzed to gain an understanding of his or her personality. As examples, see *Thematic Apperception Test* and *Children's Apperception Test*.

applied behaviour analysis, using the principles of behavioural psychology to change behaviour. These principles include (i) specifying the behaviour precisely; (ii) recording its frequency (i.e. providing *baseline data*); (iii) noting what usually precedes and follows the behaviour; (iv) planning and carrying out a *behaviour modification* programme; and (v) reviewing progress.

approved social worker, officer of the local social services authority who carries out various functions under the *Mental Health Act, 1983*. These include making applications for the compulsory admission to hospital of a mentally-disordered patient.

apraxia, inability to carry out voluntary purposeful movements when there is no paralysis or defect of muscular co-ordination. The sufferer may understand what movement is required but cannot perform it at all. For example, he or she may not be able to protrude the tongue on command; yet may freely lick ice cream from the lips. There are many different kinds of apraxia: sensory apraxia is the loss of understanding of the use of an object; motor apraxia is the inability to manipulate objects or tools to carry out a task even though the sufferer may understand the use of the object and the nature of the task to be performed; amnesic apraxia is the inability to perform an action because the sufferer is unable to remember the command to perform it.

aptitude, potential for learning a specific subject or developing a particular skill. See *ability (3)*.

aptitude test, test designed to measure *aptitude* for a particular activity such as music, mechanical engineering or clerical work, aiming to predict competence in it. Aptitude tests are used in *vocational guidance* work with school leavers.

aqueous humour, clear, watery fluid which circulates in the space between the lens and *cornea* of the eye. See *eye* illustration (p. 76).

A.R., see *initial teaching alphabet*.

Arnold-Chiari malformation, *congenital* abnormality in which parts of the lower *cerebellum* and brain stem protrude through the base of the skull; commonly found in association with *spina bifida* and *hydrocephalus*. See *neural tube defect*.

arousal level, extent to which a child shows interest in the environment and pays attention to activities. Most children readily adjust their arousal levels to those required by particular tasks, but it has been held that a *hyperactive child* is unable to do this easily. Medication, e.g. with *amphetamines*, can help some hyperactive children, but it may not be easy to find the right dosage.

arrhythmia, any disturbance in the natural rhythm of the heart. One of the causes of fatal arrhythmia is *solvent abuse*.

art therapy, creative activities using the materials and techniques of the visual arts, in which children develop a sense of achievement and identity through self-expression. Art therapy can be helpful for *emotional disturbance*: it can provide clues for understanding and solving children's problems and the sense of well-being generated by creative activity may help improve children's personal relationships and adjustment to the world around them.

arthrogryposis, variety of clinical conditions, present at birth, which result in joints which are stiff and often deformed.

Arthur Performance Scale, battery of tests suitable for children from two years upwards and for which instructions can be given in mime. It has therefore had wide use for assessing the intellectual development of young children with *hearing impairment* or *language disorders*. It was first published in 1933, but new versions have appeared since. The author was Grace Arthur.

articulation disorder, speech difficulty which results chiefly in omitting speech sounds (e.g. 'cay' for 'clay'), *lisping* or *lalling*. Substitutions, e.g. 'toof' for 'tooth', are sometimes classed as articulation disorders.

Artificial Limb and Appliance Centre (ALAC), centre where *Department of Health and Social Security* staff dispense major aids, e.g. artificial limbs, wheelchairs, tricycles and cars to the disabled. There are centres in major towns throughout the U.K.

ascertainment, process of finding out which children need *special education*, established by the legislation which followed the *Education Act, 1944*. The duty of ascertaining children in need of special education by *categories of handicap* was imposed on the *local education authority*: parents had the right to request that their child's need for special education be assessed at any time after the age of two years. The process normally included a full medical examination and psychological *assessment*, as well as a report from the child's school, if of school age. *The Warnock Report* recommended the abolition of categories of handicap, the removal of the lower age limit for ascertainment and increased emphasis on the parents' right for consultation and information. The *Education Act, 1981*, incorporates these recommendations from *The Warnock Report*.

assessment, measuring and evaluating a child's skills, capabilities and limitations. It involves gathering and interpreting information about a child, usually as a basis for the child's education. Methods of assessment used in schools include tests, homework and examinations; assessment of children with special needs, however, should take into account medical, social, psychological and educational factors. The *Education Act, 1981*, lays down detailed procedures for the formal assessment of children who may be identified as having *special educational needs*. Guidance on these procedures is given in circular 1/83, issued jointly by the *Department of Education and Science* and the *Department of Health and Social Security*. See *Statement (of special educational needs)*.

assessment centre:
(1) in *special education*, a diagnostic unit staffed by a team, usually including a teacher, *social worker*, doctor and *psychologist*, which deals with the assessment and diagnosis of children with *learning difficulties* and *behaviour disorders* in order to suggest a suitable educational programme.
(2) specifically, unit run by the local authority for the observation and assessment of children at the point of entry into care, primarily to help decide the best placement.

assisted home, see *community home*.

association test, *projection test* in which the child states the first idea that comes to mind in response to a picture or word, as in the *word-association test*. The answers help a skilled psychologist to diagnose feelings and attitudes that a child might not be able to express openly. Association tests are often used in clinical work based on psychoanalytic theory; they are used in other contexts too.

asthma, constriction of the air passages in the lungs, causing recurring attacks of wheezing on breathing out, coughing and excessive mucus. Asthma in children is sometimes associated with an *allergy*, although too much exercise or stress will occasionally trigger an attack. It has been estimated that more than one in twenty children in the U.K. suffer from some degree of asthma. Although this makes it a very common disorder it produces a significant degree of handicap in only a small number of children.

astigmatism, defect of the eye which prevents light rays from converging in a single point on the *retina*, giving rise to blurred vision. This condition may lead a child to confuse similar-looking words and letters.

Aston Index, battery of tests produced by the Language Development Research Centre at the University of Aston, to identify children who are *at risk* educationally. The tests are arranged in two groups or levels. Those at Level 1 are for *screening* young children in their first year at school: those at Level 2 are for diagnosing difficulties, particularly language difficulties, in children aged seven years and over.

asymbolia, inability to understand symbols such as words, figures, numbers, signs and gestures.

'at-risk', children identified as potentially vulnerable to social, psychological or physical handicap are sometimes called 'at-risk'. It also describes children in danger of abuse or affected by deprivation, as well as those with a specific handicap. The purpose of the label is to provide a basis for early remedial action. See *'at-risk' register*.

'at-risk' register, list of children identified as being 'at risk' in some way. There are two main types of register:
(1) register initiated by Dr Mary Sheridan to identify at birth children who may need careful supervision during the first year of life because of some handicapping disorder. This register was widely used in the 1960s but has now been abandoned by most health authorities.
(2) register kept by the *social services*, identifying children who are, or might be, in danger of emotional, physical or sexual abuse or mental cruelty within the family. Interprofessional co-operation between social workers, doctors and teachers in relation to children at risk was

stressed in the Beckford Report, 'A child in Trust'.
The *Warnock Report* recommended that 'at risk' registers for educational difficulties should be discontinued.

ataxia, poor co-ordination of the muscles involved in movement, resulting in loss of ability to perform exact movements and in poor balance, as in drunkeness. Ataxia is chiefly associated with a form of *cerebral palsy*. It is attributed to injury to the *cerebellum*, which may account for associated problems of *eye-hand co-ordination*, causing additional educational difficulties. See *Friedreich's ataxia*.

athetosis, uncontrolled, purposeless movements of fingers, hands, face, legs and other parts of the body arising from damage to the *basal ganglia*. In some cases, speech may be affected by uncontrollable movements of the tongue and other organs involved in speech. It is chiefly associated with a form of *cerebral palsy*.

atonia, absence of the normal state of *tone*, or balanced tension, in the tissues of the body, especially the muscles.

attachment, affectionate, loyal or dependent relationship with another person. These relationships tend to develop at critical periods in life. Failure to form them, through lack of opportunity or inability to relate, can contribute to the development of *personality disorders*. The first attachment between an infant and the parents, particularly the mother, is called bonding; some believe that this is of critical significance in the formation of later attachments that influence healthy emotional and psychological development.

attainment age, measure of a child's performance in an educational skill such as reading: it represents the age for which the child's performance is average. For example, if a child read at the level of an average 8-year-old, his/her attainment age for reading would be eight years, no matter what his/her *chronological age*.

attainment quotient, index of a child's attainment: an attainment quotient of 100 represents an average performance; quotients above and below 100 are above-average and below-average performances for the child's age. The attainment quotient is sometimes calculated as the ratio of *attainment age* to *chronological age*, expressed as a percentage. Thus a child with an attainment age of eight years and a chronological age of ten years would have an attainment quotient of 80 (8/10 x 100). The attainment quotient can also be expressed as a *deviation quotient*.

attainment test, test to measure competence or proficiency in a particular subject or skill. Attainment tests constitute a major category of psychological test, broadly distinguished from tests of intelligence on the one hand and personality tests on the other. Attainment tests in school subjects, particularly the basic subjects of language and number, are widely used in assessing children's *learning difficulties*.

attendance allowance, tax-free, non-means-tested allowance for adults and children over the age of two years who are severely disabled and need frequent and continuous attention and care over a period of six months or more. The allowance is given to make it easier for people to receive the necessary care. Foster parents may claim the allowance for a foster child. The allowance is not usually payable for a child in residential accommodation, such as a special school or hospital — rules governing qualification are published by the DHSS.

attendance centre, establishment to which those between 10 and 21 years of age may be required to attend for a specific number of hours. Attendance centre orders can be made in relation to any offence punishable in an adult by imprisonment. The aim is to punish the offender by deprivation of free time, usually on Saturday afternoons, for a number of weeks, which is spent chiefly in physical training, craftwork, hobbies and attending lectures

attendance officer, see *educational welfare officer*.

attendance order, order served by a *local education authority* (LEA) on parents requiring them to send their children to school regularly or otherwise satisfy the LEA that suitable educational provision has been made for the child. If the parents fail to comply, the LEA can take legal proceedings against them. See *Education Welfare Officer*.

attention span, length of time during which a child can concentrate on a given activity. It varies with age, level of development, mental and physical condition and upon how interesting the activity is for the child. See *hyperactivity*.

attentiveness rating, score on a *questionnaire* or test measuring *attention span*.

attitude scale, method of measuring the strength of an attitude, e.g. a pupil's attitude to school. Scales are often in the form of a series of carefully constructed statements, e.g.

'I always look forward to school'

agree strongly   agree   disagree   disagree strongly.

The pupil is invited to check the response that best represents his own attitude. The responses to the whole set of statements are converted into a score, which gives a measure of attitude strength. These scores can be useful in counselling pupils with *emotional and behavioural difficulties*, but there can be substantial differences between measured attitude and observed behaviour.

atypical pupil, pupil who differs markedly, physically or psychologically, from others of similar age. The term is sometimes used instead of *exceptional child*.

audio-analyser, electronic equipment used by *speech therapists* and others to identify the various sounds in a person's speech.

audio-visual aids, also audio-visual technology, umbrella term for equipment and materials which use sight (*visual aids*) or sound (*audio-aids*) or sight and sound together, e.g. film and television, to help learning.

audiogram, graph of the results of a hearing test; the results for each ear are plotted separately for *air conduction* and *bone conduction*. The audiogram shows the severity of the hearing loss (in *decibels*) and the sound *frequency* at which loss occurs. This is essential information for teaching children with *hearing impairment*.

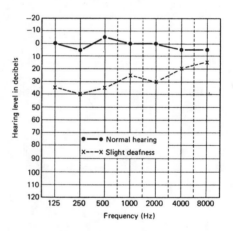

Audiogram

audiologist, person qualified to measure hearing and diagnose hearing problems, as well as to recommend and fit the most suitable hearing aid. See *audiometry*.

audiometer, electronic instrument for measuring acuity of hearing. The results are usually recorded on an *audiogram*. See *audiometry*.

audiometric screening, shortened hearing test carried out on a large scale (e.g. all school-children aged seven years in a particular local education authority) to identify those in need of further tests or specialized help.

audiometry, measurement of hearing characteristics, especially acuity, through various tests. See *acoustic impedance test, electric response audiometry, pure-tone audiometry, speech audiometry.*

auditory acuity, sharpness of hearing.

auditory aphasia, see *receptive aphasia.*

auditory closure, completing a word, phrase or sound after hearing only part of it. Poor auditory closure is associated with some *language disorders.*

auditory decoding, understanding the meaning of speech and other sounds.

auditory discrimination, ability to differentiate between sounds, e.g. in pitch and volume. Children who are unable to discriminate satisfactorily may have problems in speaking clearly.

auditory discrimination test, usually a series of pairs of sounds, often pairs of words, some of which differ slightly, e.g. 'pat' and 'pad' whereas other pairs are identical. The pairs are read out, or produced electronically, in turn. The child has to say whether each pair consists of similar or different words. Auditory discrimination can be measured by comparing the number of correct answers with the average for the age-group. The kinds of errors made can also be useful in an assessment of hearing and speech.

auditory feedback, *feedback* through sound; thus, individuals who are able to hear their own speech should be able to correct the sounds they produce accordingly. Those who are hearing impaired may not have full auditory feedback: they will be unable to hear the full range of speech sounds they produce and so lack the information to modify as they would wish. This creates obvious difficulty in learning to produce clear speech. Delayed auditory feedback involves delaying the reception of speech by the (speaker's) ear. It can be used to improve stammering.

auditory memory, ability to retain and recall information which has been heard. Children with limited auditory memory will have learning problems with many educational skills.

auditory nerve, eighth cranial nerve, which carries signals from the inner ear to the brain. See *ear* illustration (p. 66).

auditory perception, ability to register what is heard and give meaning to it. Tests of auditory perception measure characteristics such as *attention span* for words, *auditory discrimination, auditory sequential memory,* etc.

auditory sequential memory, ability to recall heard information in its correct order.

auditory training, or aural learning; instruction and exercises in the development of hearing skills and the use of *hearing aids* so that children with *hearing impairment* are able to make maximum use of their *residual hearing*, e.g. in learning to speak as clearly as possible and to recognize and interpret speech and other sounds. It can also be used to help *blind* children to develop an understanding of space and distance and to interpret common sounds of the environment.

Augmented Roman, see *initial teaching alphabet*.

aura, sensation which may be experienced at the beginning of an attack of *epilepsy* or migraine, before the onset of the main symptoms. An epileptic attack is caused by a wave of abnormal electrical activity spreading over the brain; if the wave spreads slowly, from a part of the brain associated with a sensation, then the patient feels that type of sensation (e.g. light, colours, sounds, smells) as a forewarning. The aura can be useful in enabling a child to inform the parent or teacher and to prepare for the attack. The aura of migraine varies, but often involves a feeling of sickness and blurred vision.

aural learning, see *auditory training*.

auricle, the protruding outer part of the outer ear which collects sound. See *ear* illustration (p. 66).

autism, form of childhood *psychosis* first described by Leo Kanner in 1943 as early infantile autism and sometimes known as Kanner's syndrome. It is characterized in particular by detachment from the environment, severe communication difficulties, both in *language development* and in interacting with other people, and by self-absorption. Some authorities hold that its onset occurs before 30 months of age. Its prevalence is not accurately known, partly because there is debate over its relationship with childhood *schizophrenia*, but it has been suggested that it is in the region of four or five per 10,000 live births, with a ratio of about three boys to every girl. Autism varies in severity, but all autistic children benefit from appropriate education. See *Creak's nine points*.

autistic, relating to *autism*. But the term 'autistic child' usually refers specifically to a child suffering from *early childhood autism*.

automated testing systems, computer-based systems for educational and psychological assessment. Automated testing is objective and time-saving, but does not offer the opportunity of observing personal characteristics afforded by some other testing methods. Nevertheless the application of computer technology to psychological testing is developing rapidly and automated testing systems are improving.

automatism, in *special education*:
  (1) movements or sounds such as rocking, lip-smacking, chewing and swallowing which are self-stimulating and repeated. This behaviour sometimes features prominently in severe learning difficulties and severe emotional disturbance;
  (2) behaviour without apparent conscious control or thought, as in an epileptic seizure or in sleep-walking. In the U.K. a person is not considered legally responsible for actions arising when affected in this way.

autosomal inheritance, pattern of inheritance which depends on the presence or absence of certain *genes* on the *autosomes*. Most hereditary disorders, whether resulting in physical or intellectual damage or both, are the result of a defective gene on an autosome, e.g. *cystic fibrosis, phenylketonuria, achondroplasia*. See *dominant gene, recessive gene*.

autosome, any *chromosome* that is not a sex *chromosome* and that appears in an identical pair in the human body cell. There are 22 pairs of autosomes in the normal human body cell. *Down's syndrome* is the most common chromosomal abnormality and is caused in nearly all cases by the presence of an extra autosome. See *chromosome* illustration (p. 37).

average:
  (1) arithmetic *mean*, the score obtained by totalling a set of individual scores and dividing by the number of scores. Many standardized tests are constructed so that the average score of the population on which the test was standardized is 100 points. For example, *attainment quotients* below 100 are below average, those above 100 are above average. Other measures of the central tendency of a set of scores are the *median* and the *mode*;
  (2) describes individuals whose characteristics are typical of their group e.g. average teacher.

aversion therapy, type of *behaviour therapy* in which unpleasant experiences, e.g. mild electric shock or vomiting, are used in controlled ways to reduce or eliminate unwanted behaviour. Thus an alcoholic can be made to feel nausea each time he/she takes alcohol. Aversion therapy is used for treating such problems as overeating, drug abuse and sexual perversion. It is usually restricted to adults who have agreed to its use.

avoidance behaviour, conscious or unconscious behaviour that an individual adopts to avoid or escape from an unpleasant situation, e.g. a child who dislikes a particular lesson refuses to attend school or develops sickness on the days when the lesson is timetabled.

B

babbling:
(1) stage in early development, usually beginning at about four months of age, when the baby begins to make and randomly repeat different speech sounds;
(2) exercise used in *speech therapy* to help strengthen certain muscles or develop certain sounds.

Babinski reflex, reaction causing the toes to move when the sole of the foot is tickled. The reflex is present throughout life, the toes extending upwards in the first six months or so, moving downwards thereafter, except in some pathological states.

backwardness, traditional term for educational attainments which are below those of the average child of the age group. It may refer to attainment in a single subject, e.g. backwardness in reading. The extent of backwardness is the size of the difference between the child's attainment(s) and chronological age. Thus a child with a reading age of 9 years 7 months but who is 10 years 1 month old shows six months backwardness in reading. Note that backwardness need not necessarily be serious enough to constitute a learning difficulty. Compare *retardation*.

backward chaining, technique for teaching a skill that requires a set sequence of actions, such as putting on a coat. The skill is divided into steps and the learner is placed in the position where he/she has only one step to carry out in order to complete the task, e.g. fastening the buttons of the coat. The preceding step, putting the second arm through the sleeve, is then taught and the task again completed. All the steps are taught in reverse order until the learner can repeat the actions from beginning to end. Although not suitable for all types of skill-teaching the advantages of the technique stem from the fact that the learner has frequent experience of success and knows what the result of each new step will be. Compare *forward chaining*.

ball-bounce test, test of psychomotor development, in which the child bounces and catches a tennis ball whilst sitting; it is used particularly to assess *eye-hand co-ordination*. See *psychomotor skills*.

barbiturates, large group of drugs derived from barbituric acid, that act to depress the activity of the central nervous system. Their main use is as a sedative to promote sleep; however, the more rapidly acting barbiturates (such as sodium pentothal) are given as anaesthetics, and the slow-acting ones (such as phenobarbitone) are also prescribed as day-time sedatives for the relief of tension and anxiety and for controlling attacks of epilepsy.

In young children, in particular, phenobarbitone occasionally has the opposite effect, making them bad-tempered and *hyperactive*.

basal age, an *attainment age* or *mental age* used in scoring some educational and psychological tests. In tests which group items by age, the highest age for which a child can answer all items successfully is known as his or her basal age. If, in a spelling test, a 12-year-old can correctly spell all the items designed for 10-year-olds, but fails some in the 11-year-old group, then his or her basal age on that spelling test is 10 years. But credit would also be given for items passed in the 11 year group and older age bands, even though some of these were failed, in arriving at the correct spelling age. See *ceiling (2)*.

basal ganglia, mass of nerve cells at the centre of the cerebral hemispheres which influence all motor activity. This is the area affected in athetoid *cerebral palsy* in which damage to these cells causes the purposeless involuntary movements associated with the condition.

baseline data, observations of a child's behaviour under normal conditions, which help a psychologist decide whether intervention is needed and, if so, to assess its effects. For example, in the case of a hyperactive child, the baseline data may consist of the number of times he or she leaves the room in a set period of time. This information would then provide the starting point for evaluating a programme of *behaviour modification* designed to help the child to sit still for increasing periods of time. In effect, the first A of the *ABA design* represents baseline data.

basic reading scheme, (U.S. basal reading scheme) a complete range of reading material based upon a specific scheme of teaching reading. It would normally consist of a teacher's manual, graded reading books, collections of stories and, in some cases, work books, tapes, etc. Compare *individualized reading*.

basic sight vocabulary, limited number of irregular words which appear in early reading, e.g. 'was', 'one', 'their', etc. Since they cannot be built up from sounds, children are usually taught to recognize them on sight. See also *key words*.

basic skills:
(1) skills that are central to the understanding of a particular subject, e.g. addition and subtraction are essential to an understanding of arithmetic;
(2) skills that are considered essential for everyday life. These have traditionally included the three Rs — reading, writing and arithmetic — but for the future may well include computer literacy and those *social skills* involved in coping with an increasingly complicated society.

BATPACK, Behavioural Approach to Teaching Package, inservice package for training teachers in skills such as specifying behaviour, rule-setting, effective praising, etc. The package was developed at the University of Birmingham and supports a course of six one-hour sessions, designed to be taught to groups of teachers by a trained tutor.

battered baby syndrome, pattern of non-accidental injuries suffered by a child, often at the hands of relatives. (In some instances, fractures in infancy may result from *brittle bones*.) See *child abuse*.

battery, see *test battery*.

Bayley scales of infant development, set of tests used with children from two months to two and a half years of age and with older children with *learning difficulties* to assess their psychological and physical development.

Beery Development Test of Visual-Motor Integration, for use with children aged 2–15 years and given either singly or in a group. The child has to copy a series of geometric shapes. The test is based on the premise that children with *visuo-motor disorders* may recognize the difference in geometric shapes, e.g. the difference between a square and a triangle, but may not be able to copy the shapes accurately. They cannot make their hands do what their eyes see.

behaviour analysis, see *applied behaviour analysis*.

behaviour chaining, learning a new behaviour in a series of steps, in which each step learnt serves as a stimulus to learn the next, e.g. a child learns to write his/her name letter by letter. See *backward chaining, forward chaining*.

behaviour coding, system used by psychologists to describe behaviour more precisely. Thus disruptive behaviour in class could be coded into: leaving seat; talking to neighbour; interrupting teacher, etc. Using these descriptions, *behaviour modification* programmes aimed at dealing with disruptive behaviour can be targeted more accurately and their effects measured more exactly. See *applied behaviour analysis*.

behaviour disorder, behaviour that is in some way unacceptable to parents, teachers, siblings, etc. Examples include *temper tantrums* in older children, *truancy, drug addiction*, withdrawn behaviour, etc.

behaviour modelling, learning behaviour by observing and copying someone else; i.e. following a model.

behaviour modification, form of *behaviour therapy* that relies on *operant conditioning* to change behaviour. Careful specification of the behaviour concerned and its frequency is followed by a period of systematic use of *positive reinforcement* to encourage desired behaviour, or *negative reinforcement* to discourage unwanted behaviour. The frequency of the behaviour concerned is then reassessed to check the effect of the behaviour modification programme. As an example it might be decided to try to modify the behaviour of a *hyperactive child*, focusing on the need to improve attentive behaviour during lessons. A star might be awarded for every five minutes of continuous attention to the task over a set period, and the effect of this assessed by the difference between the 'before' and 'after' measures. Programmes can be considerably more sophisticated than this and are widely used in work with children with learning and behaviour difficulties.

behaviour rating scale, list of different types of behaviour which can be used for identifying and assessing children's *behaviour disorders*. The rater usually has to indicate the seriousness of the behaviour, e.g. does the child wet the bed occasionally, about once a week or nightly?

behaviour shaping, use of *behaviour modification* techniques to develop behaviour, stage by stage. Thus, fear of dogs could be 'shaped' into liking by first rewarding handling a toy dog, then approaching a small dog, then patting the dog, etc. The skill lies in controlling the stages and the progression from one to another.

behaviour therapy, applies principles of *learning theory*, such as *conditioning*, to reduce or eliminate *emotional* and *behaviour disorders*. Behaviour therapy is a general term, covering techniques such as *behaviour modification*, *aversion therapy*, etc.

behavioural objective, precise and detailed statement of what a child is expected to learn. A behavioural objective usually states the standard to be achieved and how it is to be shown, e.g. 'Tom will be able to recognize correctly eight out of the ten new words in this reader by pronouncing them when shown on flashcards.' See *mastery learning*.

behavioural unit, special *unit* set up by *local education authorities* for disruptive pupils, providing part-time or full-time specialized help, usually in small classes. Sometimes unkindly referred to as 'sin-bins'.

bell and pad method, method of controlling bed-wetting (*enuresis*), based on *classical conditioning* principles. It consists of a bed-pad wired to sound a battery-powered bell or buzzer which wakes the child when the first drops of urine touch the pad. It is an effective approach to the problem with a success rate as high as 90%.

Bender Visual Motor Gestalt Test, nine geometric patterns for copying. The extent to which the child's copy deviates from the original design is assessed and interpreted. It has proved useful in the diagnosis of possible brain-damage in children and adults.

Bene-Anthony Test of Family Relations, *projection test* in which a child is given a standard set of statements and asked to choose which, if any, member of an imaginary family each statement best describes. A statement could be of the form 'This person is never cross with me'. The test gives a measure of a child's relationship with and feelings towards individual members of the family.

Benton Visual Retention Test, test of brain damage, designed to investigate perception of spatial relationships , *visuo-motor ability* and short-term memory. It consists of three equivalent forms, each of ten designs. Each design is shown for ten seconds and is then drawn from memory. The accuracy of the drawing in relation to that expected on the basis of age and ability is the main indicator of possible damage.

Bereiter and Engelmann Programme, North American compensatory education programme designed to make rapid improvements in the language and reasoning skills of *disadvantaged* pre-school children. The children are taught formally in small groups with little scope for creativity or self-expression. They appear to make significant improvements in their language skills and in their social and emotional behaviour, although the method has been denounced by many traditional nursery teachers and opponents of behaviourist psychology. See *Distar* and *Distar Language Scheme*.

beta-waves, one of four types of electrical waves which are recorded from the brain on an electroencephalogram. They are most obvious when the individual is mentally active.

biblio-therapy, reading material to help children gain an understanding of their own problems or identify with those of other children. Thus a story featuring adoption may be used to introduce the subject, allowing children to discuss their feelings about it with their teachers or parents.

bilingualism, ability to speak two languages fluently. In some states of the U.S.A., bilingualism is regarded as a condition requiring special education provision, though this is not so under current U.K. legislation.

binocular vision, seeing the same object with both eyes simultaneously, giving a single visual image.

birth order, the order in which children of a family are born. The position in the birth order and the spacing between *siblings* affect development to some extent. Thus it is claimed that first-born children tend to be slightly more intelligent, more conscientious, more obstinate and less aggressive than children in later positions in the birth order. One explanation for these usually slight effects is said to be the different quality and extent of parental and sibling interaction with children in different birth-order positions.

birth trauma, any injury a baby suffers during the process of birth.

blind pupils, legally defined as having 3/60 vision or less, after correction, in the better eye (though other considerations also apply). This means that in order to register as blind a person is unable to read, at a distance of three feet, a test card which people with normal vision can read at sixty feet. Very few people are totally blind; many blind people have useful amounts of residual vision. As a result of the *Education Act, 1981* blindness as a category of handicap has been replaced by *special educational needs*.

Bliss Symbol System (Blissymbolics), a language of written signs or symbols such as pictograms, which was originally designed to help international communications. Since you communicate by pointing to a sequence of symbols, high levels of *motor ability* are not required and so severely *physically handicapped* children with speech problems can use it. It has also been used successfully with children with very severe learning difficulties for other reasons.

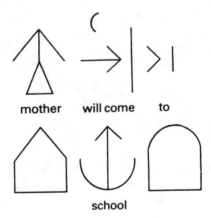

Communication using the Bliss Symbol System

block design test, a performance test of intelligence, originated by S. Koh. It usually involves using a set of coloured cubes to copy an increasingly difficult set of designs. Block design tests have been incorporated in many intelligence tests, e.g. the *Wechsler Intelligence Scale for Children*, and have uses in specialist psychological diagnosis.

Bobath method, form of *physiotherapy* devised for patients following a stroke. The Bobath Centre (see Appendix A) was set up by Dr K. Bobath and his wife in order to offer specialized help for children suffering from *cerebral palsy* and allied neurological disorders. The therapy emphasizes positioning and stimulating muscle groups used in movements needed in daily life.

bonding, see *attachment*.

bone conduction, sound reaching the *inner ear* via the bones of the skull. This is an important way of hearing if there is a blockage in the normal route, i.e. sound reaching the inner ear via the *outer ear* and *middle ear*. Compare *air conduction*. See *ear* illustration (p. 66).

braille, the most familiar reading and writing system for the blind, in which patterns of raised dots represent the letters of the alphabet. Text is read by feeling the patterns with the fingers.

brain, see *brain* illustration

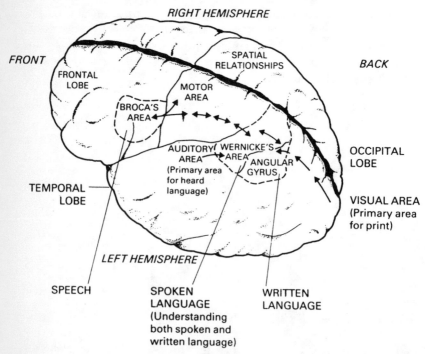

The brain

branching programme, see *linear programme*.

Bristol Social Adjustment Guides, checklists widely used (e.g The *National Child Development Study*) for assessing troubled behaviour or *maladjustment* in children aged 5–16 years. The guides are usually completed by a parent or teacher of the child whose behaviour is being investigated. They were first produced in 1958 by D.H. Stott and have been revised several times since.

British Ability Scales (B.A.S.), individual test of *intelligence*, constructed by C. Elliot, D. Murray and L. Pearson. It consists of 23 separate scales, intended to provide a profile of children's intellectual strengths and weaknesses, as well as a global *IQ*. It covers the age range 2 – 17 years and its revised version is the most recent of the major individual tests of intelligence used by *educational psychologists*. A version for use with children with *visual handicap* is being prepared.

British Picture Vocabulary Test (B.P.V.T.), see *English Picture Vocabulary Test*.

British Sign Language (B.S.L.), system of communication widely used by the profoundly deaf in the U.K. Like other sign languages it uses finger and hand positions, movements and orientations to represent concepts and ideas and the 'language' does not follow English syntax. It is held that this discrepancy may interfere with acquiring competence in handling spoken and written English, hence systems such as *signed exact English* were developed. See *Makaton*.

brittle bones, or fragilitas ossium, genetic disorder in which the bones are excessively fragile and liable to frequent fracture. Educational difficulties may arise from long periods of immobilization in hospital or in plaster and the consequent disturbance of normal schooling.

Broca's Area, area of the brain involved in speech production. Damage in Broca's Area is thought to be one of the causes of *speech* and *language disorders*, such as *aphasia*. See *brain* illustration (p. 28).

Brooklands experiment, project which demonstrated how well severely retarded children can develop given suitable encouragement and facilities. Although its findings related to one piece of work only, they helped to change public attitudes to the education and care of such children in the decade prior to the *Education Act, 1970*.

Bruininks-Oseretsky Test of Motor Proficiency, see *Oseretsky Test of Motor Proficiency*.

Bullock Report 1975, 'A Language or Life', report of the Committee of Enquiry into the Teaching of English. Among the recommendations were a number relating to pupils with reading difficulties. Thus it proposed using the term 'specific reading retardation' in place of *'dyslexia'* and recommended that every education authority should establish a reading centre or reading clinic for the minority of children with severe reading difficulties.

buphthalmas, *congenital glaucoma*, or defect of the eyes, usually present at birth and leading to severe *visual handicap*. There are no other effects.

Burt-Vernon Reading Test, *graded word reading test*, in which the child is required to read aloud single words of gradually increasing difficulty. The number of words read accurately is used to calculate a *reading age*. The test was originally constructed by C. Burt (1921) and revised by P.E. Vernon (1938). A later revision was produced in 1974 covering the age range 6–12 years.

C

calipers, splints for the leg consisting of two metal rods running from the back of a band around the thigh or from a cushioned ring around the lower portion of the pelvis. The rods are attached to a metal plate under the shoe, below the arch of the foot.

Campaign for People with Mental Handicaps, informal pressure group of parents and professionals, fighting for the *integration* of mentally handicapped people into local communities and for the closure of unsatisfactory institutions. They provide *counselling* and support for individuals. See Appendix A.

Camphill Schools, independent schools which cater for children with all kinds of handicap, but especially severe learning difficulties. They are based on the Christian Philosophy of Rudolf Steiner. The first such school in the U.K. was founded at Camphill, near Aberdeen, by Karl Konig in 1939. The schools are run as committed democratic communities, decisions being taken at general meetings. The teachers receive no salary. The *curriculum* is unorthodox, but aims to match the physical and psychological development of the children. See *curative education*.

Camphill Villages, economically self-supporting communities of handicapped and non-handicapped persons where an individual can stay for the whole of his/her adult life.

cardiac, relating to the heart.

cardiovascular system, network of structures including the heart and blood vessels that pump and convey blood through the body.

care order, order made by a *juvenile court*, usually in care proceedings brought by the police, a local authority or the N.S.P.C.C., on grounds set out in the Children's and Young Persons Act, 1969. The main grounds are neglect of the child, the child's misbehaviour, or where an offence has been committed by the child. The court may make a care order which gives the local authority rights and duties in relation to the child while the order is in force, normally the right to decide the child's placement.

careers education, 'that element in the school programme more especially concerned with preparation for living and working in the adult world'. This can be a formal part of the *curriculum*, part of a leavers' course or part of other lessons. Careers education provides information about different careers, help in making realistic choices and teaches the skills involved in getting and keeping jobs through talks, films, *work experience* and practice in interview techniques, filling in forms, etc.

careers service, service offering help in choosing employment or a course of education or training. Following the Employment and Training Act, 1973, *Local Education Authorities* are responsible for providing this service at schools and colleges whereas the Manpower Services Commission (M.S.C.) provides a service for young people in employment. It is staffed by professional careers officers who work closely with careers teachers in secondary schools. Some careers officers specialize in working with handicapped school leavers: the *Warnock Report* recommended planning for one such person per 50,000 school population and suggested that a careers officer could act as a *named person* for young people with special needs during the transition from school to adult life. See *Disablement Resettlement Officer*.

carrier:
(1) individual (or animal) who harbours and spreads an organism causing an infectious disease, without suffering personally from it;
(2) individual, male or female, whose *chromosomes* carry a *recessive gene* for one of a wide variety of hereditary disorders. Where both parents are carriers of the same recessive gene there is a one-in-four chance that one of their children will be affected by the disorder. This is the case in the vast majority of hereditary conditions. Where the *gene* is carried on the X *chromosome* it is only females who are the carriers and may transmit the disease to their sons and the carrier state to their daughters, e.g. in *Duchenne muscular dystrophy* or *haemophilia*.

CASE, Campaign for the Advancement of State Education, a national organization which campaigns for a first-class state education service throughout life, with equal educational opportunity for all and with parents and teachers working together to improve children's chances. CASE particularly champions the cause of children in poor circumstances and those with handicaps and special needs. See Appendix A.

case conference, meeting of those working with a handicapped child, often including the parents, at which diagnostic findings are shared and future plans for education and treatment are made. Regular meetings are a means of reviewing progress and pooling knowledge.

case history, accumulation of relevant data about an individual, such as family background, personal history, physical development, medical history, results of psychological and educational assessments, etc.

casework, method of treating problems which is widely used by social workers. Unlike other methods of social work it focuses on the individual person or family in difficulties, rather than perhaps attempting to change the social conditions which may have been responsible for the problems. It may draw on a variety of different theoretical perspectives, for example psychoanalytic ideas.

catalyst, in special education, someone causing or helping a change to take place, without being permanently affected. See *client-centred counselling*.

C.A.T., see *Children's Apperception Test*.

C.A.T.H., see *Children's Apperception Test*.

cataract, opacity of the *lens* of the eye, resulting in limited vision or *blindness*. Surgical removal of the lens is the most frequently used method of restoring or improving sight. In developed countries cataracts occur much more often among adults than children. In children the condition may occur as a result of *rubella*, acquired from the mother during pregnancy, but most children with cataracts are affected by a variety of hereditary disorders.

catchment area, area from which an institution draws its population: in education the area from which a school draws its pupils. Catchment areas differ in many ways, e.g. in size, in geography (town or country) and in the inhabitants' lifestyle, points which influence the aspirations and achievements of the school and its pupils. A parent can now state a preference for a school outside the accepted catchment area, and the school authority has a duty to accept that choice if certain conditions are satisfied. See *Education Act, 1980*.

Categories of handicap, means of defining types of handicap. The

Handicapped Pupils and School Health Services Regulations (1945) listed eleven such categories; the list was amended in later legislation. The *Education Act, 1981* followed the Warnock Report's recommendation to abolish categories, which have been superseded by the general term 'children with *special educational needs*'. The more important reasons for the change were the difficulties of sensibly allocating children with, often, several handicaps to a single category and the labelling effect that allocation to a category produces. See *labelling*, *classification*.

catharsis, technique for therapeutic release of pent-up or repressed feelings and emotions, perhaps by open discussion or by re-enacting a past situation. In *psychoanalysis*, *free association* is often used for this purpose, sometimes in conjunction with hypnosis and hypnotic drugs. Catharsis is sometimes used in the same sense as *abreaction*, though some distinguish method (catharsis) from product (abreaction).

Cattell Culture Fair Intelligence Tests, measures of *intelligence* which aim to reduce, as far as possible, the influence of verbal fluency, cultural climate and educational level on test performance. The tests are non-verbal, requiring only that examinees are 'able to perceive relationships in shape and figures'. See *culture-fair tests*.

Cattell 16 PF Personality Test, see *Sixteen Personality Factor Test*.

C.E.C., see *Council for Exceptional Children*.

ceiling:
(1) upper limit of ability or skill that can be measured by a test;
(2) ceiling age is the age level on a test at which a child cannot pass any more items. Thus a child may pass all items at the 8-year level on a test such as the *Stanford Binet Intelligence Scale*, some at the 9-year level but none at the 10-year level or beyond. The child's ceiling age is ten years.

central nervous system (CNS), the brain and the spinal cord. It is the main network of co-ordination and control for the entire body.

cerebellum, part of the brain which controls posture. It is attached in the back of the brain, below the cerebral hemispheres. Injury to this area can cause various problems, including difficulty in walking. See *brain* illustration (p. 28).

cerebellar ataxia, see *ataxia*, *Friedrich's ataxia*.

cerebral cortex, includes the convoluted outer surface of the brain. It integrates higher mental functions, general movement and behaviour.

cerebral dominance theory, states that some reading and speech difficulties can be linked to the location of control in the brain. It used to be believed that speech was normally controlled by the left *cerebral hemisphere*. Since in lefthanded individuals the right hemisphere was believed to control motor activities it was argued that this 'division of responsibilities' could be the cause of some language difficulties for lefthanders. Similar explanations were constructed for language difficulties in children who showed *'crossed dominance'*. It is now known that this is a far too simple — and incorrect — view of speech and reading problems.

cerebral dysfunction, often used in preference to 'brain damage'. It applies both to damage to a previously normal brain and to disorders in which the brain has never functioned normally.

cerebral hemisphere, one of the halves of the *cerebrum*. See *brain* illustration (p. 28).

cerebral palsy, inability to control body movements and posture normally, due to damage to the brain. The damage usually occurs during the birth process or shortly afterwards and the site of the damage partly determines the type of cerebral palsy. The three main types are (i) spasticity, in which the muscles become very stiff and resistant to attempts to move them; (ii) athetosis, in which uncontrollable movements (often slow and continuous) occur; and (iii) ataxia, in which the sense of balance is affected. (This is a classification based on motor ability: cerebral palsy can also be classified by limbs affected, e.g. *hemiplegia; paraplegia;* etc.) *Spatial ability* is often affected, too. These difficulties of movement, perception and learning etc. can lead to major *special educational needs*, sometimes met through intensive programmes such as *conductive education*. The main forms of medical treatment include surgery, drugs to relax muscles, *physiotherapy*, including the *Bobath method, speech therapy,* and *occupational therapy*. The incidence of cerebral palsy has been estimated at two or less per thousand live births. See *Spastics Society* in Appendix A.

cerebrospinal fluid (CSF), liquid that surrounds the brain and spinal cord.

cerebrum, the main part of the *brain* consisting of two *cerebral hemispheres*.

chaining, method of linking two or more items of *behaviour* based on *behaviour modification* principles. Thus, at its simplest, in teaching a child to dress, the reward for putting on a sock leads to another reward after the appropriate shoe is put on next. Quite complicated sequences of behaviour can be developed in this way. See *backward chaining, forward chaining*.

CHES, see *Child Health and Education Survey*.

child abuse, physical or mental injury, sexual abuse, negligent treatment or maltreatment of a child under 18 years of age by a person responsible for the child's welfare. Criminal proceedings may be instituted by police officers against an adult alleged to have abused a child; Social Services Departments and other authorized persons, such as inspectors of the National Society for the Prevention of Cruelty to Children can institute civil proceedings in respect of a child thought to be at risk for this reason. A *care order* or *place of safety order* for the protection of a child may be made.

child advocate, person or group speaking for a child's rights: in the U.S.A. such a person often makes the case for the child in legal proceedings over the educational rights of handicapped children.

child guidance, helping children showing signs of difficulties, particularly in personal relationships, at home or school. The professional child guidance team normally consists of a *child psychiatrist*, *educational psychologist*, and *psychiatric social worker*, but it is often broadened to include a *psychotherapist*, a teacher etc. Specialized treatment was and still is provided at a *child guidance clinic* but modern child guidance is increasingly involved in preventive work in schools and other community organizations.

child guidance clinic, facility housing child guidance team; the base from which intensive *child guidance* work is provided. See *School Psychological Service*.

Child Health and Education Survey (CHES), *longitudinal study* of the development of all children — over 15,000 — born in England, Scotland and Wales during the week of 5th – 11th April, 1970. It is the third of three such studies and like the others provides information on the incidence and nature of special educational needs. See *National Child Development Study*, *National Survey of Health and Development of Children*.

child minder, person who is paid (in cash or in kind) for looking after one or more children under 5 years old in the child minder's own home for two or more hours a day or for any longer period not exceeding six days. Responsibility for registration and inspection of child minders lies with the local social services authority and some authorities offer a training programme for child minders.

child observation schedule, method of recording details of a child's behaviour. The kind of behaviour to be noted is usually carefully specified and in some schedules the observations are to be made at set intervals. In this way an objective record of a child's behaviour can be obtained. See *behaviour coding*.

child psychiatrist, *psychiatrist* specializing in children's emotional problems in particular and *psychiatric disorders* in general.

child psychologist, *psychologist* specializing in the scientific study of children's behaviour and thought processes.

children in care, children who have been admitted into the care of a local authority and who will remain there until the age of 18, or exceptionally 19 years, unless they are discharged from care earlier. The local authority is obliged to review their cases regularly. Recent practice emphasizes greater use of support systems at home before a child is taken into care. See *care order, Children's Acts*.

Children's Acts, all Acts refer to England and Wales.

Children and Young Persons Act, 1933, governs the protection of juveniles in criminal proceedings and provides emergency procedures for protecting juveniles through the issue of a warrant to remove him/her to a place of safety.

Children and Young Persons Act, 1969, sets out methods of protecting and caring for juveniles who have either been neglected or found guilty of an offence (excluding homicide), by bringing them before a *juvenile court* in care proceedings. If the necessary grounds are established, the juvenile court can make, for example, a care or supervision order.

Children's Act, 1975, in conjunction with the Adoption Act, 1958, sets out rules relating to *adoption* and to *custodianship*.

Child Care Act, 1980, sets out the powers and duties of local authorities in:
(1) promoting the welfare of children,
(2) receiving children into care and
(3) the treatment, maintenance and accommodation of children *in care*.

Children's Apperception Test (C.A.T.), *projective technique* in which children aged three to ten years are asked to tell stories to pictures of nursery-tale animals in different situations. Their own problems and anxieties are assumed to be projected in their stories. There is a variation using humans instead of animals, (C.A.T.H.) which can be used with those older children who do not respond well to animal pictures.

Children's Behaviour Questionnaire, widely used *questionnaire*, often forming part of a procedure for screening children with *emotional and behavioural disorders*. It is available in two forms, one for completion by parents, one by teachers. The questionnaire provides a measure both of the severity of the behaviour and of its nature.

chorea, disorder of the *central nervous system*, associated with *rheumatic fever* and characterized by spasmodic twitching of muscles (St. Vitus Dance). In some cases the child is emotionally unstable. The disease may present serious obstacles to the child's educational progress, but is now extremely rare in Western Europe. This disorder of childhood should not be confused with Huntington's Chorea, a hereditary disorder of middle-age.

choreiform movements, sudden short, spasmodic, jerky movements which occur irregularly in different muscles. The child has difficulty keeping arms outstretched while his/her eyes are closed.

chromosome, threadlike structure which occurs in the body cell, and which carries the *genes* or hereditary characteristics. In humans the body cells normally contain forty-six chromosomes arranged in twenty-two pairs plus two sex chromosomes. Irregularity in the number or occasionally the structure of chromosomes (chromosomal anomaly) may be present in some children with special needs, (e.g. in children with *Down's syndrome*).

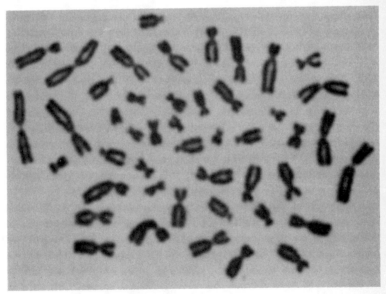

Chromosomes (from a single male cell)

chronic, continuous or recurring and of long duration: usually used to describe a disease, condition, habit or situation.

Chronically Sick and Disabled Person's Act, 1970, aimed to provide services for disabled people at home and in the community. The Act required local authorities to identify the number and needs of disabled people and to inform them of the help which it is the authority's duty to supply where needed, e.g. meals, help in obtaining a telephone, special equipment, taking holidays, access to public places and suitable toilets. There has been increasing concern about the lack of proper individual assessment under the Act, which led to the Disabled Persons (Services, Consultation and Representation) Act, 1986. This Act, not yet in force, aims to improve assessment arrangements and provides a framework for advocacy on behalf of disabled people.

chronological age, the time (in years and months) that has elapsed since an individual's birth, i.e. 'age' in the ordinary sense. Compare with *mental age, developmental age*.

classical conditioning, learning to link inborn behaviour to a stimulus that is not naturally linked to it. An example is learning bladder. control. Urination is inborn behaviour naturally linked to the stimulus of bladder pressure. When bladder pressure is regularly paired with the potty, this itself becomes a stimulus for urination. See *bell and pad method*; compare *operant conditioning*.

classification, controversial procedure which has been widely used in special education. The *Warnock Report* recommended that the *categories of handicap* which had been used in classifying children should be abolished, on two main grounds:
(1) the illogicality of assigning a child with several different special needs to one category of handicap
and
(2) the dangers of *labelling* to which classification gives rise.
The *Education Act, 1981* legally abolished categories of handicap. Classification is found useful elsewhere. Thus the *World Health Organization* recommended a 'multi-axial' approach to classification in child psychiatry, in which the disorder, not the child, is described in the following ways: (i) clinical psychiatric syndrome; (ii) intellectual level; (iii) biological factors; (iv) aetiological factors; (v) developmental disorders.
The International Classification of Diseases and the Manual on Terminology and Classification of the American Association on Mental Deficiency are two examples of other systems of classification sometimes encountered.

cleft lip, or *hare lip*, split in the upper lip. This is a *congenital condition* which may occur on its own or in association with *cleft palate* or other congenital conditions. Like cleft palate it affects speech and can also be disfiguring unless repaired. It is normally treated by surgery in infancy.

cleft palate, opening in the roof of the mouth, either partially or completely through both hard and soft palates. The condition, which is present at birth, results in nasal speech and *articulation disorders*.

client-centred counselling, *counselling* where the client determines the content and direction of the discussion with very little guidance from the counsellor, who creates a warm accepting atmosphere but does not offer advice. The technique assumes that the client possesses the potential for constructive personality change, while the counsellor acts mainly as a *catalyst*.

clinical psychologist, *psychologist* usually employed in the Health Service, and who can work with children or adults or both.

closure (school), closure of *special schools* is now subject to the same conditions of notice, appeal, etc. as other schools. This was not so prior to the *Education Act, 1981*.

cloze procedure, method of determining *readability* of books, etc. Words are systematically deleted from samples of the text and the extent to which they can be correctly guessed is taken as an index of readability. This helps to match reading material to a child's developing reading skills. The method can also be used to measure a pupil's comprehension of material read, which is a more proper use for it. See *readability formulae, GAP reading comprehension test*.

club foot, or talipes, *congenital abnormality* in which the foot is turned downward and inward at the ankle. Splints and casts in infancy should produce complete correction.

clumsy child syndrome, pattern of poor coordination in motor activities such as walking, throwing, dressing, etc., which can be associated with *perceptual disorder* and may be associated with difficulties in writing neatly, for example. It may occur for various reasons, for example it is one of the characteristics of *minimal brain damage* and may be helped to some extent by *motor therapy*.

cluttering, or agitolalia or agitophasia, speech disorder characterized by rapid, confused, incoherent delivery. It may be associated with other *language disorders*, e.g. difficulty in learning to speak, read and spell, and with some personality and behavioural problems.

cochlea, organ of hearing in the *inner ear*, a conical, bony structure, resembling a tiny snail shell. It changes sound vibrations into tiny nerve impulses. See *ear* illustration (p. 66).

Cocktail Party Syndrome, ready repetition of words and phrases heard, without necessarily understanding them. It is said to be characteristic of some children with *hydrocephalus* or *spina bifida*.

coefficient of correlation, see *correlation coefficient*.

coeliac disease, permanent disorder of childhood in which the child is sensitive to one of the constituents (gluten) in wheat, rye and oat flour, and therefore has to live on a diet which totally excludes these. With careful control of diet, normal physical and mental growth can be achieved.

cognitive development, progressive growth in a child's ability to understand concepts and explain relationships: usually equivalent to intellectual growth. Many psychologists believe that a child's cognitive development can best be described as a series of stages, each building on the preceding one. For a child with learning difficulties, assessing cognitive development is often a central part of an assessment procedure, explored by educational psychologists in various ways. Many psychologists hold that learning potential is equally if not more important to assess. See *Learning Potential Assessment Device*.

cognitive modifiability, principle underlying Feuerstein's *Instrumental Enrichment*, belief that it is possible to alter a child's thinking processes so as to make substantial changes in his/her intellectual development. Such changes are called structural changes and the ability to change, the cognitive modifiability, is measured by the *Learning Potential Assessment Device*.

Coleman Report 1966, U.S.A. survey to determine the extent of educational inequality within, and discrimination against children from low income backgrounds. The report revealed that within broad geographic regions, for each racial and ethnic group, the physical and economic resources going into a school bore little relationship to the achievement of pupils coming out of it: e.g. Coleman found that the teacher–pupil ratio showed a consistently poor relationship to achievements for all groups under all conditions. The implication that increasing resources for education will produce little or no benefit has been strongly challenged.

College of Special Education, institution set up in 1966 by the Guild of Teachers of Backward Children. It has an advisory and information centre and presents lectures, short courses and exhibitions.

colour blindness, inability to distinguish certain colours. The only common form of this disorder is the hereditary inability to distinguish red from green, occurring almost entirely in boys and inherited via the mother, who is a *carrier*(2).

colour-coding, method of helping children learn to read: colour clues indicate the relationship between specific letters and their sounds. Thus long vowels could always be printed in red. The principle of colour-coding has been used in several reading schemes, e.g. *Words in Colour*.

Coloured Progressive Matrices, see *Raven's Progressive Matrices*.

Columbia Mental Maturity Scale, individual *performance test* especially suitable for assessing the intelligence of children from 3 to 12 years with severe motor problems. The child has to choose one inappropriate figure in a set of drawings on a single card. Choice can be made by simply pointing or nodding.

Committee of Enquiry into Special Education, see *Warnock Report*.

Committee of Enquiry into Special Education of Handicapped Children and Young People, see *Warnock Report*.

communication aids centre, funded by the DHSS in hospitals and Health Service units to offer information and advice on developments in communication technology. Unlike *A.C.E. Centres* and *SEMERCs* they are not intended primarily for schools and teachers.

community care, support which enables an individual to live in the community rather than in a special social, medical or educational institution. It covers services provided by both the local authority and by the health service.

community home, home provided, managed and equipped by a local authority or provided by a voluntary organization but designated by the local authority as either 'controlled' or 'assisted'. A controlled home is managed, equipped and maintained by the local authority, which also nominates two-thirds of the home's management committee; an assisted home is managed, equipped and maintained by a voluntary organization with the local authority nominating one-third of the management committee. Children *in care* can be placed in a community home.

compensation, reacting to feelings of inadequacy or incompetence in one activity by concentrating on achievement in another. Thus a child with poor co-ordination may compensate for poor sports performance by striving for academic success. The term is also used for body movements which restore equilibrium.

compensatory education, educational programme designed to reduce the intellectual and other handicaps that children growing up in deprived environments are believed to suffer. The *Head Start Programme* is the best-known example. Good programmes involve the parents and work intensively with young, preschool children. See *deprivation*, *Swansea Project*.

comprehension — reading, see *reading comprehension*.

comprehension test:
(1) test which assesses how well a child can interpret or judge a situation presented in words or pictures. Some intelligence tests use comprehension tests as single items or whole sub-tests, e.g. *Wechsler Intelligence Scale for Children*;
(2) in reading, a test to determine how well a child understands what he/she has read, usually by answering questions on it.

compulsory education, legal requirement that children aged 5 – 16 years must attend school. Until 1972–3, the upper age-limit of compulsory education was 15 years for most children, but 16 years for those attending special schools. The limits are now the same for all children.

computer-aided instruction (CAI), learning through drill and practice computer programmes which take the learner through a series of steps to a well-defined skill, e.g. typing, with testing at intervals to check how well the material is being assimilated. CAI is also regarded as a branch of *computer-assisted learning*, a broader term.

computer-assisted learning (CAL), any learning from computer programmes which not only cover the more mechanical skills of computer-assisted instruction but also involve the learner in experiences and discovery in order to develop understanding of complex ideas. See *SEMERC*.

concept keyboard, board of touch-sensitive switches and pads used with a microcomputer. The keyboard can be programmed to perform various tasks. It is particularly useful for children with impaired motor control.

concept sorting test, assesses a child's ability to sort objects, or pictures of objects, into meaningful groups and to explain the reasons for this grouping. For example, a child may be given a variety of shapes of different colours, in order to see whether he or she can sort by more than one principle, the concept of shape (circle, rectangle, etc.) the concept of colour (red, green, etc.). The explanation for the sorting gives insight into the child's intellectual development.

conditioned reflex, piece of behaviour which has been learnt through *classical conditioning*.

conditioning, central explanation of learning offered by behaviourist psychology. It implies that behaviour depends on (or is conditional on) reacting with the environment. The two main forms of conditioning, both of which have applications in the education of children with special needs, are *classical conditioning* and *operant conditioning*.

conduct disorder, kind of *behaviour disorder* which gives rise to social disapproval, e.g. aggressive or destructive behaviour, bullying. It is more frequent in boys than girls.

conductive hearing loss, hearing loss due to poor functioning in the *outer* or *middle ear*. It is usually characterized by poor hearing at all levels of pitch, i.e. 'flat' hearing loss, rarely exceeding a maximum of 60dB. The condition can often be improved by surgery and/or a *hearing aid*, depending on the cause: temporary conductive hearing losses often occur in association with colds, catarrh, etc. See *grommet, hearing impairment*, Contrast *sensorineural hearing loss*.

conductive education, or Peto method, system for teaching people with motor disorders to function in society: intensive integrated programme of physical and intellectual education for children with severe physical handicaps. It emphasizes teaching children to recover control of their afflicted limbs rather than to cope with their handicap through the use of aids and devices. Individual programmes are prepared daily and the specially trained *conductor* encourages the children to take responsibility for their progress and to develop motivation by talking about their movements and activities as these are attempted. The approach originated in Hungary, where it is claimed that 70% of pupils learn to enter the normal setting of school or work without aids, wheelchairs, ramps, etc. See *Foundation for Conductive Education* in Appendix A.

conductor, leader of a class of children being taught by *conductive education*, The conductor takes on the role of teacher, *physiotherapist*, *speech therapist*, etc. as appropriate. It is claimed that contact with one person instead of different professionals helps to promote the children's development.

congenital abnormality, abnormality present at birth: classical examples are *cleft palate* or *club foot*.

congenital amputation, being born without some or all of a limb or limbs.

conjoint family therapy, see *family group therapy*.

consonant digraph, combination of two consonants which results in one speech sound, e.g. 'sh'.

contextual clue, help towards recognising a word from the sense of surrounding words in the passage. Children with poor reading ability can benefit from particular training in the use of contextual clues.

contingency, relationship between behaviour and its consequences. Thus, regularly following ten minutes of quiet working with praise is an example of a *reinforcement* contingency which could be used in *contingency management*.

contingency management, arranging contingencies in such a way that desired behaviour is encouraged and undesired behaviour reduced: the central principle of *behaviour modification*, widely used in treating behaviour difficulties.

continuing education, learning opportunities for young people and adults who are normally beyond school-leaving age. Usually these programmes cover specific areas of knowledge and skills rather than the traditional *curriculum* and can be provided in schools as well as in colleges and other establishments of *further* and *higher education*. The *Warnock Report* recommended that young people with special needs should be given the opportunity to stay on at school after the age of sixteen or should have access to sixth form colleges; that establishments of *further education* should provide courses of training in social competence and independence; that *Universities* and polytechnics should formulate and publicise a policy for the admission of disabled students and that *adult training centres* should include an educational element as part of the programme.

continuum of reproductive casualty, the view that there is a range of damage that can occur at birth, more severe damage leading to overt disease like *cerebral palsy*, while less severe damage perhaps causes minor *learning difficulties*.

contract therapy, treatment based on a contract between the client and a therapist. The principles of contracting have been used outside therapy, for example in the classroom. They include negotiating the contract (between child and teacher), recording the contract clearly in order to avoid misunderstanding, reviewing the contract to check for problems and clearing the contract on completion, leading to a speedy reward.

control group, group of individuals which matches, as nearly as possible, a similar group or groups who are the subjects of experimental research. The control group is not given the experimental treatment and so it provides a reference with which the experimental groups can be compared.

controlled home, see *community home*.

convulsion, alternative word for *'fit'* or *'seizure'*. When a convulsion occurs there is a sudden rapid electrical discharge in the brain. What the outside observer sees is either a *'grand mal'* fit, in which the patient loses consciousness, falls, moves his limbs violently and is often incontinent, or various lesser froms of 'grand mal' where one limb or the face are involved, or other variations. *'Petit mal'*, where the sufferer does not fall or move but goes into a brief state of inattention, sometimes at frequent intervals, occurs more rarely. True 'grand mal' convulsions can occur in otherwise normal children who have high fever; they also occur in various cerebral disorders including *cerebral palsy*. See *epilepsy*.

convulsive disorder, clinical syndrome which is characterized by frequent seizures, causing the body to thrash about in an uncontrolled manner. Children with *mental handicap* are said to be about twice as likely to have *fits* or *convulsions* as children of normal *intelligence*. For some children a tolerable degree of control can be achieved with *drug therapy*. See *epilepsy*.

Copewell System, set of curriculum materials designed at the *Hester Adrian Research Centre* for use in *Adult Training Centres* and with handicapped adolescents generally. The materials cover four areas, self-help skills, social and academic skills, interpersonal skills and vocational skills. As well as the curriculum descriptions the system includes teaching packages and assessment and recording materials.

Copy Forms Test, the child has to copy shapes such as a circle, square, triangle, divided rectangle and diamond. The accuracy with which the shape is copied, its position on the page, etc. give useful information about the child's development.

cornea, transparent outer coat of the eyeball in front of the *iris* and lens. See *eye* illustration (p. 76).

corrective braces, supports usually used to help in straightening leg bones; they allow joints to move by supporting part of the body weight. See *calipers*.

corrective reading, reading programme using *Distar* methods but designed for 11-year-olds and over who have made a start with reading. The programme follows behavioural principles and provides specific lesson plans which define the teacher's contribution in detail.

correlation, the way in which sets of measures vary together, e.g. younger children tend to be lighter and older children heavier: in other words there is a correlation between age and weight. The correlation in this case is positive, since low values of one set of measures (age) tend to go with low values of the other (weight): but if low values of one variable tend to go with high values of the other, as in the relationship between age and dependency on parents, the correlation is said to be negative.

correlation coefficient, index of how well sets of measures relate to each other. It is expressed in decimals from +1.00 indicating perfect positive correlation, to −1.00 indicating perfect negative correlation. Zero indicates the absence of any regular relationship.

cortisone, hormone from the cortex of the adrenal gland, which belongs to a chemical group known as steroids. Cortisone can be synthetically prepared and is prescribed as an anti-inflammatory agent reducing allergic and rheumatic reactions.

coryza, common cold.

Council for Exceptional Children, C.E.C., U.S. organization concerned with the education of children with special needs. Membership consists mainly of teachers, administrators and other staff engaged in special education. C.E.C. is a large structure with over 40,000 members organized into a number of divisions.

counselling, relationship between two people where the counsellor provides help and support for the client, aiding the client to gain insight into problems and to change ways of dealing with stress. While informal counselling takes place in many settings, counsellors with professional training are employed in schools to help students with personal anxieties or concerns over academic progress or career opportunities. In the U.K. school counsellors are usually trained and experienced teachers with additional training in counselling. Various counselling techniques have been developed. For example behavioural counselling is based on behaviourist psychology whereas *non-directive counselling* is based on the humanistic psychology of Carl Rogers.

counter-conditioning, reducing the unpleasant feeling which has become attached to certain stimuli by associating them with positive experiences, e.g. fear of bathing might be reduced by associating water with pleasant experiences. It is an example of one of the techniques used in *behaviour therapy*.

Court Report 1976, 'Fit for the Future', the report of the Committee of Enquiry into Child Health Services under the chairmanship of Professor Donald Court. It was set up to review health services for children after the 1973 reorganization of the National Health Service. The report recommended that there should be one integrated child health service following the child's development from early pre-school years through school and adolescence; a primary health care team linked to a district service should offer preventive and therapeutic services. Recommendations relating to *handicapped* children included proposals for support for parents from *district handicap teams* in each health district. These teams would provide diagnostic assessment and treatment facilities. The report met opposition from much of the medical profession.

CPK, creatine phosphokinase; chemical in the bloodstream. High levels are associated with muscular dystrophy, thus permitting an early diagnosis to be made, before physical symptoms appear. Carriers can be identified in the same way.

cranial abnormalities, malformations of the skull, often, but not always, associated with *mental retardation*, ranging from mild to severe. See *acrocephaly; hydrocephaly, microcephaly*.

craniostenosis, deformity of the skull caused by the cranial bones closing too soon, producing irregularities in the shape of the head.

Creak's 9 points, criteria for diagnosing *autism* in children, established by Dr. Mildred Creak; the three main indicators of the nine are:
(1) that the child relates to things rather than forming normal relationships with people;
(2) retardation and abnormalities in speech;
(3) ritualistic and compulsive phenomena, e.g. being obsessed with apples.
Other diagnostic criteria have since been developed. See *autism*.

cretinism, or hypothyroidism, condition resulting from inadequate action of the thyroid gland in early life. This produces varying degrees of mental retardation, with short stature and a variety of less serious symptoms. Early diagnosis and treatment can result in virtually normal physical growth and negligible or very minor mental retardation. Routine screening of new-born infants by blood tests helps to detect the disorder, which is now very rare in Western Europe.

Crichton Vocabulary Scale, test devised by J. C. Raven at the Crichton hospital, designed to measure the vocabulary of children aged four and a half to eleven years, by asking them to define a sample of words arranged in order of difficulty and given orally by the tester. Together with *Raven's Progressive Matrices* it is used as a measure of aspects of *intelligence*.

criterion-referenced test, scale which measures an individual's performance in relation to set standards. An example is the driving test, which assesses mastery of set roadcraft skills. This procedure emphasizes the individual's own performance, not whether the individual is better or worse than the average of the group. Thus a criterion-referenced reading test measures how well a child has mastered specific skills, such as recognizing and pronouncing correctly a specified set of *initial blends*, *digraphs*, etc. rather than measuring reading performance in relation to other children. It is thus as much an assessment of the success of teaching as of the child's learning. Contrast with *norm-referenced test*. See *precision teaching*.

critical periods:
(1) times of life when, given the right experiences, children normally develop or learn particular skills. It is believed that if the right experiences are not then available, the skill will be more difficult to gain later;
(2) times in the development of the unborn child when it is vulnerable to damage in particular ways. Thus the critical period for causing deafness, etc., due to *rubella* is usually the first three months of pregnancy.

crossed-dominance, see *dominance (2)*.

cross laterality, the preferred use of different sides of the body for different purposes. It is often used specifically for crossed hand/eye laterality, e.g. *left-handedness* in a person who prefers to use the right eye for sighting, etc. This has been regarded by some researchers as a contributory factor to children's *learning difficulties*, and reading difficulties in particular, but clear evidence is hard to find.

cross-sectional study, collecting information on aspects of child development from groups of children of different ages. The information (on the development of height or of reading skills, for example) is collected at or about the same time. Thus the method is quick, but does not permit the development of individuals to be studied. Contrast *longitudinal study*.

Croydon Check List, method of screening young children for learning problems based on systematic observation of their behaviour and progress. It includes items assessing speech, perceptual, motor, emotional and social development. It suggests helpful exercises and activities covering the development of listening skills, the use and understanding of words and concepts, etc.

CSF, see *cerebrospinal fluid*.

cued speech, the use of manual gestures to help lip-readers distinguish between sounds which are ambiguous (e.g. p and b) or invisible (e.g. k).

cultural deprivation, some loss of the normal experiences of childhood through crowded conditions, poverty at home, lack of adult interest, etc. This may restrict intellectual growth in particular. Concern over the effects of cultural deprivation on children's educational progress led to the launching of the *Head Start* program in the U.S.A. and *compensatory education programmes* in the U.K. While cultural deprivation was originally seen as primarily a problem of poor, inner-city children, neither poverty nor urban life are necessary conditions, for children from wealthy homes and children living in rural areas can also be culturally deprived.

cultural handicap, the effects of *cultural deprivation*.

cultural-familial retardation, also familial mental retardation, mild to moderate *retardation* with *IQ* mainly in the 50 – 70 range, which is not caused by *neurological impairment*, but by the interaction of heredity and environment. This level of mental retardation is more frequently found at the lower end of the socio–economic scale than elsewhere: it is held that low ability leads to unskilled, poorly paid work and, in turn, to inadequate nutrition and medical care of the children, poor educational opportunities and limited experiences, as well as to other factors which together can constitute a self-perpetuating syndrome. See *cycles of deprivation*.

culture-fair test, test, often of intelligence, which claims to be equally valid for children from any cultural background. In theory this does away with unfair results obtained, for example, by giving a test of intelligence constructed in the U.S.A. to children from, say, the North of England. In practice, culture-fair tests are very difficult to devise.

culture-free test, test with supposedly no cultural content.

cumulative record, school's account of each child's educational experiences, including performance in academic subjects, health, background and social adjustments. Information is collected through examinations, observation, interviews with parents, tests, etc. It is used in planning a child's future education.

curative education, aims to produce a harmonious relationship between a child and the outside world. Forms of handicap are thought to reveal the imbalances in a child's personality and spiritual condition, e.g. *hydrocephalic* children are said to display 'heady' traits, dreaminess and aloofness. Curative education involves making these children aware of their limbs and solid, earthy qualities. *Music therapy* plays an important part in curative education, which is associated with the Rudolf Steiner movement. See *Camphill Schools*.

curriculum, structured content of an educational course. Three broad curriculum types have been identified for children with special needs. They are explained below, in the order and words of the *Department of Education and Science*:

(1) mainstream with support, 'curriculum provided in ordinary schools, but with the provision of additional support which may be in the form

of additional resources, e.g. aids, small group teaching, ancillary help';

(2) modified, 'curriculum similar to that provided in ordinary schools but, while not restricted in its expectations, has objectives more appropriate to children with moderate learning difficulties';

(3) developmental, 'range of educational experiences but more selectively and sharply focused on the development of personal autonomy and social skills with precisely defined objectives and designed for children with severe learning difficulties'.

cursive writing, letters linked with flowing lines, rather than separate, printed letters. Children with *perceptual disorders* are often taught cursive handwriting only, instead of being first taught to print letters.

custodianship, legal order which may be awarded by a court to a non-parent, such as a relative, step-parent or foster-parent. If granted, custodianship vests 'legal custody' over the child in the applicant.

cycles of deprivation, idea that *deprivation* persists in certain areas of society despite economic progress: the view that deprivation often stays with a family for successive generations, linked with poverty, unemployment, poor housing, poor health, poor educational attainment, crime, inadequate parenting and a series of problem families.

cystic fibrosis, inherited disorder affecting the mucous glands in the body, which produce abnormally thick secretions, thus obstructing bodily functions and causing deterioration of body organs. Treatment is directed mainly at the prevention of respiratory infections. It also includes special diets.

D

dactylology, see *finger spelling*.

Daniels and Diack Standard Reading Tests, see *Standard Test of Reading Skills*.

DATAPAC, Daily Teaching and Assessment for Primary Age Children, a programme of individual education, based on close integration of teaching and *assessment*. The pack contains guides for teaching basic language and maths skills and appropriate assessments. It is used in the education of younger children with *learning difficulties*.

day care, day centre, day hospital, social facilities, education, training or medical care provided on a daily basis by health and social services departments or voluntary organizations. Day care for some handicapped young people consists of education and vocational training at a training centre; other types of day care include social facilities and contact for the handicapped who might otherwise be housebound and isolated.

day nursery, *day care* provided by social services departments, voluntary organizations or individuals for children from 6 weeks to 5 years old. Day nurseries must conform to recognized standards and have to be registered with and inspected by the local authority. Some take a quota of children with *special educational needs* while a few are designed specifically for them. The *Warnock Report* recommended an expansion in facilities and an increase in the provision of combined day nurseries and *nursery schools* for children with special educational needs.

deaf aid, see *hearing aid*.

deaf-blind, children whose hearing and vision are both severely impaired. These children have to learn methods of communication different from those used with the deaf or the blind: the sense of touch and *kinaesthetic feed back* are used to supplement *residual hearing* and *residual vision*. See *SENSE* in Appendix A.

deafness, complete or partial loss of hearing in which the person affected cannot interpret human speech without some help. There are two main forms of deafness: transmission or *conductive deafness* caused by an obstruction of abnormality in the *outer* or *middle ear*, and *sensorineural* or *nerve deafness* caused by an abnormality of the *inner ear* or of the *auditory nerve*. Deafness may be present at birth, caused perhaps by a virus infection (particularly *rubella*) of the mother during pregnancy, or by an inherited defect, responsible for a high proportion of children with severe *hearing loss*. It may also occur after the development of normal speech, as a result of an illness or accident. See *ear* illustration (p. 66), *hearing impairment, high-tone deafness*.

deaf pupils, were defined by the '*Handicapped Pupils and Special Schools Regulations*,' 1959, (as amended) as those 'with impaired hearing who require education by methods suitable for those with little or no naturally acquired speech or language'. As a result of the *Education Act 1981*, this legal category of handicapped pupils was abolished.

decibel (dB), unit for measuring the intensity (loudness) of sound—a whisper registers about 20dB and normal conversation 60dB. It is used in measuring *hearing loss*. See *hearing impairment*.

decoding, perceiving and interpreting signals in order to understand their meaning. Listening and reading are decoding skills: in listening to someone, the signals consist not only of the sounds but also their intonation, stress, sequence and context, as well as accompanying gestures and facial expresssion: in reading, the signals are groups of letters and words arranged in sequence and context. Inability to decode leads to misunderstanding and will affect the *encoding* skills of speaking and writing (including spelling). If these difficulties are severe, special educational help is needed.

defectology, term used in the U.S.S.R. for the interdisciplinary study of all aspects of *handicap*. The Scientific Research Institute of Defectology in Moscow is the body with main responsibility for planning and co-ordinating research on handicapped children and for training teachers for *special schools* in the U.S.S.R.

defence mechanism, term used by Sigmund Freud to describe the ways by which all individuals protect themselves, often unconsciously, from hurt and loss of self-esteem. Major defence mechanisms include *repression*, *projection*, *regression (1)*, and *sublimation*. However, if a child continually uses defence mechanisms to avoid facing reality, then ineffectiveness and escapism may result.

delayed auditory feedback, see *auditory feedback*.

delayed speech, speech which is significantly below the *norm* for the child's *chronological age*. It may occur for a number of reasons, e.g. low *intelligence*, *hearing impairment*, damage to the *central nervous system*, *emotional disorder*, certain types of illness and adverse environmental conditions. It may also be a temporary condition. See *developmental delay*, *speech therapy*.

delicate pupil, originally, a child suffering from *tuberculosis* or *malnutrition* and who needed to attend open-air school. The '*Handicapped Pupils and School Health Services Regulations*', *1945,* listed delicate pupils as a separate category and defined them as 'pupils not falling under any other category who by reason of impaired physical conditions need a change of environment or cannot, without risk to their health or educational development, be educated under the normal regime of ordinary schools'. The improvement in living standards and health since World War II has reduced the need for this type of provision. However, some children with problems were classed as 'delicate' because more suitable facilities were not available or because they did not readily fall into any other category of handicap. This is no longer possible: following the recommendation of the *Warnock Report*, the *Education Act, 1981,* abolished the category system and replaced it with the all-embracing term 'children with *special educational needs*'.

delinquency, see *juvenile delinquency, maladjustment, Jesness Inventory*.

Delinqency Prediction Instrument, test procedure designed by D. H. Stott to identify potential juvenile delinquents. It is based on the *Bristol Social Adjustment Guides*.

delta wave, the slowest of four types of electrical activity of the brain commonly known as brain waves. Delta waves are usually associated with a state of deep, dreamless sleep from which an individual is not easily aroused, but in certain circumstances may also indicate brain disease. They are recorded on an *electroencephalogram*.

dementia, mental deterioration in a previously normal person, caused by infection, injury, chronic poisoning, degeneration of the arterial system, or a wide variety of rare hereditary biochemical disorders in which the brain cells gradually deteriorate.

dentition, development, arrangement and character of teeth, sometimes important in the *assessment* of *speech difficulty*.

Department of Education and Science (DES), government department responsible for education, including *special education*, in England and for government policy towards the universities in England, Scotland and Wales. The DES is headed by the Secretary of State supported by the Minister of State for the Arts and two Parliamentary Under Secretaries of State. The DES formulates general education policy and influences local authorities to carry it out through the control of resources and independent inspectorate and expert advice services. In Scotland and Wales, the Scottish Office and the Welsh Office have responsibility respectively for all aspects of education except the universities. See *Her Majesty's Inspectorate*.

Department of Employment, government department responsible for implementing government policies affecting the conditions of employment of the country's present and future workforce. Some of the department's executive functions and services, including some concerned with the employment of young people who have special needs, have been transferred to bodies which are independent of the Department but responsible to the Secretary of State for Employment. See *Disablement Resettlement Officer, Employment Rehabilitation Centre*.

Department of Health and Social Security (DHSS), government department responsible for health and social services and the administration of social security benefits and state pensions in the U.K. It is headed by the Secretary of State for Health and Social Security, supported by the Minister of State for social Security and the Disabled, the Minister of State for Health, and by two Parliamentary Under Secretaries of State, one joint Parliamentary Under Secretary of State and one Ministerial Adviser. In Scotland and Wales the responsibilities for health and social services lie with the Scottish and Welsh offices respectively.

dependency, physical and emotional reliance upon another person or substance, for example, being dependent on drugs.

depression, common term for feeling dejected: more serious depressions are properly termed *depressive disorders*.

depressive disorder, abnormal emotional state characterized by exaggerated feelings of sadness, dejection, worthlessness and emptiness that are out of proportion to reality. In adolescents and adults depressive disorders are usually associated with loss of appetite, sleeplessness, loss of interest and concentration and frequently with preoccupation with physical complaints. In children, before the age of puberty, depressive disorders are less common, tend to be tied to specific situations and are less frequently accompanied by weight loss or reduced physical activity. *Antidepressant* drugs may be prescribed: although they do not cure, they provide relief from distressing symptoms and allow the patient to cope until the underlying disorder resolves itself, or responds more positively to *therapy*.

deprivation, complex concept suggesting that there is a minimum standard of life which is regarded as acceptable and that those falling below it suffer from deprivation. In 1972 the Secretary of State for the Social Services referred to the *'cycle of deprivation'*, the process whereby deprivation is perpetuated from generation to generation. There is no clearly defined group of children who may be classed as deprived nor are there clear-cut characteristics. However, children may suffer from deprivation in a variety of ways: at home they may suffer from the effects of poverty, poor housing conditions or parental neglect; they may be socially isolated and unable to develop the affectionate relationships essential to emotional growth; in school deprivation may take the form of inadequate facilities, poor teaching and deficient learning experiences; outside school they may lack the basic facilities for play, recreation and cultural stimulation. Different types of deprivation will have different effects on a child's response. See *compensatory education, deprived area, cultural deprivation*.

deprivation, maternal, separation of mother and child, especially in the early years. It was believed that this caused serious emotional problems for the child. However, separation is not inevitably followed by adverse effects; the outcome is affected by factors such as the age of the child, the quality of the mother-child relationship, the nature and extent of the separation, together with the child's capability to form a close relationship with another person.

deprivation, sensory, limited stimulation of the senses. Children with *hearing impairment* and *visual impairment* are most obviously at risk, but so are other children who are deprived of experiences such as handling materials and toys, an interesting and varied environment, conversation, etc. Unless recognized and actively combatted, severe sensory deprivation can lead to poor *perception* in particular and poor *cognitive development* in general.

deprived area, area which falls below approved standards in education, social amenities and quality of life. Such areas are characterized typically by poor housing conditions and overcrowding; high unemployment and low income; high levels of *juvenile delinquency*; poor school attendance; high incidence of children with *special educational needs*. See *educational priority area*.

Derbyshire Language Scheme, set of activities designed to improve children's language skills. It is aimed particularly at children with learning difficulties whose language development is below a four-and-a-half year level. The scheme emphasizes the use of play and adult-child interaction and the activities suggested are linked to assessments of the child's *expressive* and *receptive language*.

DES, see *Department of Education and Science*.

desensitization:
(1) form of *behaviour therapy* in which an individual is gradually but regularly presented with a frightening situation, either in fantasy form or reality, with the aim of reducing the fear through regular extensive encounters with the situation. Compare *flooding treatment*;
(2) in counselling, the process of reducing an individual's sensitivity to various situations, e.g. sensitivity to being handicapped, by skilled discussion;
(3) the treatment of certain conditions, e.g. *asthma*, hay fever, *allergy* to certain foods, by giving the patient increasing doses of *allergen* over a long period of time to establish partial or complete immunity.

detention centre, establishment where male offenders over 14 but under 21 years of age can be sent under a court order for a period of between 3 weeks and 4 months, following conviction for an offence for which an adult could have been imprisoned. Detention centres are of two kinds: junior centres for those under 17 years of age and senior centres for older offenders.

development chart, illustration of the sequence of stages of normal child development, which helps parents to estimate their child's present level of development.

developmental age, description of a child's level of maturity. It sometimes refers to physical development only, in which case a child would have a developmental age of nine years if physical development (height, weight, etc.) had reached the level of the average 9-year-old, notwithstanding the child's *chronological age*. It can also refer to all-round development, in which case qualities such as intellectual and social skills would also be taken into account.

developmental assessment, *assessment* which provides information on a child's level of development, usually in several different areas, e.g. physical, intellectual, social or language development. See *developmental age*.

developmental curriculum, see *curriculum*.

developmental delay, delay in the acquisition of skills, e.g. crawling, walking and speech, which would usually have appeared by the child's *chronological age*. Delays can vary in length: most delays, e.g. minor differences in the ages at which children learn to walk, are regarded as acceptable variations in normal development; serious delays need investigation.

developmental quotient (DQ), measure of physical and mental development, usually obtained by expressing *developmental age* as a percentage of *chronological age*. Thus a 10-year-old child with a developmental age of eight years would have a developmental quotient of 80 (8/10 x 100). It can also be expressed as a *deviation quotient*, in which case it indicates more precisely how the child's development compares with that of others in the same age group.

developmental word deafness, delay in understanding the spoken word, not due to *hearing loss*, and resulting in speech which is slow to develop and often distorted, mispronounced and ungrammatical. A form of *aphasia*.

deviant behaviour, *behaviour* which differs markedly from the moral *norms* or commonly held values of society; it is usually applied to disapproved behaviour, such as *truancy*.

deviation IQ, *intelligence quotient* obtained from relating a child's performance on an *intelligence test* to that of others in the same age group. It may be contrasted with a classical *intelligence quotient* calculated from *mental age*, in which a child's performance is related to the average performances of children in other age groups. Thus a deviation *IQ* of 130 on the *Wechsler Intelligence Scale for Children* indicates a test score which is better than 97.5% of children in that age group, but gives no indication of *mental age*.

deviation quotient, score obtained on a *standardized test* which indicates performance in relation to others in the same age group. It is a form of *standardized score*. See *deviation IQ*.

dextrality, preferred use of the right side of the body. See *laterality*: compare *sinistrality*.

DHSS, see *Department of Health and Social Security*.

diabetes (mellitus), condition characterized by high levels of sugar in both blood and urine due to a deficiency of the hormone insulin. There is no cure for this condition, but it can be controlled by *diet*, anti-diabetic drugs or regular injections of insulin. It is very unusual for childhood diabetes to respond to anti-diabetic drugs and most children and young people require regular injections of insulin. There is no reason why sufferers should not lead a normal life and attend an ordinary school, though teachers have to be sensitive to the child's pattern of insulin treatment, diet and exercise.

diabetic coma, also known as hyperglycemic coma, relatively slow disturbance of consciousness caused by unrecognized diabetes or by failure to carry out adequate treatment subsequently.

diacritical marking system, marks added to letters (*graphemes*) to indicate pronounciation values (*phonemes*); used in teaching children to read and in particular to help overcome the difficulty some experience when the letters or groups of letters in written English do not correspond to the sounds of the spoken language. In this system the spelling is unaltered but special marks are added: e.g. letters which are not pronounced are crossed out (happen∉d); two consonants which are pronounced as one sound have a bar under them (shut); a long vowel is marked with a bar over it (mē). There are 17 marks altogether. Selective use of this system may help a child with a particular reading difficulty.

diagnostic test, aims to identify and analyse problems or weaknesses, perhaps medical, psychological or educational. Thus diagnostic tests are used to identify childhood diseases, or colour blindness, or reading difficulties. There is a sense in which any test can be regarded as a diagnostic test if its purpose is the identification of problems, but in special education the term tends to be reserved for tests which are heavily used for locating areas of weakness in the basic subjects in particular, with teaching procedures built on their findings.

diagnostic unit, see *assessment centre (1)*.

diagraph, see *digraph*.

diet, consumption of food which provides the raw material for the growth and health of the body. A balanced diet provides balanced proportions of the essential elements of protein, carbohydrate, fat, vitamins and minerals. Conditions caused by deficiency in any of these elements may be improved by correcting the diet. Some conditions, including *diabetes*, *coeliac disease* and enzyme deficiencies, e.g. *phenylketonuria*, may require a special diet. There is a body of opinion that some behaviour and learning difficulties in children, such as *hyperactivity* may be relieved by careful regulation of carbohydrate and blood-glucose levels and adhering to a special diet free of synthetic chemical additives. See *Feingold diet*.

differential diagnosis, listing the possible diagnoses when presented with a child with certain symptoms and eliminating the incorrect ones in order to reach the correct one. See *medical model*.

digit repetition test, test in which the subject is asked to repeat a series of numbers after hearing them once. The longest series successfully repeated is the subject's 'digit span'. Versions of the digit repetition test appear in some *intelligence tests*.

digraph, or diagraph, two letters representing one sound, e.g. 'sh', 'ea'. One diagraph may have more than one pronunciation, but the letter combination results in a single sound in each case, e.g. 'ch' in character, choose and chauffeur. The sound values of digraphs are taught in the *phonetic* method of teaching reading, often used with pupils with *learning difficulties*.

diopter (dioptre), unit for measuring the refractive power of a lens used in testing eyes and prescribing spectacles.

diplegia, broadly, paralysis of both sides of a part of the body: specifically, in *cerebral palsy* it refers to spasticity in both legs, usually with some weakness in both arms. Compare *hemiplegia*, *paraplegia*, *quadriplegia*.

diplopia, double vision: the images of a single object on each *retina* are not fused to create a single image.

direct instruction, teaching method originating in work with disadvantaged children, such as the *Bereiter and Engelmann Programme*. It emphasizes careful organization and planning of lessons, which are often scripted, with constant checking of children's learning. The *Distar* materials have been developed on these principles.

directionality, awareness of position together with the ability to perceive directions, e.g. left–right, front–back and up–down. Some children with learning problems have a poorly developed sense of directionality, e.g. it is said that one of the symptoms of *dyslexia* is difficulty in distinguishing left from right. Text is read from left to right whereas addition of numbers is usually carried out from right to left: hence the ability to distinguish left from right is important in learning the basic subjects.

disability, funtional limitation of an individual's *ability* to carry out the normal *activities of daily living* caused by either a permanent physical or mental impairment or a *chronic* clinical condition such as *epilepsy*, bronchitis or *schizophrenia*. Thus it is implied that there is a standard of activity which is normal and those who fall below it are regarded as disabled. The McCorquodale Committee on the Assessment of Disablement referred to the principle that assessment should be determined by 'means of a comparison between the condition of the disabled person and that of a normal healthy person'. Disability is sometimes used synonymously with handicap, but this is inaccurate: handicap is the effect of disability in restricting *achievement* and causing social disadvantage: e.g. chronic bronchitis is a disability since the sufferer would not be able to take part in activities involving moderate exercise; a sedentary worker living in a bungalow would be much less *handicapped* by it than a labourer living in an upstairs flat. Similarly a boy with a leg amputated suffers gross disability, but may not be academically handicapped at all.

Disabled Graduates Data Bank, service, established at the University of Nottingham, offering careers guidance to disabled students and graduates and help for their advisers and employers on all matters concerned with career choice and planning. See Appendix A.

Disabled Persons' (Employment) Acts, 1944, 1958, legislation making special arrangements for the employment of the disabled. Every company with more than twenty employees should employ a quota (3% of its total work-force) of workers recruited from the *Register of Disabled Persons*. However, it is possible for employers to apply for exemption from these regulations if there are insufficient workers available on the register, and there is considerable concern about the effectiveness of the regulations.

Disablement Resettlement Officer, (DRO), official employed by the Employment Services Division of the *Manpower Services Commission* to advise and assist disabled people wishing to enter or retain employment and advise employers about jobs which might be suitable for them. The DROs maintain the *Register of Disabled Persons*, organise training and rehabilitation courses and arrange to provide any special aids and facilities needed. The blind and some partially sighted people are served by their own Blind Persons Resettlement Officers.

disadvantage, burden placed on children growing up in adverse social and economic conditions; roughly equivalent to *deprivation*. However, many educationalists have broadened it to describe the situation of children who are prevented in any way from fulfilling their potential. Others see disadvantage as a relative term: any child whose life-chances, i.e. opportunities for income, health, etc., fall below those customary in society, is seen as disadvantaged.

discrimination:
(1) recognizing differences, e.g. *auditory discrimination*, *visual discrimination*;
(2) differential treatment of individuals, typically through restrictions against them in housing, public services and employment, usually on grounds of race, religion or sex. It is argued that handicapped individuals are discriminated against because, for example, public buildings are not always designed to make them easily accessible. Educating handicapped children in *special schools* and hence separating them from the non-handicapped is also regarded by some as a form of discrimination. Discrimination of the grounds of colour, race or national origin was made illegal in 1968 and 1976 by the Race Relations Acts. The Sex Discrimination Act 1975, applies similar principles to discrimination on the grounds of sex;
(3) positive discrimination involves deliberately improving the opportunities of some sections of society, e.g. by seeking to appoint a proportion of black teachers, or providing better pupil-teacher ratio, more resources, etc. for schools in a deprived area. See *education priority area*.

discrimination index, measure of the extent to which a test item distinguishes between high- and low-scoring candidates. It is used in deciding which trial items to include and which to reject in constructing an educational or psychological test.

disruptive behaviour, problem or difficult behaviour on the part of individuals or groups. Unlike *emotional and behavioural disorders* the term usually refers specifically to *antisocial behaviour* in the classroom or school.

Distar, or *D*irect *i*nstruction *s*ystem for *t*eaching *a*nd *r*emediation (some times given as *D*irect *i*nstructional *s*ystem for *t*eaching *a*rithmetic and *r*eading). North American series of prescribed lessons for use by teachers with children in the 5 to 8-year-old range. It emphasizes clear aims and systematic teaching. It was originally designed for use in *compensatory education* programmes in North America, but has been used in special education in British settings. There are Distar programmes for teaching language, reading and arithmetic. See *Corrective Reading*.

distractor, one of a number of incorrect but usually plausible answers to a test *item*, so providing a choice of answers. Such items are known as multiple choice items. The greater the number of distractors the less the likelihood that a correct answer will be given by guessing.

distractibility, marked inability to concentrate on one activity for any length of time, associated sometimes with *hyperactivity*. Children with disorders of the *central nervous system* may show serious distractibility but it may also occur for other reasons.

district handicap team, group of professionals usually including a *paediatrician*, a nursing officer for handicapped children, a specialist *social worker*, a *psychologist*, a *speech therapist*, a *physiotherapist* and a teacher, with the function of identifying and assessing more seriously handicapped children and recommend treatment. The setting up of these teams was reommended in the 'Report of the Committee on Child Health Services,' 1976 (the *Court Report*), and endorsed by the Warnock Report, which added the rider that, except for the most complex disorders, the team should not need to meet in hospital.

district health authority, one of 192 administrative units in England and Wales, responsible for the planning and provision of hospital and community health services within its area.

dizygotic twins, non-identical twins; children born of the same pregnancy and developed from separate eggs which have been fertilized by two separate sperm. The twins are no more alike genetically than ordinary brothers and sisters. Compare *monozygotic twins*.

Doman-Delacato method, controversial programme for the treatment and education of children with *cerebral palsy* and other types of handicap, developed by Doman and Delacato at the Institute for the Achievement of Human Potential, Philadelphia U.S.A., and based on the idea that when part of the brain is damaged, surviving cells can be patterned or trained to resume lost functions. The programme requires systematic and intensive training in such *motor skills* as rolling, creeping, crawling, walking. See *British Institute for Brain Injured Children*, in Appendix B.

dominance:
(1) control exercised by one or other of the two *cerebral hemispheres*, or *cerebral dominance*;
(2) preferred use of one side of the body; in this usage it is similar to laterality. Thus a child who prefers the right hand for throwing, the right foot for kicking, the right eye for sighting, etc. can be described as right-side dominant. The preferred use of different sides of the body for different tasks is known as crossed dominance, a term often used in relation to crossed hand and eye dominance, e.g. a right-

handed child whose left eye is dominant. The lack of clear preference is known as mixed dominance: thus an *ambidextrous* child can be said to show mixed hand dominance. There has been considerable research into the relationship between dominance patterns of various kinds and educational difficulties, but the findings have not been clear cut. Clearly, left-handed children will not usually find writing quite so easy to master as right-handers, if only because the writing hand moves across the fresh writing. (Forced use of the right hand is not recommended.) See *laterality* and *crossed laterality*.

dominant gene, *gene* which always produces the characteristic it carries; i.e. if one parent gives a dominant gene to a a child then the child will show that characteristic, irrespective of the gene contributed by the other parent. Contrast *recessive gene*.

dominant hemisphere, see *dominance* (1).

Down's syndrome, also trisomy 21, type of *mental retardation* evident at birth, first identified in 1866 by J. Langdon Down who named it mongolism because of certain physical characteristics, viz. slanting eyes resembling an Oriental face. The preferred term however is Down's syndrome. Other physical characteristics include broad, short head, small depressed nose, large furrowed tongue and small squared hands. Typically, a Down's syndrome child may have poor muscle control and be susceptible to respiratory complaints: about one in four suffer from heart conditions. In the vast majority of cases Down's syndrome is caused by an extra *chromosome* 21; the remainder arise as a result of *translocation* of chromosomes. The incidence is approximately one in seven hundred. The risk of giving birth to a Down's syndrome child increases (though not steadily) with maternal age. The extent of *retardation* varies considerably so that while many Down's syndrome children show severe learning difficulties, some hold their own in the ordinary curriculum. Education should begin as early as possible and continue as long as possible. It is a myth that all Down's syndrome children are simply lovable, happy and friendly: in fact, they appear to possess the same range of personality traits as other children. See *Down's Syndrome Association* in Appendix A.

DQ, see *developmental quotient*.

drama therapy, use of acting as a therapeutic activity. The experience of drama benefits many children and takes several different forms. Techniques employing movement, music, dance and improvisation are adapted to the needs and abilities of the children. Drama is considered to have special therapeutic value for emotionally disturbed children because it is a type of *role-play* in which children portray characters in changing moods, emotions and situations; by absorbing themselves in other roles, children may be able temporarily to ease their own problems and release emotional pressures. For the severely handicapped the experience may consist of responding to music or other stimuli; for deaf pupils the techniques of mime are particularly appropriate; and for *blind* or *partially-sighted* pupils drama may be used to develop the other senses and encourage confidence in movement.

Draw-a-Man Test, *intelligence test* designed by Florence Goodenough. The child's drawing of a man is marked for its accuracy of observation and detail rather than artistic merit; this mark is then converted to an *IQ*. The test was revised in 1963 by Dale Harris and became the *Harris-Goodenough Drawing Test of Psychological Maturity*.

D.R.O., see *Disablement Resettlement Officer*.

drug addiction, according to the *World Health Organization* a condition with four characteristics; first, intolerable craving for the drug: secondly, increasing tolerance so that larger quantities of the drug are necessary to produce the same effect; thirdly, physical dependence on the drug so that it becomes an essential part of modified chemical processes in the body, leading to the physical illness and distress known as withdrawal symptoms when it is discontinued; fourthly, harmful effects upon the user's mental and physical health, together with long-term social problems. Narcotics such as heroin and opium can satisfy all the conditions of this definition. Other drugs, such as cocaine, cannabis, the hallucinogens and *amphetamines*, do not cause physical dependence and so do not satisfy the four conditions listed. However, the psychological dependence that they induce is regarded by some authorities as equally dangerous and likely to cause mental disturbance. Many agencies exist to help drug-users break their addiction but true addiction is difficult to cure: there is little chance of success unless the addict is totally committed to the treatment. See *addiction*.

dual sensory impairment, see *deaf–blind*.

Duchenne muscular dystrophy, also known as progressive muscular dystrophy, or pseudohypertrophic muscular dystrophy, inherited disease in which the muscles gradually waste away or are replaced by fat. This condition is one of the commonest sex-linked hereditary disorders, carried by the female and affecting males only. It was first described by the French neurologist G. B. A. Duchenne, in 1868. It can be identified at birth but it does not usually become apparent until after the age of two years and usually spreads from the leg and pelvic muscles to the rest of the body, eventually reaching the heart and lungs. There is no known cure. Most children with this condition need a wheelchair by the age of 10 years or thereabouts and are likely to die in adolescence or early adulthood from heart failure or lung infection. The condition is managed by *physiotherapy* and some regular exercise, especially swimming, wherever possible, and conditions in the home adapted so that life is made as comfortable and enjoyable as possible. The children can, and should attend nursery and primary schools, but most fall in the low average *intelligence quotient* range; this, together with their clumsiness and lack of co-ordination, may lead to unnecessary, frustrating testing and treatment in an attempt to help them learn. By secondary-school age, a *special school*, where specialist staff and the necessary facilities are available, is sometimes considered necessary; at all stages of education teachers should remember that the children's health is gradually deteriorating. See *CPK*.

dwarfism, severe failure of growth resulting in reduced body height: it may also involve various other defects, including *mental retardation*. There is no absolute height at which an individual may be classified as a dwarf. The most common cause of dwarfism in a European population is *achondroplasia*.

Dyfed Bilingual Screening Test of Articulation and Language, *speech therapy* screening test for children aged between three and eight years whose first language is Welsh, designed to be used by doctors, health visitors and teachers.

dys-prefix, see *a- and dys- prefixes*.

dyscalculia, see *acalculia*.

dysarthria, see *speech difficulty*.

dysgraphia, see *agraphia*.

dyskinesia, or akinesia, lack of control and co-ordination of the voluntary muscles resulting in clumsy movements or inability to execute some movements at all. *Chorea* (rapid, jerky movements) and *athetosis* (slow, purposeless, sinuous movements) are both dyskinetic muscle disorders.

dyslalia, see *speech difficulty*.

dyslexia, general term for impairment of the ability to read. It was originally a medical term for the reading difficulty of those who had suffered certain types of brain damage; this condition is now described by the terms *alexia*, acquired dyslexia or traumatic dyslexia. Specific developmental dyslexia is used to describe the learning disorder of children who have difficulty in acquiring reading skills. Dyslexia is a controversial condition. Some authorities regard it as a misleading label and think that the condition is a combination of reading problems, each of which should be isolated by appropriate tests, and that the children should be described as having a *specific learning difficulty* in reading rather than as dyslexic. However, other authorities have identified a number of symptoms, existing separately or in combination, in children who have reading difficulties even though they have high intellectual ability. The symptoms include the confusion of left and right; clumsy and poorly constructed writing; inability clearly to distinguish letter sequences in written words; difficulties in repeating a sequence of digits in reverse order; and slowness and difficulty with numerical concepts. It is claimed that symptoms such as these indicate specific developmental dyslexia. There is a growing body of research that considers specific developmental dyslexia to be connected to an unusual pattern of brain organization involving the language centres and in particular the relative *dominance* of the right and left *hemispheres*. Dyslexic children can make great improvements in their reading with appropriate *remedial education*. In 1981 the Minister of State for Education summed up the situation: 'Whatever the cause or nature of the condition commonly called dyslexia . . . the degree of difficulty should be revealed by *assessment*, and local education authorities will have to make appropriate arrangements for meeting the individual educational needs of children . . .'.

dyslogia, ideas can be expressed in speech only with great difficulty. The condition is associated with certain kinds of psychoses and brain damage. See *aphasia*.

dysmetria, inability to control and direct movement, a sign of *minimal brain dysfunction*, in which the child may have difficulty directing the finger to the nose with eyes closed, for example. See *finger-to-nose test*.

dysnomia, see *nominal aphasia*.

dysphasia, impairment of speech caused by brain damage. Some authorities use the term to describe a mild form of *aphasia*.

dysphonia, see *speech difficulty*.

dyspraxia, partial loss of the power to co-ordinate movements. The terms *apraxia* and *ataxia* are generally preferred.

dystrophy, see *Duchenne muscular dystrophy*.

E

ear, see illustration.

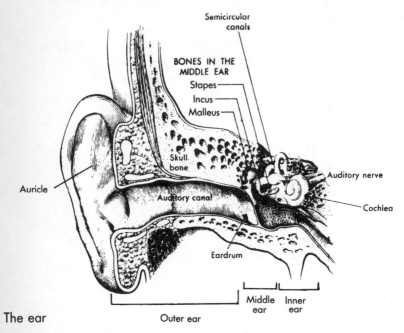

Semicircular
canals

**BONES IN THE
MIDDLE EAR**

Stapes

Incus

Malleus

Skull
bone

Auditory nerve

Auricle

Auditory canal

Cochlea

Eardrum

Middle   Inner
ear   ear

The ear   Outer ear

eardrum, or tympanic membrane, thin membrane that transmits sound
vibrations from the *outer ear* to the *middle ear*. See *ear* illustration.

early childhood autism, see *autism*.

early infantile autism, see *autism*.

Early Learning Skills Analysis (ELSA), scheme designed to identify a
child's skills in those curriculum areas important in the early stages of
schooling, e.g. various language, number and motor skills. The scheme
provides clear objectives for each area with the skills required defined and
graded. A criterion for success is specified and must be reached before
progressing to the next stage.

ear mould, part of a *hearing aid* moulded to fit the shape of the individual's
outer ear. An exact fit is essential for the wearer's comfort and to help
prevent the occurrence of *acoustic feed back*.

earshotting, technique designed to help a maladjusted or retarded child
develop desirable behavioural patterns. It involves deliberately speaking

positively about some behaviour of the child within the child's hearing. If John has been noisy in class then his teacher may say to a visitor within John's earshot 'John is working well and is much quieter'. This helps to build up a child's self-concept.

ear–voice reflex, stage in children's development occurring normally at about six months when their *nervous systems* are sufficiently mature for the sound of their own voices to stimulate their hearing, which in turn stimulates the voice to produce the sounds again. See *lallation*.

e.b.d., see *emotional and behavioural disorders*.

echo-box memory, process describing the way *autistic* children, with language difficulties, appear to store words and phrases in their memories, which they repeat parrot fashion without any understanding. See *echolalia*.

echocardiography, use of ultrasound waves to study the structure and rhythm of the heart, as an aid to the diagnosis of defects and disease.

echoencephalogram, recording produced by ultrasound techniques which enables the inner areas of the skull to be studied. It is especially useful as a means of assessing the damage caused by fractures of the skull.

echolalia, automatic repetition of words or phrases without fully understanding their meaning. The imitation of any sounds and words is a normal stage in a young child's speech development, occuring at about one year old. It is during this period that the sound patterns of the child's native language are acquired and form the basis of adult speech. However, echolalia is also a characteristic of some *speech disorders* and other conditions. Thus it occurs in some *autistic* children who may repeat parrot fashion, without understanding, phrases just heard and in the case of delayed echolalia, heard hours or even days previously. See *echo-box memory*.

echolocation, technique which uses sound waves to locate objects and which is incorporated in some aids for the blind. A hand held device emits high frequency sound waves which bounce back from objects, producing a signal whose loudness indicates their size and whose pitch their distance away.

Edinburgh Articulation Test, assesses the production of English consonant sounds by children aged three to six years. It is used as one means of identifying children whose articulation of speech sounds may need specialized help. The test is *norm-referenced*.

Education Acts, all acts refer to England and Wales unless otherwise stated.

Education Act, 1944, has since formed the basis of the education system in England and Wales, emphasizing that the education provided should suit a pupil's age, ability and aptitude. It laid down responsibilities for providing *special education*, which have been amended since, in particular by the *Education (Handicapped Children) Act, 1970*, and then by the *Education Act, 1981*, which repealed the provisions of the Education Acts relating to special educational treatment.

Education (Handicapped Children) Act, 1970, transferred the responsibility for mentally handicapped children from the Health Service to *local education authorities*, thus endorsing the right of all children to be educated. The transfer took place on 1st April 1971 and involved the development of *junior training centres* into *special schools* and training arrangements to confer qualified teacher status on their staff. See *Scott Report*.

Education Act, 1976, dealt mainly with the reorganization of secondary schools into comprehensive schools. But the House of Lords introduced Section 10, which required *special education* to be provided in ordinary schools, apart from certain provisos. This section was never implemented; it was superseded by the *Education Act, 1981*.

Education Act, 1980, among other provisions, this act compelled all schools including *special schools* to have parent and teacher governors, though in most cases these will form a minority of the governing body, the majority being appointed by local education authorities. It gave all parents (except the parents of children attending either special or nursery schools) the right to express some preference over their choice of school.

Education Act, 1981, came into force on 1st April 1983, repealing all provisions of the Education Acts which related to special educational treatment. It established a new framework for *special education*: this included the idea of defined *special educational needs*; the abolition of *categories of handicap*; the duty of a *local education authority* to provide special education for children as young as two years of age and from birth at parental request; the provision of special education in ordinary schools wherever possible; rules for the conduct of the *assessments* of children; extensions of the rights and responsibilities of parents, etc. For teachers, the central effect is an increased awareness of the educational needs of children with *learning difficulties* in ordinary classrooms; for parents the central effect is a much closer involvement with the education of their children from the earliest years. See *integration (1)*.

Education (Scotland) Act, 1946, established the basis of the current education system in Scotland, including the legal framework for special education, since modified by later Scottish education acts.

Education (Mentally Handicapped Children) (Scotland) Act, 1974, introduced legislation broadly similar to that provided for England and Wales by the *Education (Handicapped Children) Act, 1970*.

Education (Scotland) Act, 1981, came into force on 1st January, 1983. Like the *Education Act, 1981*, it repealed earlier legislation relating to special education. Its effects are broadly similar in principle and spirit, but there are a number of differences in detail reflecting the particular characteristics of the Scottish legal and educational systems.

Education Authority, the Scottish equivalent of Local Education Authority in England and Wales, with broadly similar responsibilities for special education.

Education (Northern Ireland) Order, 1984, aims to provide a system of education for handicapped children based on principles broadly similar to those established in the legislation for England and Wales. See *special care schools*.

Educational Disadvantage Unit (EDU), body set up by the *Department of Education and Science* to study the problems of educationally disadvantaged children, particularly immigrant children, and ways of dealing with these problems, including the appropriate allocation of resources.

educational guidance, advice and *counselling* over such matters as choice of school, choice of course or subjects, etc., provided by specialists such as *school counsellors*, *educational psychologists* and others.

educationally subnormal, (ESN), obsolete term used to describe the largest category of educational handicap, subdividing into ESN moderate and ESN severe. The *Handicapped Pupils and Special School Regulations 1959* defined ESN pupils as those who as a result of limited ability or other conditions require some specialized form of education, which may take place within a *special school*, a remedial class or a regular class in an ordinary school. *The Warnock Report* recommended that statutory categorization of *handicapped* pupils should be abolished and as a result of the *Education Act 1981* those children who were categorized as ESN are now described by the more general term 'children with *learning difficulties*.'

educational priority area (EPA), set up as a result of the *Plowden Report*, which recommended a policy of positive *discrimination (3)* for schools in *deprived areas*. An area was given EPA status if it fulfilled certain conditions such as high levels of supplementary benefit, poor standard of housing, poor conditions of school buildings or a high proportion of handicapped and immigrant children. Between 1969–71 action research projects were set up to develop positive discrimination in favour of schools in these areas and funds were allocated for new school buildings and teachers' allowances. These EPA projects were given the objectives of raising children's educational performance, improving teachers' morale, increasing parental involvement in their children's education and extending people's sense of community responsibility. The published results of these projects are known as the *Halsey Report*. See *Swansea Project*.

educational psychologist, professionally qualified and experienced teacher with a degree in psychology and post graduate qualifications in educational psychology who studies the intellectual, emotional, social and physical development of children and young people. Educational psychologists are responsible, among other activities, for carrying out *assessments* which help to decide the educational programme for children with special needs. They work closely with teachers and parents and may thus be consulted over a suitable programme for a child with a persistent learning difficulty, or a suitable *behaviour modification* programme for dealing with undesirable *behaviour*. They work mainly for *local education authorities*. See *school psychological service*.

educational welfare officer, person employed by *local education authority*, originally to investigate absence from school. Duties have since broadened to include such matters as investigating applications for free school meals, financial help with school uniforms, etc. and social work generally. Sometimes called *attendance officer* or educational *social worker*.

EDY, Education of the Developmentally Young, project and training programme in *behaviour modification* for staff working with children with severe *learning difficulties*. It trained educational psychologists and special education advisers to disseminate such skills as *operant conditioning*, *shaping*, *time-out*, by running workshops in their own areas. Certificates are awarded to those who complete the training programme satisfactorily.

ego:
(1) the self, the individual's awareness and idea of himself;
(2) in Freudian theory that part of the personality which restrains and organizes the instinctive drives of the *id* in the light of the demands of the *superego* and environment.

egocentric sequences, spoken language including the words 'I think' or the equivalent, as opposed to sociocentric sequences which include such phrases as 'wouldn't it', 'isn't it'.

elective mutism, see *mutism, elective*.

Electra complex, Freud's term for a daughter's attachment to her father and antagonism to and jealousy of her mother's relationship with her father, normally resolved in childhood. See *Oedipus complex*.

electrocardiogram (ECG), record of the electrical activity of the heart muscles as detected by an electrocardiograph. The ECG can reveal disturbances in rhythm — *arrhythmia* — and conditions where the heart muscle is damaged.

electrical response audiometry, variety of techniques for assessing hearing, based on recording and analyzing the slight electrical activity that is generated when sound reaches the ear. The techniques are specialized and may make use of an *electroencephalograph* for picking up changes in brain-wave patterns and a computer for processing them.

electroencephalogram (EEG), record of the brain's electrical activity as detected by an *electroencephalograph*. Regular wave patterns coincide with different types of brain activity and have been named *alpha, beta, delta* and *theta rhythms*. Although there is controversy about the interpretation of EEGs they have an important use in some methods of assessing hearing, in diagnosing and distinguishing between the different types of *epilepsy* as well as locating areas of brain damage.

electroencephalograph, instrument for recording the brain's electrical activity. Electrodes taped to different areas of the scalp pick up and amplify the minute electrical waves generated in different areas of the brain. These patterns are recorded on a chart and are referred to as the *electroencephalogram*.

electromyogram (EMG), record of the electrical activity generated by skeletal muscle. Electrodes attached to the surface of the muscle measure the electricity generated by the nerve impulses and the responding muscle. The resulting record, the EMG, is used in the diagnosis of neuromuscular diseases, such as *muscular dystrophy*.

elongation of tendo-achilles, surgical operation which may be performed on a child suffering from *cerebral palsy* in which the tendon connecting the main calf muscle to the heel is made longer to reduce flexion and to improve the child's ability to walk.

emotional and behavioural disorders (e.b.d.), sometimes emotional and behavioural difficulties, term which is increasingly used to replace *maladjustment*. It includes both *neurotic* and *antisocial behaviour* and is perhaps most clearly characterized by poor personal relationships. This is the main advantage of the rather cumbersome term: it focuses attention on behaviour and possible reasons for it, whereas it is argued that maladjustment implies a condition that the child possesses and so focuses attention on the child, to the possible neglect of other contributory factors. E.b.d. are usually managed in variations of two main ways, through changing the environment (e.g. placing the child in a special class) or changing the child (e.g. psychotherapy). Both methods can of course be used together. See *school psychological service*.

emotional deprivation, lack of or removal of loving care, particularly the mother's, in a growing child's life. Such *deprivation* can arise from special circumstances, e.g. death or divorce, from the inadequate personalities of the parents or from intolerable social conditions; it can harm a child's development, and lead to *emotional and behavioural disorder*.

Employment Rehabilitation Centre (ERC), formerly *Industrial Rehabilitation Unit*, offers vocational *assessment* followed by short, individually tailored retraining courses, to those who are finding difficulty in obtaining a job, including the handicapped. Their main purposes are to improve physical skills, develop confidence and make suitable recommendations for work. Some ERCs also run work-preparation courses for handicapped school leavers.

Employment Service Division (ESD), formerly known as the Employment Service Agency, a section of the Manpower Services Commission responsible, among other activities, for running *Employment Rehabilitation Centres* and keeping the *Register of Disabled Persons*.

encephalitis, acute inflammation of the brain, usually caused by one of a group of viruses, some of which are rare and cause encephalitis only, whereas others, e.g. mumps, *measles* and chickenpox are common but only occasionally behave in this way. Encephalitis leads to variable degrees of brain damage with very many different types of outcome. The vast majority of virus conditions are not progressive; once the acute illness is over there may well be some recovery from the apparent disability and certainly no deterioration.

encephalocele, like *spina bifida*, but the defect is in the back of the skull; a small portion of brain projects here and has to be removed. There is usually a variable degree of *nervous system* disturbance after removal.

encephalopathy, any disease of the brain, especially one which shows physical changes of the tissue brought about by causes other than inflammation, e.g. *lead poisoning*.

encoding, putting one's thoughts, experience or impressions into symbols which can be understood by other people. Speaking and writing are the basic encoding processes but other forms of expression, e.g. gesture, song, drawing, written symbols other than *language*, may also help to convey meaning. Compare *decoding*.

encoding test, any test designed to assess a child's ability to put ideas into understandable words or gestures, etc., for example one of the subtests of the *Illinois Test of Psycholinguistic Abilities*.

encopresis, inability to control one's bowels, not caused by organic damage or illness. There are three main types of encopresis:
(1) failure to learn bowel control;
(2) partial bowel blockage with secondary overflow of loose motions;
(3) soiling started as part of a psychiatric disturbance after bowel control has been established.

English Picture Vocabulary Test, (EPVT), adaptation of the U.S. Peabody Picture Vocabulary Test for use with English children. It is now being itself replaced by the newer (1982) British Picture Vocabulary Test, standardized on an age-range from just under three to just over eighteen years. Both tests measure comprehension or receptive vocabulary. The tester says a word and the child chooses which one of several pictures corresponds to it: as the test progresses words of increasing difficulty and abstraction are used. Since the only response required is pointing to a picture the test is useful in assessing the vocabulary development of children with speech impairments.

enrichment:
(1) stimulating deprived children by a teaching approach which intro-duces normal situations and activities they have failed to experience;
(2) extending the *curriculum* for *gifted children* by including extra activities and subjects taught at a greater depth in order to develop abilities without the feelings of frustration and boredom at being held back by less able classmates.

enuresis, incontinence of urine, particularly at night, when it is called nocturnal enuresis. Primary enuresis usually means that a child has never been 'dry' while secondary enuresis refers to the child who has learnt bladder control but becomes incontinent again. Children are not able to gain urinary control until their bladders are sufficiently developed to hold a night's production of urine; this happens usually by the age of 4, though often earlier. A child who is slow to develop control may be helped by restricting fluid intake, being woken at night and by other training based on encouragement. *Aids* to training include the use of various *drugs* or *behaviour therapy* which often involves an alarm system to wake the child when urine is released. A child who suddenly loses bladder control, when there is no apparent physical cause, may have some emotional disorder, associated with *anxiety* at school or stress within the family, perhaps; when the problem is resolved the child will be able to regain bladder control. See *bell and pad method*.

epilepsy, group of disorders of the *central nervous system* which are characterized by loss of consciousness and *convulsions* together with disturbances of feeling or behaviour. There are about half a million epileptics in Britain and it has been estimated that about 5% of children suffer an epileptic fit at some time, but in only a tenth of these is it serious enough for the children to be considered epileptics. In a small number of cases the cause may be linked to brain damage or disease but usually there is no recognizable cause and no symptoms other than the convulsion. There are several types of epilepsy. '*Petit mal*' involves attacks of no more than a few seconds, without *convulsions*, the brief loss of consciousness often passing unnoticed. '*Grand mal*' is more severe, involving longer loss of consciousness and muscle spasm, the child finally falling into a deep sleep. In *focal epilepsy*, the convulsions are restricted to the muscles in one part of the body and there is usually no loss of consciousness. The flickering of a visual display unit or television screen or sudden changes in colour patterns may sometimes trigger off an epileptic fit in children with no previous history of the condition. Although there is no cure for epilepsy, it is possible for the fits to be controlled by various drugs and most sufferers are able to lead a normal life. See *epileptic pupils*.

epileptic pupils, most children with epilepsy are educated in ordinary schools. However, where the convulsions are difficult to control by drugs or where there is an associated handicap the child may need special schooling in one of the small number of schools specializing in the education of epileptic pupils. The *Warnock Report* recommended that these schools should be developed as *resource centres* to help and advise on the *assessment*, health care and education of all epileptic children in the area. *Anti-convulsant* drugs taken to control the *epilepsy* have a sedative effect which reduces the child's ability to concentrate in school. It is thus essential that teachers in ordinary schools are aware of the particular difficulties an epileptic child faces. Children are no longer categorized as epileptic for educational purposes, but may be children with special educational needs.

epileptogenic foci, areas of the brain apparently related to attacks of *epilepsy*.

epiloia, tuberous sclerosis, hereditary disease of the *central nervous system* which may occur in a severe form in one generation and a milder form in another. The disease is characterized by *epilepsy*, skin disorders, tumours of the brain and other body organs with progressively severe *mental retardation*. It is sometimes known as Bourneville's disease.

EPVT, see English Picture Vocabulary Test.

erythroblastosis foetalis, *anaemia* in the new born originating before birth, usually as a result of the incompatibility of the mother's and baby's blood. The baby's red blood cells are damaged by the mother's antibodies and where damage is extensive the baby either may not survive or develop severe *jaundice* after birth with possible brain damage. The standard treatment of an exchange blood transfusion at birth saves over 95% of affected babies. The condition itself is now largely preventable by treatment of the mother.

eugenics, science of improving the characteristics of a species through selective breeding. The eugenics movement of the early part of the 20th century made largely unfounded claims that hereditary *mental retardation* was the main cause of a series of social ills ranging from prostitution to poverty and their theories influenced attitudes towards the handicapped and retarded and the kind of institutional care provided for them. Modern advances made in the field of *genetics* and the possibility of genetic engineering have provided a more scientific basis for eugenics. One aim is to prevent the inheritance of fatal and crippling diseases by genetic couselling, for example.

exceptional child, North American term for a child who differs significantly from the *average* of the age group in one or a combination of several mental, physical and social characteristics; the extent of the difference is such that *special education* is needed. The term includes both the child who is unable to perform up to the level of the average, for whatever reason, and the *gifted chi* whose level of performance is consistently much higher than the average.

excluded child:
(1) pupil who is barred from attending school on medical grounds because he/she has an infectious disease or is carrying parasites such as head lice;
(2) pupil who has been temporarily suspended from school on disciplinary grounds.

experience chart, teaching aid consisting of a large sheet of paper upon which the teacher writes down a shared experience as described by the class. The chart is developed as a group effort and grows out of the children's activities. It may be adapted for use with all types of teaching material, e.g. as a means of introducing new words or teaching logical patterns of thought.

expressive aphasia, inability to make the movements needed to produce a word, even though the sufferer knows the word intended. See *aphasia*; contrast *receptive aphasia*.

expressive language, *language* produced by the child, usually speech or writing. Contrast *receptive language*.

expressive language disorders, usually difficulties in producing spoken *language*, leading to limited use of words and reliance on pointing and gesture. See *aphasia*; compare *receptive language disorders*.

extended work time, concept used to cover various ways in which extra provision can be made for *gifted children*, e.g. extended activities groups, homework, lengthening the school day and shortening the school holidays.

external auditory canal, or external auditory meatus, passageway in the *ear*, stretching nearly one inch from the floor of the *auricle* on the outside of the head, to the eardrum, where it ends blindly. Sounds collected in the auricle are transmitted along the canal and absorbed by the eardrum which is then set in motion. See *ear* illustration (p. 66).

extinction, getting rid of unwanted behaviour by removing that which is acting as a *reinforcer*. Thus if a child's disruptive behaviour is being reinforced by the attention given to it by the teacher, ignoring the behaviour would offer a strategy for extinguishing it.

eye, see diagram.

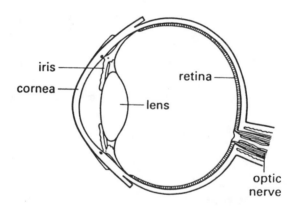

The eye

eye contact, meeting another person's gaze, so creating a means of communication. It is an important factor in bonding between mother and child and there is some evidence that eye-to-eye contact may be responsible for stimulating the maternal instinct. *Autistic* children's withdrawal from personal relationships may be partially related to their inability to look at other people with a steady gaze and special training is used to foster their development of eye contact.

eye dominance, preference for the use of one eye rather than the other. See *left-eyedness*.

eye-hand co-ordination, ability underlying manipulative skills which involve the simultaneous use of eyes and hands, e.g. ball-catching. Eye-hand co-ordination normally begins to develop at about 3 months when a baby intently watches the movements of its own hands. Eye-hand co-ordination may be poorly developed in some handicapped children either through damage to the central nervous system, or limited experiences, or other reasons.

eye-movement, left-to-right movement of the eye as it follows print while reading. The movement is punctuated by tiny pauses, or fixation-pauses during which recognition of words takes place. If this recognition is faulty or incomplete, then the eye will make a backward or regressive movement in order to read the word again. A poor reader makes many more fixations and regressions per line than a good reader. See *saccadic eye movements*.

eye-pointing, method of communication used by *physically handicapped* children and children with severe learning difficulties, which involves directing their gaze to a particular point, e.g. to indicate a correct answer from a choice of questions, pictures or to indicate a need. This form of communication may take time to develop and may not be readily used with strangers.

F

facilitator, person who helps members of groups, especially therapeutic groups, interact in order to achieve their aims. See *group therapy*.

factor, term generally used for a real or imaginary entity which simplifies the relationships between qualities. Thus, it is possible to explain most of the many qualities which characterise children's reading skills — fluency, interpretation, meaningfulnesss, confidence, hesitancy, etc. — as combinations of three facors, viz. reading speed, accuracy and comprehension.

factor analysis, statistical technique for reducing a large number of related variables to a relatively small number of underlying hypothetical *factors* on the basis of the *correlations* between the variables. Thus, the many human intellectual qualities were reduced by L. L. Thurstone to nine primary mental abilities, through the use of factor analysis. It is widely used in constructing many of the psychological and educational tests which are used to assess children's development.

fading:
(1) gradually withdrawing the cues and prompts which help a pupil to learn the correct response to a situation or problem until the response can be made unaided;
(2) more specifically, helping children with *learning difficulties* develop perceptual discrimination and learn concepts. For example, in a film showing objects differing in colour and shape, the differences in the shapes of the objects would be highlighted by gradually fading out their colours;
(3) weakening association between a stimulus and its response owing to lack of *reinforcement*, usually through lack of successful practice.

false-negative, missed identification or diagnosis: e.g. a child known to be maladjusted who is not identified as such by a screening procedure.

false-positive, incorrect identification or diagnosis: e.g. a child known not to be maladjusted who is nevertheless identified as such by a screening procedure.

familial mental retardation, see *cultural-familial retardation*.

Family Fund, also known as the Rowntree Family Fund, government fund, administered by the Joseph Rowntree Memorial Trust, providing help in the form of goods, services and grants for families with severely handicapped children under 16 years of age, where need is related to the handicap and is not covered by statutory provisions. Assistance is discretionary and is not subject to a means test, although circumstances are taken into account. The kind of help given includes laundry equipment, family holidays, outings, driving lessons, clothing, bedding, recreational and other items.

family group therapy, form of *group therapy* which recognizes that some children's problems are family-centred and in which the family as a group meets a *therapist* to discuss its problems. It can be contrasted with methods of child psychotherapy which assume that the difficulties are mainly child-centred and emphasize treating the child. It is also known as conjoint family therapy when there are two or more therapists present. Used in *child guidance clinics*.

family help units, centres run by the Spastics Society offering short-term care and accommodation for children with *cerebral palsy*, so that their parents can enjoy short breaks. It is one example of a general service of short-term and respite care provided by a number of voluntary organizations and local authorities.

Family Relations Indicator, *projection test* in which the child is encouraged to make matter-of-fact statements about pictures representing family members in various face-to-face domestic situations. Analysis of the responses is held to throw light on the child's view of attitudes and relationships in his/her own family. See *family relations, tests of*.

family relations, test of, tests designed to explore a child's views about his relations with members of his family. These tests include the *Bene-Anthony Test of Family Relations*, the *Family Relations Indicator* and the *London Doll-Play Technique*, for example.

Family Service Units, voluntary organization working intensively with families with multiple problems. Their objective is to keep a family together and they are often effective where official help is rejected. Over a hundred centres work at any one time with over a thousand families. They were started during the second world war by Quaker conscientious objectors but are now maintained by local authorities or voluntary organizations. See *problem families*.

family therapy, see *family group therapy*.

farsightedness, see *hyperopia*.

father figure, originally a person (usually a psychoanalyst) who, as a result of a *transference (3)* relationship, is seen in the light of a father and attracts similar feelings: now more widely used to describe an older person, e.g. a teacher, placed in a paternal role. A good father figure can be particularly important in work with some children with emotional disorders.

fauces, narrow opening between the mouth and throat, bounded by the soft palate above, the tongue below and on either side by the tonsils; its condition will affect the tonal quality of speech and the *articulation* of sound.

feeblemindedness, outdated term for mild mental retardation, replaced in the *Education Act, 1944* by the broader idea of educational subnormality, which has in turn been replaced by the idea of *learning difficulty*.

Feingold diet, special diet devised in 1973 by Dr Ben Feingold, which, though controversial, is used in the treatment of hyperactivity and children with learning difficulties. The diet eliminates all food that contains artificial colouring and flavours as well as two preservatives; the antioxidants butylated hydroxytoluene and butylated hydroxyanisole. It also recommends the elimination of fresh fruits and vegetables which contain natural salicylates, e.g. apples and tomatoes.

Fernald method, see *VAKT method*.

FIE, see *Instrumental Enrichment*.

filtering, the selection of the critical parts of a mass or collection (of data, sensory stimuli, etc.). The term has many specific applications, e.g.

(1) neural filtering occurs when the nervous system chooses from the array of sensations normally received those relevant to a particular task. *Hyperactivity* is sometimes thought to be due to poor neural filtering.

(2) acoustic filtering involves removing or diminishing sounds at particular levels of frequency or pitch from human speech. In this way the distorted human voice as heard by children suffering from high-frequency deafness, for example, can be simulated. This helps parents and teachers to appreciate the problems posed by this condition. See *audiogram*.

fine motor skills, complex movements of the hands and fingers which require practice to accomplish, e.g. holding a pencil or fastening buttons. Contrast with *gross motor skills*. See *psychomotor skills*.

finger agnosia, inability to recognize which finger has been touched (see *finger localization test*). Finger agnosia, in the sense of inability to move the relevant finger when it is named, is said to be a symptom in the *Gerstmann syndrome* and sometimes associated with reading difficulties such as *dyslexia* and *alexia*.

finger-localization test, test of the awareness of the position and number of fingers touched by another person, whilst the subject is not allowed to witness the action. It is said to be related to basic *language skills*, such as reading, writing and spelling. It has also been held to be an effective predictor of future reading performance among children at a pre-reading level. See *finger agnosia*.

finger opposition test, or finger-to-thumb test, test of psychomotor development, in which the child touches each finger to the thumb with his eyes open or closed, depending on age; it is used particularly to show *synkinesis*.

finger-pointing test, test of psychomotor development in which the child must touch the examiner's fingertip with his own, straight out from his/her body; it is used particularly to show small-muscle control.

finger spelling, or dactylology, manual method of communication used by the deaf in which the finger alphabet is used with one hand (U.S.) or two (U.K.) to spell out individual words of the written language, letter by letter. It may be used alone, or in conjunction with speech and *lip-reading* (a combined method). Compare with *Paget-Gorman sign-system*; *cued speech*.

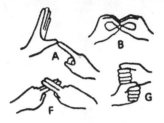

Finger spelling

finger-to-nose test, test of psychomotor development in which the child touches the tip of the index finger to the tip of the nose, with his eyes shut; it is used particularly to show small-muscle control.

finger-to-thumb test, see *finger opposition test*.

Fish Report 1985, 'Educational Opportunities for All?', probably the best-known of the consultative documents on special needs, policies and provisions produced by education authorities (in this case for the ILEA) in the wake of the *Warnock Report* and the *Education Act, 1981*. It took a firmer stance on *integration* than the Warnock Report, following the line that children with special needs were children first and foremost, with similar needs to their peers. Their special needs should be met in the light of this view. It thus defined special educational provision as the technology and methodology needed to provide access to the comprehensive curriculum and emotional and social climate in which education takes place. It stressed that these matters are the concern of every teacher since every teacher is a teacher of pupils with special needs.

fistula, abnormal channel between a natural cavity or canal and the surface of the body, or between one natural cavity or canal and another. A fistula normally arises as a result of injury or disease, or it may be present as a birth defect, as when a baby is born with a channel from near one of the tonsils to the surface of the neck. Fistulae may also be surgically constructed to overcome certain conditions.

fits, usually synonymous with a *convulsion* but occasionally used to describe an hysterial fit, i.e. a purely psychological disturbance.

fixation:
(1) focusing one or both eyes upon an object or particular point (fixation point) so that its image falls on the most sensitive part of the retina;

    (2) in some *learning theories*, the law of fixation holds that if learning is continued far enough beyond the threshold of understanding it becomes permanent;

    (3) arrest of development at a particular stage, so that behaviour or emotions associated with that stage become, in psychoanalytical terms, 'fixated'.

fixation pause, pause in the movement of the eyes to allow the reader to absorb what has been read. See *eye-movement*.

fixation point, see *fixation (1)*.

fixation time, length of time it takes for the eyes to fix on the word or object to be recognized.

fixed-interval reinforcement, see *interval reinforcement*.

fixed-ratio reinforcement, see *ratio reinforcement*.

flashcards, *visual aids*; cards which are shown briefly (a few seconds at a time) to pupils to increase their speed of recognition of the material printed on them. They are used most frequently as a means of developing and increasing speed of word recognition, often in remedial work. Since pupils are not allowed sufficient time to examine the word's constituent letters, the technique is aimed at speedy word recognition and complements the *look-and-say* or *whole-word* methods of teaching reading; alternatively, cards with sentences on them are used to assist whole-sentence recognition.

flooding , form of *behaviour therapy* used particularly in treating *phobias*. The therapist either places the subject in a feared situation for a period or helps the subject imagine him/herself in a 'most feared' situation. The purpose of the therapy is gradually to remove the phobia by demonstrating, with skilled help, that the fear is in reality groundless and no harm ensues.

Flying Start, teaching material designed to help children learn how to learn and so reduce learning difficulties. It was prepared by D. H. Stott and intended for young primary school children with mild and moderate *learning difficulties*. It has also been used with children and adults with severe learning difficulties.

focal epilepsy, see *epilepsy*.

foetal alcohol syndrome, condition in newborn babies, characterized by facial deformities and poor mental and physical development associated with excessive consumption of alcohol by mother during pregnancy.

Fog index, method of assessing the difficulty of reading material. For a few sample passages of 100 words, calculate (a) the average sentence length in words and (b) the percentage of words of three or more syllables. (a + b) x 0.4 is said to be the index of the *grade equivalent* (U.S.) for which the material is suitable, To find the approximate *reading age*, in years, add 5.0. See *cloze procedure, smog index.*

Fokus Society, Swedish voluntary organization which built flats designed and equipped for severely disabled people as integral parts of housing units shared with people who are not disabled. The government has taken over this programme and is building flats throughout the country, with at least one unit in every town. The programme rests on the belief that the government has a responsibility to cater for the needs of the disabled, of which the disabled themselves are the best judges.

fonator, electronic device that converts speech into patterns of vibrations. A hearing-impaired child can feel these and associate them with a written version of the same words, thus helping to identify and understand them.

fontanel(le), soft areas of membranous tissue in the top of a baby's skull, where bone formation is not complete. These areas gradually ossify until by the age of about 18 months the skull is entirely bone; there is considerable variation in the age at which the fontanel in normal children closes over. *Hydrocephalus* tends to cause the fontanel to bulge.

footprints technique, method of teaching a child how to recognize similarities and differences by comparing his own footprints with those made by others.

forearm-rotation test, test of psychomotor development in which the child, standing with one arm relaxed, rotates the other forearm as quickly as possible. It is used particularly to detect *synkinesis* in the opposite arm.

forward chaining, method of teaching a pattern of behaviour. The behaviour to be learnt is first analysed into its constituent parts. These are then taught, beginning with the first and adding each part in sequence until the pupil has built up the full behaviour pattern and can reproduce it as a whole. Rewards are given as sequences of parts are learned. Contrast with *backward chaining.*

foster child:
(1) child in the care of the local authority who has been boarded out by the authority with *foster parents;*

(2) any child below the age of 16 whose care and maintenance are undertaken by someone who is not a relative, guardian or custodian (Foster Children Act, 1980). There is no need for any reward to be paid. The Act excludes children who are fostered for not more than six days or, when they are being looked after by someone who is not a 'regular' foster parent, for more than 27 days. Certain children looked after in some other contexts are also excluded.

foster parents, those with whom a child has been boarded out by a local authority (if the child is *in care*) or placed by parents (if it is a private fostering within the meaning of the Foster Act, 1980). Foster parents sometimes seek to acquire wider powers and responsibilities toward the child, mainly by means of *adoption* and *custodianship*.

fragilitas ossium, genetic disorder in which the bones are excessively fragile and subject to frequent fracture. Educational difficulties may arise from long periods of immobilization in hospital or in plaster and the consequent disturbance of normal schooling.

F-ratio, statistic named after its originator, Sir Ronald Fisher; technically, the key statistic calculated in an *analysis of variance*.

free association:
(1) basic psychoanalytic technique, developed by Sigmund Freud, in which subjects talk spontaneously and unreservedly about their thoughts and feelings in order to help to reveal unconscious mental processes;
(2) tests, sometimes used in clinical work with disturbed children, in which subjects report whatever they first think of when presented with a word or picture. See *word association test*.

Freeman's chart, diagnostic chart for evaluating the quality of handwriting and diagnosing faults.

free schools, schools that have an unstructured *curriculum* and an informal relationship between students and staff; some cater for pupils who have been persistent truants from conventional schools.

frequency, rate of vibration usually measured as cycles per second (c.p.s.) or Hertz (Hz). High frequencies are perceived as high-pitched sounds, low frequencies as low-pitched sounds. The highest sound that a young person with good hearing can normally hear is said to be a frequency of about 16,000 c.p.s., the lowest about 60 c.p.s. The approximate frequencies of some speech sounds are given in the illustration on p. 85. See *high-frequency deafness*.

Freudian theory of psychosexual development, set of ideas, part of

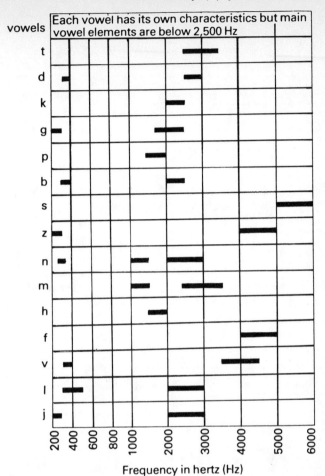

vowels — Each vowel has its own characteristics but main vowel elements are below 2,500 Hz

Frequency in hertz (Hz)

It should be remembered that this diagram is only a rough guide to the frequencies contained in the various sounds

Frequencies of Speech Sounds

the theory of psychoanalysis, which describes the growth of personality through five main stages of development;

(1) *oral stage*, when the mouth region is the focus of the baby's attention.

(2) *anal stage*, which occurs towards the end of the first year, when the infant is said to experience a sense of power and achievement either by expelling the faeces aggressively or by retaining them.

(3) *early genital or phallic stage*, when interest begins to centre on the genitals about the end of the third year.

(4) *latency period*, when sexuality is assumed to be in suspension: the period separating infantile from normal adolescent sexuality.

(5) *adult genital stage*, starting at puberty, when normal sexual activity becomes possible.

Freud and his followers believed that much psychological illness in adults originates in difficulties experienced in moving through these psycho-sexual stages. The theory also incorporates many explanations of other features of human development. See *Oedipus complex*, for example.

Friedreich's ataxia, inherited disease, with its onset in childhood or adolescence, in which there is degeneration of nerve tracts in the spinal cord and brainstem. The main symptoms, initially, are unsteadiness of gait and stumbling, progressing eventually to inability to walk or to speak intelligibly.

Frohlich's syndrome, disorder found mainly in adolescent boys, characterized by underdevelopment of the sexual organs and *obesity*, with female distribution of fat.

frontal lobe, division of the *cerebrum*, situated directly behind the forehead, occupying the forward portion of each *cerebral hemisphere*. The motor cortex, which controls voluntary muscular activities, is located in the frontal lobe, as is *Broca's area*, which is associated with *language* functions. See *brain* illustration (p. 28).

Frostig Development Test of Visual Perception (DTVP), pencil-and-paper test, constructed by Marianne Frostig and intended for children aged 4 – 8 years. It measures five *visual perception* skills and is used in diagnostic work with children with *learning difficulties* in particular. The kinds of perceptual problems revealed are tackled by the *Frostig Visual Perception Training Program*.

Frostig Visual Perception Training Program, set of exercises designed to remedy perceptual weakness revealed by the Frostig Developmental Test of Visual Perception in particular. It is claimed that the program can benefit some children whose learning difficulties are linked to perceptual problems.

fugue reaction, or fugue state, a protracted and severe loss of memory and physical flight from the customary environment, which may have physical origins (e.g. as a symptom associated with *epilepsy*) or may be a means of escape from a situation of intolerable conflict, stress or emotional pain. The fugue may last for days, weeks or, more rarely, years, during which time the sufferer may acquire a new identity, whilst retaining his basic knowledge and skills. On recovery, the sufferer is not usually able to remember much about events of the fugue period, merely those happening prior to its onset.

functional assessment, evaluating the extent of a person's handicap in terms of ability to perform the tasks needed to live normally. This helps to identify skills which need to be developed by training. It can be contrasted with psychological or medical *assessment*. See *activities of daily living* and *adaptive behaviour*.

functional curriculum, programme of education which emphasizes *social competence*, learning how to cope with recurring problems of living and how to adapt successfully to life within the community.

functional hearing loss, inability to hear arising from psychological causes rather than from organic defect of the ear, *auditory nerve* or brain.

functional literacy, sufficient competence in reading and writing for effective functioning in one's group and community. Since societies vary considerably in their complexity and demands, functional literacy is a relative term. Many find this a more satisfactory way of defining literacy than a score on a standardised test. See *literacy (1)*.

further education, includes three main areas of post-secondary education. First, vocational education, which covers courses for vocational qualifications linked to specific fields of employment and is normally based at colleges of further education and polytechnics. Secondly, non-vocational *adult education*, which covers all other types of classes for adults and is provided mainly in evening classes. Thirdly, educational, social and recreational activities for young people during their leisure hours which are organized through the Youth Service. Further education is provided mainly by *local education authorities*; however, other bodies play a significant part, e.g. university departments of extra-mural studies, as well as voluntary organizations and clubs.

Since 1978, the Manpower Services Commission (MSC) has been involved in further education with its programmes of training and work experience for unemployed school-leavers. Further education for young people with special needs is in a developing state: the range of provision varies widely in extent and quality between different local education authorities. However, suitable curricula are being designed — and a young person up to the age of 19 years has a right to full-time education. *The Education Act 1981*, lays down the duty of education authorities to provide special educational facilities, as specified in statements of *special educational needs*, for young persons to the age of 19 years. The *Warnock Report* specifically recommended that colleges of further education should develop courses suited to the requirements of young people with special needs; it also recommended that in each region there should be a special unit, based on a college of further education, providing courses for young people with severe disabilities.

G

'g' (general factor), general ability or general *intelligence*, first described by Spearman in 1904 as the common factor in performance on tests of different abilities. A person with high 'g' would be expected to perform well on most tasks. 'g' was held to be inborn, a controversial view that has been strongly attacked. Contrast with *'s' factor*.

galactosaemia, hereditary disease in which the body cannot convert sugar for use in the normal way. If it is not identified and treated soon after birth by a controlled *diet*, *mental retardation* and sometimes *cataracts* and liver damage, can result.

Gallaudet College, pioneer U.S. institution for educating the post-school hearing-impaired.

GAP reading comprehension test, is intended for children aged eight to twelve years. Reading comprehension is measured by a form of *cloze procedure*: the children have to complete the gaps (44 in all) in a piece of text, a different method from usual. See *comprehension test (2)*.

Gates reading tests, classic U.S. reading tests, occasionally used in the U.K., and prepared by A. I. Gates for testing all aspects of reading skills. Beginning at the *reading readiness* level they also include, *word recognition*, paragraph reading, speed of reading, accuracy of comprehension and *reading vocabulary* tests.

Gates-McKillop Reading Diagnostic Tests, U.S. tests designed to assess a child's reading and writing skills in order to provide a profile of ability in reading and related areas. They are intended primarily for 6–12-year-olds but may be used for older children with reading difficulties.

Gaussian curve, see *normal curve*.

gene, unit of biological material which helps to transmit characteristics from parents to children. Hereditary factors are carried in the *chromosomes*, where the genes are distributed in a predetermined sequence along the length of the chromosomes, half the genes coming fom each parent. Most physical characteristics of children are genetically determined, as are some illnesses (e.g. *muscular dystrophy*) but there is controversy over the extent to which psychological characteristics (e.g. *intelligence*, aggression) are also transmitted by genes.

general intelligence, *general ability*: see *'g'*.

genetics, science of *heredity*, the principles governing the transmission of characteristics from parents to their children.

genetic counselling, part of family planning counselling, where there is concern that children might inherit a disabling condition. The objectives are:
(1) to give accurate information to parents or prospective parents about the risks of a disease occurring in children, or in further children;
(2) to alert the medical profession to any special risks of disease, before birth;
(3) to reduce, through early diagnosis and treatment, the incidence of disorders which are wholly or partly genetically determined. Techniques such as *amniocentesis* can be used in diagnosis.

geneticist, person who has specialized in the study of *genetics* and understands the way in which children will inherit characteristics from their parents.

genital stage, the final phase of the *Freudian theory of psychosexual development*; full maturity is said to be reached through the establishment of a stable heterosexual relationship.

genius, see *gifted children*.

German measles, see *rubella*.

Gerstmann syndrome, four symptoms, viz. difficulty in identifying fingers correctly; confusion between right and left; writing difficulties; arithmetical difficulties. These four symptoms, first described by Gerstmann in 1927, may together indicate damage to the *angular gyrus*.

Gesell tests, U.S. schedules, designed by A. Gesell, which assess four areas of child development:
(1) motor behaviour, including postural reactions, head balance, standing, creeping, walking and fine *motor co-ordination*.
(2) *adaptive behaviour*, covering *eye-hand co-ordination* e.g. handling objects, ringing a bell, simple drawing.
(3) *language* behaviour, covering all means of communication e.g. facial expression, *gesture*, postural movements.
(4) personal social behaviour, covering the child's personal reactions to the social culture in which he lives, e.g. feeding, toilet training, play.
The tests, which are usually used with infants and young children, involve careful observation and are usually supplemented by an interview with the child's mother.

gifted children, outstandingly talented children; originally defined as children with a particularly high intelligence quotient, but more recently as children who have demonstrated high achievement and/or potential in a particular field or fields. Those usually mentioned include general intellectual ability, specific academic aptitude, creative or productive thinking, leadership ability, visual and performing arts and psychomotor ability. These children may require special educational programmes and/or services beyond those normally provided in order to realize their exceptional gifts. There are three main methods of offering suitable special education, through *special classes, acceleration* and *enrichment*.

Gillingham method, similar to the Fernald method of teaching reading in that it is a *VAKT* technique, but different in that it emphasizes a highly structured, phonic approach. Several variations of the Gillingham method have been developed.

Gittins Report 1967, 'Primary Education in Wales', report produced by a committee whose members were drawn from the Central Advisory Council for Education (Wales) under the Chairmanship of Professor Charles Gittins. Many of its conclusions and recommendations were similar to those of the *Plowden Report* but the two reports differed chiefly in that the Gittins Report emphasized *inservice training* for teachers, argued for freedom from the school *curriculum* and favoured a fully bilingual education. For children with *learning difficulties* in primary schools the report recommended increased provision for special *units* and classes to be integrated into the main school. It also argued for provision for flexible transfer between ordinary and *special schools*.

glaucoma, abnormal condition of the eye in which a severe rise in the internal pressure seriously affects vision. The common form of glaucoma is only found in late adult life, but rarer forms occur congenitally.

glue ear, form of *otitis media*, fluid in the *middle ear*, often associated with minor infections, colds, etc., and leading to some *hearing impairment*. This is often temporary only, but episodes, which often occur in the first five or six years of life, may hold back learning.

Goodenough Draw-a-Man-Test, see *Draw-a-Man Test*.

grade equivalent, U.S. measure of educational performance, based on attainment of 'grades' in the U.S. school system. In most States children enter Grade 1 at the age of 6+ years and normally progress by one grade each year until they enter the last year of High School, or Grade 12, at age 17+ years. Thus a reading performance of grade equivalent 3.5 is the average performance of children halfway through grade 3, roughly similar to that of 8½–9-year-olds.

graded reader, book for pupils at a particular level of attainment, or *reading age*. Graded readers are usually the component books of a reading series or reading scheme which offers a gradually increasing level of reading difficulty.

graded word reading test, word recognition test in which a child reads aloud a number of increasingly difficult words. The number of words correctly pronounced is usually converted into a reading age. Because they are quick and relatively simple to administer, graded word reading tests are widely used as measures of children's reading performance, though they clearly do not assess important reading skills such as comprehension or fluency.

grand mal, severe *convulsion*, occurring for various reasons, in particular in true *epilepsy*. The patient loses consciousness, falls and goes stiff, and may have difficulty in breathing. Incontinence frequently occurs.

grant-aided residential special schools, Scottish term for residential *special schools* provided by voluntary bodies; known in England and Wales as *non-maintained special schools*. These schools are not under the control of *local education authorities*.

grapheme, one or more written letters used to represent a particular speech sound or *phoneme*; a written symbol.

grapheme-phoneme correspondence, relationship between the written symbol and spoken sound. In languages where this relationship is consistent, reading is easier than in languages where it is not. English is an example of a language in which grapheme-phoneme correspondence is highly irregular: the *grapheme* 'o' corresponds to several different *phonemes* as in ton; tone; not; for example. This inconsistency can lead to considerable difficulty in learning to read. See *initial teaching alphabet*.

Griffiths Mental Development Scale, an extended version (1970) of the *Griffiths Scale of Infant Development*, so that children between the ages of three months and eight years can be assessed. A sixth scale (Practical Reasoning) has been added.

Griffiths Scale of Infant Development, produced by Ruth Griffiths and used over the age-range three months to two years. It has five subscales:
A The Locomotor Scale   D Hand and Eye Development
B The Personal-Social Scale   E Performance
C Hearing and Speech

grommet, small tube placed in the *eardrum* to help a malfunctioning *middle ear* operate more efficiently, so reducing *conductive deafness*.

grooming aids, specially designed implements to assist *physically handicapped* children in managing their grooming and toileting independently; e.g. a rod curved at an angle of 70 degrees, with a standard plastic comb screwed to it, may facilitate hair combing when arm movement is limited.

gross motor skills, skills which involve large muscle activity, e.g. rolling, crawling, walking, running, throwing and jumping.

group dynamics, study of behaviour of groups of people, and of the interaction of members of a group; in particular the study of the development of common perceptions through the sharing of emotions and experiences.

group factor, ability that is said to underlie performance in a group of related skills; broader than an '*s*' factor but not as comprehensive as the '*g*' factor. See *k.m.*; *v.ed.*

group tests, tests which can be administered to a group of children at the same time; the advantages of economy have to be set against the loss of information to be gained from individual contact.

group therapy, treatment in which a group of people with similar problems or needs are brought together to help each other by discussion under the guidance of a skilled but unobtrusive leader, usually a professional *therapist*.

'Guess Who' technique, type of rating procedure used in obtaining children's *assessment* of each other. The children are given a number of brief 'word pictures', and asked to write under each the name of every classmate who might fit the description, e.g. 'this is a nice chap, friendly with everyone,' or 'this one is disagreeable, always picking on others and annoying them'. The procedure is sometimes used in identifying and investigating emotional and behavioural disorders.

H

habit disorders, *behaviour disorder* involving habits, e.g. *enuresis*, sleepwalking food fads.

haemophilia, inherited disorder, in which the blood fails to clot normally. This disease is carried by the female and found only in the male. Haemophilia is characterized by excessive bleeding, both internal and external, from even slight injuries and affects the large joints of the limbs in particular.

halfway house, temporary place of residence, usually run by an institution, with the aim of preparing individuals from the institution to live independently within the community.

halo effect, tendency to be biased in the rating of an individual or group by some irrrelevant characteristic, with the result that the assessor's estimates are consistently too high or too low. Thus it has been suggested that some teachers are biased by pupils' docility, rating obedient pupils more highly for '*intelligence*', for example, and disruptive pupils lower, than either group deserves.

Halsey Report 1972, description of a three year action-research project which took place in four *educational priority areas*, Birmingham, Liverpool, London and the West Riding of Yorkshire.

handedness, preferred use of either the left or right hand. There is some evidence that handedness has a genetic basis, but factors such as the attitude of society to left-handedness, the child's temperament and environment may influence the choice of hand.

handicap, general term for the effect of intellectual, social, emotional or physical disabilities preventing individuals from living a normal life and in particular hindering children from learning in the normal educational environment. The *Handicapped Pupils and School Health Service Regulations, 1945*, listed eleven *categories of handicap*, since amended and now replaced by the general term *special educational needs*. See *disability*.

Handicapped Guides and Scouts, the Guides Association has extension units mainly based in *special schools* and hospitals for *handicapped* girls who can understand the 'Promise'. A postal service is available for any handicapped girl unable to get to a unit and the guide handbook is available in *braille* and large print. The Scout Association publishes a leaflet on how activities may be adjusted to meet the needs of any specific handicap.

Handicapped Pupils and School Health Service Regulations, 1945, defined eleven categories of pupils: *blind, partially sighted*, deaf, *partially deaf, delicate*, diabetic (see *diabetes*), *educationally subnormal, epileptic, maladjusted, physically handicapped* and those with *speech defects* (see *speech difficulty*). Delicate and diabetic children had previously been treated as physically handicapped. Speech defects and *maladjustment* were entirely new categories. The regulations prescribed that blind, deaf, epileptic, physically handicapped pupils and pupils with aphasia must be educated in *special schools*. Children with other disabilities might attend ordinary schools if adequate provision was available for them. See *Warnock Report*.

Handicapped Pupils and Special Schools Regulations, 1959, amended the categories of pupil requiring *special education*, replacing *'partially deaf'* by *'partially hearing'* and deleting the category 'diabetic'. These amended regulations were in force up to 1981. See *Handicapped Pupils and School Health Service Regulations, 1945*.

handicap register, under the *Chronically Sick and Disabled Persons Act, 1970*, the local authority social services committees were obliged to seek out any such persons living in their area and to include them in a handicap register, kept by the social services department. Registration is not a precondition for providing services.

HARC, see *Hester Adrian Research Centre*.

hard neurological sign, firm evidence of organic damage to the brain and/or *central nervous system* gathered from changes in reflexes, sensations, or muscular strength and *co-ordination*.

Hargreaves Report (1984), 'Improving Secondary Schools' report of a committee charged by the ILEA with considering the curriculum and organization of secondary schools, with special reference to underachieving pupils. Its main recommendation for meeting pupils' special needs was that in-class support was a more productive way of offering help than special units and schools, but it also recognized that the different personalities of pupils and teachers might lead to other arrangements having to be made. See *achievement*.

Haringey Project:
(1) early experiment in integrating partially-hearing children, initiated by D.M.C. Dale. Some children were placed in units attached to ordinary schools, while a few were taught in ordinary classes with part-time specialist teaching support;
(2) scheme for helping children learn to read through involving parents in a planned and systematic way; instituted in the London Borough of Haringey. See *paired reading*.

Harris-Goodenough Drawing Test of Psychological Maturity, 1963 revision of the earlier *Goodenough Draw-a-Man Test*, measuring *intelligence* through assessing a child's drawing skills. The child is asked to draw a picture of a man, a woman, and optionally him/herself. The characteristics of the drawings are assessed according to dimensional representation, accuracy of proportion, clothing etc. rather than artistic merit. The average score is then converted to an *intelligence quotient*. See *Draw-a-Man Test*.

Harrison-Stroud Reading Readiness Profiles, U.S. scale, standardized on 6-year-olds, intended to measure whether a child has the skills necessary for starting formal reading lessons. The first five of the six subtests are group tests where the child uses symbols, makes *visual discriminations*, selects an appropriate drawing, makes *auditory discriminations*, uses contextual and auditory cues. In the sixth subtest the child names the upper and lower case letters of the alphabet.

Harris Test of Lateral Dominance, measures of eye, hand and foot *dominance (2)* in children from seven years old upwards.

headpointer, apparatus for typing, using the head. It consists of a headband or cap with an adjustable pointer or wand attached. The typist nods the head to depress the key with the pointer.

Head Start, nationally funded U.S. programme started in the 1960s which originally provided disadvantaged pre-school children with medical, nutritional and social benefits as well as early education to enable them to learn more effectively once they reached school. Early evaluation cast doubt on its effectiveness but more recent work suggests that children paticipating in the Head Start programme derived long-term benefits which could be detected in adolescence. The scope of the programme has since expanded considerably. See *compensatory education, sleeper effect*.

health visitor, state registered nurse with intensive extra training. Their main functions lie in preventive medicine, visiting all homes where there is a child under five years of age, screening and identifying handicap, counselling parents, giving information about health and welfare services, and generally providing informed reassurance and support for families. They are a very important link between families with handicapped children and their schools, doctors etc. The *Warnock Report* suggested that a health visitor could act as a '*Named Person*', i.e. be a point of contact between families with a young handicapped child and all professional authorities concerned with the child's wellbeing.

hearing aid, device to increase hearing efficiency by focusing and/or amplifying sound waves. Aids fall broadly into two main groups, those placed behind the ear to increase bone conduction, so by-passing a damaged *middle ear*, and those inserted into the ear to amplify air-conducted sound.

hearing aid centres, *units* attached to N.H.S. hospitals, in which *audiologists* fit suitable *hearing aids*.

hearing impairment, loss of the ability to hear normally; usually measured in *decibels* (dB). The degree of *hearing loss* is usually categorized as slight — up to 40 dB loss; moderate — 41 to 70 dB loss; severe — 71 to 95 dB loss or greater losses acquired after 18 months; profound — 96 or more dB loss, if present before 18 months of age. There are two main types of hearing impairment, *conductive* and *sensorineural*: the latter is usually a more intractable condition. Temporary conductive hearing loss due to heavy colds, ear infections, blockages, etc. occurs quite often in childhood and can affect educational progress significantly. See *glue ear, otitis media, audiogram* illustration (p. 18).

hearing loss, see *hearing impairment*.

hearing, islands of, See *islands of hearing*.

hearing test, usually an audiometric test to determine the hearing threshold for *pure tones* and/or speech. See *acoustic impedance test*, *pure-tone audiometry*, *speech audiometrey*.

hearing threshold, level (loudness) at which an individual can just perceive a sound. Hearing threshold is measured in *decibels* (dB) on an *audiometer*, and varies according to the *frequency* of the sound.

hemiplegia, paralysis affecting one side of the body. Compare *diplegia, quadriplegia, paraplegia*. See *cerebral palsy*.

hemispheric dominance, or cerebral dominance , control of body movement by one *cerebral hemisphere* rather than the other resulting in the preferred use of left or right limbs, etc. See *cerebral dominance theory*.

heredity, transmission of physical and mental characteristics from parents to offspring by the *genes*. Some conditions requiring *special education* are hereditary, but both sufferers and *carriers* of a disorder can seek *genetic counselling* when considering becoming parents. The role of *heredity* in the development of *intelligence* is a particularly controversial issue. See *eugenics, genetics, chromosomes*.

Her Majesty's Inspectorate, in England, body of about 500 inspectors, (HMIs) based on the *Department of Education and Science* and responsible for the inspection of schools and other educational establishments such as colleges and polytechnics. Inspectors assess course content, teaching methods and working conditions, and act as advisers. They give professional advice to the *DES*, run courses for teachers and prepare some publications. One of the Chief Inspectors (CIs) has particular responsibility for special education. The *Warnock Report* recommended that they should be increasingly involved in monitoring standards of education of the handicapped in *non-maintained special schools* and also in specialist teacher training for teachers of children with severe learning difficulties. Similar functions are carried out by the Inspectorate in Scotland and Wales, whose members are based on the Scottish and Welsh Offices respectively.

Hester Adrian Research Centre, (HARC), centre for research into the psychological, social and educational research into the psychological, social and educational factors that affect the development of mentally handicapped children and adults and into the services provided for them. The centre was established in 1968, at Manchester University. It holds parents' workshops, courses, etc., but cannot help with specific inquiries relating to individual problems. It publishes a wide range of research reports and other material aimed at parents and professionals. Latterly the centre has emphasized work with adults, rather than children.

high-frequency deafness, see *high-tone deafness*.

high-tone deafness, reduced ability to hear high-frequency sounds, particularly the sounds of the consonants and consonant *digraphs*, f, s, z, ch, sh, th. High-tone deafness is a handicapping condition which is easily overlooked and *audiometry* is needed to determine the extent and nature of the *hearing loss*. It is often found in association with athetosis, particularly where this has been caused by neonatal *jaundice*.

higher education, advanced education beyond school. Some institutions, e.g. the *Open University* and Sussex University (which has facilities for the deaf and *physically handicapped*) make special provision for handicapped students. The *Warnock Report* recommended that all universities and polytechnics should develop and publicise policies for the admission of students with disabilities or significant difficulties. See *National Bureau for Handicapped Students* in Appendix A.

hip, congenital dislocation of, condition present at birth, but which can be treated so as to allow the child a normal life.

Holborn Reading Scale, individual test measuring a child's progress in word recognition and comprehension of sentences. The scale consists of 33 sentences graded in order of difficulty and the child's performance is measured as a *reading age*.

Holtzman Inkblot Technique, *personality test* developed from the *Rorschach Inkblots Test*. The subject has to give a single response to each of forty-five cards, which contain a wide variety of inkblot forms. Unlike the Rorschach test, the scoring is objective and it can be given in group format.

homebound, originally a North American term for children who are unable to attend school for reasons such as periods of illness, orthopaedic operations which may involve long periods in plaster, or other handicaps. *Local education authorities* have to make appropriate educational provision for such children, usually through *home tuition*.

home-school liaison teacher, teacher responsible for working with parents of pupils who have special needs and sometimes for maintaining the school's links with other services.

homes, short-stay holiday, parents can obtain information about holidays for handicapped children through their *social worker* or local voluntary organizations.

home tuition, teaching at home by a teacher employed by a *local education authority*, usually up to five half-days a week. Home tuition was originally simply teaching at home, but it has since developed into a co-operative exercise between teacher, child and parents, programmes being planned jointly and parents being helped to teach activities arranged between teacher visits. See *Portage project*.

Honeylands, pioneer family help unit within the Exeter district general hospital paediatric service which helps families with handicapped or chronically sick children or children who are socially disadvantaged. It provides babysitting facilities and short term stays, as well as medical care. There is an infant unit where mothers can stay and learn how to handle their handicapped baby. Educational facilities are available for the chronically sick and daytime activities are co-ordinated by a *play therapist*, the main aim being to return a child to the family and the care of the normal community services.

hospital school, established for education in hospital. Education is the right of every child over five years old whether living at home or in hospital, and under the *Education Act 1944* it may be provided in hospital special schools, maintained by the *local education authority*. The *Warnock Report* recommended that all children entering hospital, for however long or short a duration, should receive some education as soon as possible. It also expressed the wish that, wherever practicable, long-stay children in hospital should attend school in the community.

hostel, residential facility; in particular provided for handicapped school leavers under the *Mental Health Act, 1959*. Local authorities have to provide residential homes and hostels in order to keep school-leavers with severe *learning difficulties* in the community rather than in hospital.

hydrocephalus, also known as water on the brain, enlargement of the skull due to excessive *cerebrospinal fluid,* which if unrelieved, can lead to *severe learning difficulties.* It is often found in association with spina bifida. See *neural tube defects, shunt.*

hydrotherapy, *physiotherapy* in water. It is used to help children with physical handicaps.

hyperactivity, or hyperkinesis, behaviour characterised by poor attention span, chronic distractibility, and excessive restlessness. Some experts restrict the use of the term hyperactivity to describe the behaviour of some children with *epilepsy,* low *IQ* and recognizable neurological problems. In the U.S.A. the term is often used for a behaviour pattern that includes antisocial behaviour, aggression and disobedience. Various possible causes have been identified (recently, lead poisoning has been emphasized). Treatment depends on the cause, but treatment with drugs may have some success in controlling hyperactivity as may the use of the *Feingold Diet,* though this is still a matter of controversy. See *filtering (1).*

hypercalcaemia, inborn disorder in which the child seems unable to process calcium properly, possibly leading to minor but significant *mental retardation.* Treatment with a *diet* low in calcium is helpful but not a cure.

hyperkinesis, see *hyperactivity.*

hypermetropia, see *hyperopia.*

hypernasal, speech through the nose, e.g. as in *cleft-palate* speech.

hyperopia, also hypermetropia, a form of farsightedness, term used for defective vision in which the images of objects are focused behind the *retina,* in effect because the length of the eyeball is too short; the retinal image is therefore blurred. The alternative term, farsightedness, does not mean that a person with this kind of vision necessarily sees distant objects more clearly than a normally sighted person does, merely that such objects are more easily brought to focus on the retina than near ones. Hyperopia, like other refractive errors, is genetically determined. It is corrected by wearing spectacles with convex lenses. Contrast *myopia.* See *eye* illustration (p. 76).

hypertonia, unusually high muscular tension.

hypoglycaemia, low glucose level in the blood. The condition may result in weakness, behavioural changes and if not rapidly treated, uncon-sciousness. There are many minor causes, but the only significant one is a dose of insulin (in a diabetic) not accompanied by sufficient intake of food.

hyponasal, speech characterized by lack of *resonance* in the voice as a result of obstruction in the nose.

hypotonia, decreased muscle tension, affecting posture. Hypertonic muscles are seen in some forms of *cerebral palsy.*

hypothyroidism, see *cretinism.*

hypoxia, see *anoxaemia.*

hysteria, form of *neurosis* characterized by emotional instability and the presence of symptoms with no physical cause; e.g. hysterical paralysis is a paralysis due to psychological causes.

I

id, used by Freud to signify the sum of the instinctual needs, e.g. the needs for drink, food, sexual satisfaction, sleep, warmth, etc. One of the three divisions of the psyche proposed by Freud. See *ego, superego.*

IDDM, *insulin-dependent diabetes mellitus.*

identification:
(1) particularly as used in education, recognition, specifically the recognition of children with special needs, perhaps as a result of *screening;*
(2) particularly as used in *Freudian theory*, a *defence mechanism* by which a child associates him/herself with others in an attempt to feel less threatened or more secure;
(3) particularly as used by some schools of psychoanalysis, a deliberate or subconscious process by which a child incorporates into his/her own personality aspects of the behaviour or *attitudes* of someone admired or loved.

identity crisis, upsurge of doubt during which abilities, aims and values are questioned in an attempt to establish an inner confidence and authority, often accompanied by experiments with different roles. Identity crises often occur in adolescence. For children who are handicapped in any way this can be a particularly testing time.

idioglossia, or idiolalia, private or invented *language*, often so distorted or indistinct as to be incomprehensible.

idiopathic, condition without a cause, as in idiopathic speech, a *speech disorder* for which no cause can be found.

IEP, see *Individualized Education Programme*.

idiot savant, individual of very low general *intelligence* (an idiot was formerly a term for a person with an IQ of less than 20) who nevertheless shows a remarkable ability in a particular area, perhaps in mental arithmetic, remembering dates or playing a musical instrument.

ILEA, See Inner London Education Authority.

Illinois Test of Psycholinguistic Abilities (ITPA), U.S. test which assesses a young child's competence in ten different language skills, e.g. *auditory sequential memory*, vocal encoding, etc. It has been standardized on children aged three to ten years and provides a language age overall, and for each of the different skills. It has been widely used to provide a basis for remedial programmes aimed at improving language performance by training weaknesses revealed by the test. The authors were Kirk and McCarthy.

illiteracy, inability to read and write as well as society expects. Illiteracy is a relative term, defined by the *norms* of the education system: an adult whose reading age was below seven years on U.K. tests would usually be regarded as illiterate there. Concern about the extent of illiteracy prompted the government to launch the adult literacy campaign. See *Adult Literacy Resource Agency, functional literacy, literacy*.

immigrant education, special programmes of education for immigrant children, originally emphasizing English language, communication and *social skills*, taught at *reception centres* and by *peripatetic teachers*. During the 1960s and 1970s many immigrant parents were concerned at the relatively high proportion of their children being placed in special classes and schools for the *educationally subnormal* and *maladjusted*. This was a major influence in establishing the committees which produced the *Rampton Report* and the *Swann Report*. Latterly, emphasis has been placed on teaching initially through home language and culture, stressing the different needs of a multi-ethnic population.

immunisation, process which creates or increases resistance to an infectious disease. See *vaccination, vaccine-damaged*.

impairment, general term for any injury, damage or defect which prevents normal physical or mental functioning, e.g. *strabismus* is a *visual impairment*. Compare *disability, handicap*.

impedance audiometry, see *acoustic impedance test*.

in care, term applied to a child who has been admitted into the care of a local authority, usually under section 2 of the Child Care Act, 1980, or by means of a care order made under section 1 (2) of the *Children and Young Person's Act, 1969*. The right to decide upon a child's placement while in care is normally vested in the local authority.

incidence, relative frequency of an event, e.g. the incidence of *spina bifida* has been estimated as 2 to 3 new cases per 1,000 live births. It is often used as equivalent to prevalence, but should be distinguished from it. Prevalence is used in the sense of frequency of all existing cases, new and old, in a population.

inconsequential behaviour, D. H. Stott's term for the *behaviour* of a child who is very easily distracted and unable to concentrate on any purposeful activity. This sometimes results in the child being wrongly described as unintelligent.

incontinence aids, equipment to help those who suffer from incontinence manage with the problem. They include protective pants, pads, urinary appliances and adapted toilets which in some cases local authorities provide free of charge. Some associations provide practical advice and help for sufferers and their families. See *Disabled Living Foundation* in Appendix A.

incus, one of the three ossicles in the *middle ear*, which resembles an anvil. It transmits sound vibrations from the *malleus* to the *stapes*. See *ear* illustration (p. 66).

Independent Living Movement, U.S. organization set up partly by disabled people and partly by concerned professionals to help severely disabled individuals seek a more fulfilling life for themselves in an able-bodied society. It has been responsible for setting up facilities for university students with severe physical disabilities and also for numerous groups of purpose-built housing units. The Movement has also been responsible for pressing for legislation on accessibility to public buildings and public services, e.g. transport.

Individualized Education Program (IEP), written individual education programme for handicapped children as specified in U.S. *Public Law 94–142*. The programme should include details of the child's present level of educational performance, short-term and long-term aims for the child, any special services needed and the date these will begin. The programme is drawn up by a team of people, including parents; the IEP is paralleled in the U.K. by the *Statement (of special educational need)*.

individualized reading, programme for teaching reading in which each child in a class has a different book and progresses at a separate rate. The teacher provides books of varying degrees of difficulty and covering a variety of subjects. Each child chooses and reads a book until the teacher calls upon the child to read. During this time the teacher will check the number of pages the child has read, question him/her on the contents and meaning of the story, give help where needed and plan suitable follow-up activities. It is a different approach from the use of basic reading scheme for the class, though both approaches are complementary, not alternative.

inductive coupler, electronic device which can be fitted to telephones, enabling users of certain *hearing aids* to tune directly to the telephone, thus cutting out background noise.

ineducable children, obsolete category of children who were excluded from the education system by the *Education Act,1944*, which described them as having 'a disability of mind of such a nature and to such an extent as to make them incapable of receiving education at school'. In England and Wales, these children were the responsibility of the local health authority until 1971, when the legislation following the Education Act, 1970, required that all children should be educated. See *learning difficulties, severe, Education (Mentally Handicapped Children) (Scotland) Act, 1974, special care school*.

infant mortality rate, the average number of infants in every thousand live births who die before they are a year old.

infantile paralysis, see *poliomyelitis*.

inferiority complex, feelings of inferiority and inadequacy arising from the conflict between the urge to achieve recognition through self-expression and accomplishment and the fear of hurt or frustration experienced in the past in similar situations. The feelings of inferiority are wholly or partly unconscious and may give rise to aggressive, boastful behaviour in compensation. Some children who are *handicapped* may feel unable to cope with the situations of everyday life and develop an inferiority complex. The term, which was introduced by Adler, is now used loosely to mean a sense of inadequacy.

informal reading inventory (IRI), analysis of a child's reading level, based on observation of performance. The child reads aloud a series of paragraphs and answers questions about these. The teacher is able to assess the child's word recognition and comprehension, while at the same time observing him/her. The procedure is informal and not *norm-referenced*. The child is placed at one of three levels: independent (can read the material for pleasure); instructional (needs some help); frustration (material too difficult).

information handbook, publication providing details of *special education* within an area which is produced by some *local education authorities*. The

Warnock Report recommended that each area should produce a handbook for parents containing details of the types of special education it provides, as well as related services, together with information about the local activities of voluntary organizations and societies.

initial blends, first (usually first two) sounds of a word, combined. Thus the first two sounds of 'sting', 's' and 't' are blended to make 'st'. The initial blend 'st' begins many words; once these are recognized and learnt, children's reading skills improve. Learning initial blends is an aspect of the *phonic* method of teaching reading.

initial teaching alphabet (i.t.a.), an early version of which was known as Augmented Roman (AR), medium for reading and writing devised by Sir James Pitman. Although less widely used than in the 1960s it is claimed to be very helpful, especially with children who are experiencing difficulties in learning to read. These difficulties are often caused by the vagaries of traditional English spelling, where 26 letters inconsistently represent some 44 sounds. I.t.a. keeps 24 of the traditional small ('lower case') letters, dropping 'x' and 'q', and adds 20 new symbols. Each of these 44 *graphemes* consistently represents only one of the 44 sounds. It is a system for use in the initial stages of learning to read and is phased out when children are ready to change to normal spelling, or *t.o.*

injury, non-accidental, see *battered baby syndrome*.

in loco parentis, legal term, (from the Latin), which means 'in place of the parent'. It is applied to teachers, who are expected to behave as responsible parents when pupils are in their care.

inner ear or internal ear, organ which transmits sound vibrations from the *middle ear*, through the *semi-circular canals* changing them into electrical energy in the *cochlea* to permit hearing.

Inner London Education Authority, (ILEA) the largest local education authority in the U.K., with responsibility for the education of children from a wide variety of ethnic and social backgrounds. (According to the *Hargreaves Report*, one third of ILEA pupils qualify for free meals, 26% live in one-parent families and they speak 147 different languages.) In recent years the ILEA has produced three major reports on education, one of which, the *Fish Report*, dealt with special education. See also *Hargreaves Report, Thomas Report, 1985.*

insecurity, feelings of *anxiety* linked to lack of confidence or uncertainty. Some children's behavioural problems may be traced to a deep and continuing sense of insecurity, perhaps caused by their uncertainty about their parents' affections towards them

In-Service Education of Teachers (INSET), provision of courses for practising teachers to enable them to update their skills and be aware of new techniques and developments in education. Special education is one of the areas to which priority has been attached by the *Department of Education and Science*.

INSET, see In-Service Education of Teachers.

insight:
(1) ability rapidly to understand and solve a problem, often found in *gifted children*;
(2) term used in *psychotherapy* to describe an individual's ability to understand and accept the reasons for feelings and behaviour.

Inspectors of Special Education, see *Her Majesty's Inspectorate*.

institutionalization, process whereby an individual's development may be damaged as a result of placement in a large organization such as a hospital or orphanage, for example. Early studies of institutionalized children revealed a higher incidence of behaviour problems such as unforthcomingness, restlessness and distractibility, associated with lack of stimulation and individual loving care and attention. Present policy emphasizes placing children for fostering within families.

institutionalized personality, child or adult who has spent much of his/her life in a residential institution such as a hospital, mental home, *community home* etc. and who has adopted the pattern of *behaviour* and values peculiar to the institution. Such individuals experience great difficulty in adapting to the conditions of life in the outside world and in developing an independent life style.

Instrumental Enrichment, FIE, Feuerstein Instrumental Enrichment, a programme of more than 500 pencil and paper exercises, divided into 15 sections, or 'instruments', designed by R. Feuerstein. The programme is based on the author's belief (and experience of working with immigrants to Israel) that many children with learning difficulties function at a low level because they have never learnt how to learn. The exercises of the instrumental enrichment programme are designed to remedy this. Essentially, they require the learner to carry out a wide variety of intellectual exercises (e.g. finding patterns) in content-free material (e.g. dots) to try to modify thinking skills. Instrumental Enrichment is not seen as a substitute for, but a supplement to normal school lessons. Although it can be used in its entirety, selected instruments can be used to target particular weaknesses in a pupil's thinking. These are revealed by the *Learning Potential Assessment Device*.

insulin shock, reaction suffered by diabetics when they have had too much insulin, insufficient food or excessive exercise. It is characterized by feelings of hunger, trembling, perspiration and muscular contractions. Diabetics are taught to recognize the symptoms which, in the early stages, may be relieved by eating sugar to increase the glucose level of the blood; if uncorrected the shock condition can lead to *convulsion, coma* (sometimes known as hypoglycaemic coma) and death.

integration:

(1) educating handicapped and other children together as part of the general principle that where possible the handicapped should share the same opportunities as the rest of society. The *Education Act, 1981*, based on the recommendations of the *Warnock Report*, placed a duty upon *LEAs* to ensure that children with special needs should be educated as far as possible in their local primary and secondary schools. The *Warnock Report* distinguished three main kinds of integration:

(i) locational, where children with special needs are educated on the same site as others, but in separate *units* or schools, and hence have little contact;

(ii) social, where regular social interchange occurs, for example at mealtimes, in play-areas and out-of-school activities, although formal education is separate;

(iii) functional, where children with special needs attend regular classes and participate in other activities. The curriculum is shared.

The report emphasized that if integration was to be successful it had to be 'patiently nurtured' and positive *discrimination* (3) made in favour of children with special needs.

The *Education Act, 1981* placed a duty on *local education authorities* to ensure that children with special educational needs were educated in their local primary and secondary schools provided that the parents were in agreement, that it was practicable, that it was educationally efficient, and that it was not unreasonably expensive. See *mainstreaming, normalization*.

(2) term used to describe the way in which an immigrant group adapts to the customs and behaviour of its adopted country.

integrated day, school day where the traditional timetabling for the allocation of set subjects has been replaced by a more flexible approach to teaching and learning. The children are involved in activities such as project work, which may extend over a long period. The principle behind the integrated day is that each child should be treated as an individual: thus it can be a particularly appropriate teaching strategy for children with *learning difficulties*.

intelligence, the ability to learn, to solve problems and deal with new situations. Some believe that intelligence is largely inherited and varies little throughout life: others believe that intelligence is heavily influenced by the child's experiences. All accept that heredity and environment both play a part in determining intelligence; there has been controversy over the relative contribution of each and also over whether it is sensible or helpful to attempt to allocate relative contributions. There has also been controversy over the wisdom of continuing to use a term which, some believe, misrepresents through oversimplifying complex aspects of human development.

intelligence quotient (IQ), index of a person's *intelligence*, originally defined as the ratio of *mental age* to *chronological age*, multiplied by 100. Nowadays a different principle is usually used: an intelligence quotient now indicates the extent to which an individual performance on a particular *intelligence test* differs from that of others of the same chronological age. An IQ of 100 represents *average* performance; on most tests about two-thirds of scores lie between IQ 85 and IQ 115.

intelligence test, standardized method of measuring intelligence, widely used by teachers and psychologists in assessing children's special needs. Some tests measure verbal intelligence or non-verbal intelligence only; nearly all tests are designed for specified age-groups and are norm-referenced. Performance is usually represented by an *intelligence quotient*. Intelligence tests are controversial instruments and their use in assessing children's special needs has been opposed in some quarters, perhaps most strongly in parts of the U.S.A. There are various reasons for this — as examples the unskilled use of an intelligence quotient may lead to labelling; the use of inappropriate tests, as in the assessment of children from a different cultural background from those for whom a test was intended, can lead to bad decisions. Intelligence tests, more than most procedures, need to be used sensitively and their results interpreted with care.

interference, sometimes called 'negative transfer', impaired ability to remember a word, fact or skill because of something else that has been learned. An example is mother-tongue interference, occurring in ethnic minority children, when words and ideas of the native culture may make it difficult to learn English.

Intermediate Treatment (IT), requirement inserted into a supervision order made under the *Children and Young Person's Act, 1969*, through which the juvenile can be required to take part in a programme of activities, which may include a number of days on a residential course. Intermediate Treatment is a half-way house between removing a young person from his/her family or community and leaving him/her in an unchanged environment.

International Year of the Disabled, the calendar year 1981, designated by many governments throughout the world as a period during which special efforts were to be made to focus the public's attention on the difficulties and frustrations experienced by disabled people in their attempts to live a normal life in the community. To improve inadequate facilities for disabled people, governments set aside additional funds and voluntary organizations and individuals raised money for many special projects.

interval reinforcement, technique used in *behaviour modification*; suitable behaviour is rewarded after periods of time. When the time intervals are equal, as when a child is rewarded after every five minutes spent on a task, the procedure is called fixed interval reinforcement: when the intervals are varied, so that the child will not know when to expect a reward, the procedure is called variable interval reinforcement. The choice of procedure depends on considerations such as practicability, the child's personality characteristics, etc. Contrast *ratio reinforcement*.

intra-uterine development, growth of the foetus in the uterus between conception and birth, a most important period. Normal inter-uterine development is promoted by good health and good *diet* in the mother but abnormalities may arise from maternal infection (such as *rubella*), maternal *smoking*, and drinking alcohol or maternal *diabetes*, for example.

inverse square law, principle of special significance in sight and hearing: when a stimulus reaches a sense receptor, e.g. the eye or ear, from a distance, its intensity varies inversely as the square of the distance between the source of the stimulus and the receptor, e.g. sound heard from a distance of two feet will be nine times as loud as the same sound heard from a distance of six feet. ($6/2 = 3: 3^2 = 9$)

IQ, see *intelligence quotient*.

Irlen lens, tinted non-refracting lens, claimed to alleviate some reading difficulties. Irlen believes that in some persons the retina is unduly sensitive to light of certain colours, resulting in visual distortions, especially apparent with the high black and white contrast of print. Irlen claims that these distortions are reduced by using lenses that filter out those particular colours to which a person is sensitive and that this improves reading performance. The procedure is still being validated, but it is worth noting that a sensitive retina has now been proposed as one cause of *dyslexia* and that this is not measured in routine eye examinations. Covering the page with a coloured overlay is said to be as effective as using a lens.

Ishihara (or Ishihari) Colour Test, used to identify and measure *colour blindness*. It consists of a series of plates on which are printed numerous dots in different colours and patterns. People with normal colour vision can identify a particular number or pattern on the plates, while those with defective colour vision are unable to do so, or sometimes see a different number or pattern.

islands of hearing, hearing in children who are deaf across most of the frequency range but have some hearing at particular points.

Isle of Wight Survey, series of enquiries carried out in 1964 and 1965 into the education, health and behaviour of 9–12-year-old children living on the Isle of Wight, together with a more intensive study of the health of children in the whole of the then compulsory school age range, 5–15 years. The main objective of the study was to discover the full picture of three types of handicap among the children;
(1) intellectual or educational *retardation*;
(2) *emotional and behavioural disorders*;
(3) *chronic* or recurrent physical disorders, including neurological conditions.
Its main conclusion was that, in the child population studied, which was somewhat above *average* in *intelligence* and standards of living, one child in six had a *chronic* handicap of moderate or severe intensity. The conclusions of the study were extremely valuable in helping to frame policy for the education of children with *special educational needs*.

isolate, loner, one who makes no relationship with members of his/her social group and who is, in turn, not chosen as a friend by any of them. The term is used in *sociometry*. (See illustration on p. 184).

isolation booth, small room or area, large enough to accommodate a small group without crowding, sometimes used for teaching brain damaged or emotionally disturbed children who have *learning difficulties*. In an attempt to prevent the pupils from being distracted, furniture is sparse and simple and each pupil has a given working area, which may be divided off by screens, and an individual learning programme.

IT, see *intermediate treatment*.

i.t.a., see *initial teaching alphabet*.

item, name given to each question or problem in a *standardized test*.

item bank, large collection of test questions or problems, in a particular subject area or at a particular level, which is constantly being added to and from which can be drawn fresh combinations of items to make up new tests.

itinerant teacher, term used in the U.S.A. (and elsewhere) for *peripatetic teacher*.

ITPA, see *Illinois Test of Psycholinguistic Abilities*.

J

Jacksonian epilepsy/fit/seizure, focal *seizure* affecting first described by Hughlings Jackson, a British *neurologist*. Typically, it begins with twitching of one part of an extremity, e.g. the toes on one foot, or the side of the face, and spreads progressively, first to other muscles on the same side, usually without loss of consciousness.

Jacobson method of progressive relaxation, method of teaching a child how consciously to reduce excess muscular tension as an aid to developing good muscle synchronization and emotional control, developed by E. Jacobson. The child is first taught how to become fully aware of excess tension and then how to reduce it by focusing full attention on relaxing it; the main techniques used are relaxation through fantasy and muscle tension release exercises.

jaundice, condition in which the blood contains too much bilirubin (a brownish yellow bile pigment) which passes into the tissues, giving rise to the characteristic yellowing of the skin and whites of the eyes. It has three main causes: excessive breakdown of the red blood cells, liver disease and blockage of the bile duct. In new-born babies severe jaundice (usually arising as a result of maternal-foetal blood group incompatibility) may lead to a form of brain-damage known as *kernicterus*. See *Rh factor* and *erythroblastosis foetalis*.

Jay Report 1979, Report of the Committee of Enquiry into Mental Handicap and Nursing Care. The Committee recommended that all mentally handicapped people should live in the community, receiving help and support from professional services. It also proposed a common Training Certificate in Social Service. This arrangement was intended to replace the existing *mental handicap* nurse training, but the proposal was rejected by the government. In the 1981 Green Paper on *mental handicap* and *community care* a policy statement was made that no children would be admitted into *hospitals* for mental handicap and those already there would move into community-based homes wherever possible.

Jesness inventory, designed not only to provide a basis for distinguishing between delinquents and non-delinquents, but also to offer a profile of social behaviour in 8–18-year-olds. It consists of 155 true/false questions which explore reactions to a wide range of situations. The inventory was devised by Dr. Carl F. Jesness in the U.S.A. but has been adapted for use elsewhere, including the U.K.

'Jim's People', language kit designed for teaching communication and *language skills* Developed from work carried out at the *Hester Adrian Research Centre* in conjunction with teachers, it was a forerunner in the field of language programmes for children with severe learning difficulties. The graded teaching materials are now used more generally with children with communication difficulties.

John Tracy Clinic, associated with the University of Southern California, Los Angeles, organizes correspondence courses for the guidance of parents and families of pre-school deaf children, to which those living outside the U.S. may subscribe. The clinic stresses the role of the parents in helping the child.

Joint Commission on International Aspects of Mental Retardation, commission formed by two international organizations concerned with the welfare of handicapped people, viz. the International League of Societies for the Mentally Handicapped and the International Association for the Scientific Study of Mental Deficiency; the commission has consultative status with the *World Health Organization*.

joint consultative committees, committees set up by area (now district) health authorities and local authorities under the National Health Service Acts to advise the health, education and social services on the planning, provision and co-ordination of arrangements in their areas, especially in fields of activity where the services have overlapping responsibilities, e.g. school health. The *Warnock Report* considered that these committees are in a key position to co-ordinate and develop services for children and young people with special needs; it recommended that their influence in this field should be increased.

Joseph P. Kennedy Jr. Foundation, U.S. foundation which makes international awards for research, leadership and service in the field of *mental retardation*.

jumbulance, purpose-built and specially equipped bus provided by Across Trust for severely *handicapped* and chronically sick individuals to travel to Lourdes, as well as on tours of the U.K. and Europe; about half of their 22 passengers are qualified voluntary helpers. Across Trust also hires its jumbulances to other organizations.

Junior Multi-Disabled Games, indoor and outdoor sports and track events, held each summer at Stoke Mandeville by the *British Sports*

Association for the Disabled (see Appendix) on behalf of affiliated organizations. They are open to children aged 10–16 years whatever their *disability*.

junior occupational centre, institution in Scotland, controlled by the *local education authority* and staffed mainly by instructors, which, from 1947 – 1975 was responsible for the care and training of those severely mentally retarded children who were deemed to be 'ineducable but trainable'. With the implementation of the *Education (Mentally Handicapped Children) (Scotland) Act, 1974*, these centres were renamed schools; moreover, as a result of this Act, children who had been previously described as 'ineducable and untrainable' came within the full scope of the education service. Compare with *junior training centre* and *adult training centre*. See *educationally subnormal*.

junior training centre, centre administered by the local health authority, which cared for the majority of severely mentally retarded *(ESN(S))* children prior to 1971. Children in these centres had been deemed unsuitable for education at school and excluded from the education system. Criticism of these arrangements led to the *Education (Handicapped Children) Act, 1970*, which transferred responsibility for junior training centres from the Health authorities to the Education authorities. The junior training centres were designated *special schools* and all mentally retarded children came within the scope of the education system. Compare with *junior occupational centre* and *adult training centre*. See *educationally subnormal*.

juvenile court, court consisting of local magistrates, appointed to the juvenile court panel as especially qualified to deal with proceedings involving juveniles. These include care proceedings and criminal proceedings between the ages of ten and seventeen years. The court procedure is intended to be informal and suited to children's needs and the public are excluded. In Scotland most of the functions of the juvenile court have been replaced by children's panels. See *care order, place of safety order, Intermediate Treatment*.

juvenile delinquency, term for the criminal behaviour of a juvenile, but often used loosely to include general *anti-social behaviour*.

juvenile liaison scheme, scheme introduced by some police authorities in the early 1960s, with the aim of identifying and cautioning young first offenders without involving the *juvenile court*; it involves close liaison between police, parents, teachers and *social workers*.

K

k, symbol used by factor analysts for spatial abilities, i.e. competence at manipulating two-and three-dimensional shapes. The factor was first extracted by El Koussy.

Kanner's syndrome, see *autism*.

KDK — Oseretsky Test, modified form of the *Oseretsky Test of Motor Proficiency*, introduced by Kershner and Dusewicz for use with *mentally retarded* children.

Kelvin Spelling Test, Scottish *standardized test* of spelling.

keratitis, inflammation of the *cornea*.

kernicterus, damage caused by *jaundice*, encountered chiefly in new-born infants whose blood is not compatible with that of the mother. It can be prevented by exchange blood transfusions in the first two days after birth, but if untreated may lead to athetosis, *deafness* and possibly some degree of *mental retardation*. See *Rh. factor* and *erythroblastosis foetalis*

key words, the most frequently used words. Two hundred key words are said to comprise half to three-quarters of the running words occurring in everyday reading matter. these are usually the words which children learn first when learning to read. Various games and activities can be devised, e.g. using *flashcards* — to provide practice with them.

kinaesthesis, sense of position and movement of the body, derived through nerves from the muscles, joints and tendons.

kinaesthetic method, general term for teaching techniques which use *kinaesthesis* and kinaesthetic *feedback (3)* to supplement and reinforce other sensory stimuli. This method is used some reading approaches, e.g. the *VAKT method*, in which kinaesthetic feedback from tracing the shape of the letters of the word to be learnt reinforces impressions of the word gained from other senses.

kleptomania, a persistent and obsessive impulse to steal which does not arise from the monetary or practical value of the articles. Treatment usually consists of *psychotherapy* to uncover the underlying *emotional disorder*.

k.m., symbol for the spatial-mechanical category of abilities, one of the two major groupings or group factors into which intellectual abilities are usually divided. It comprises abilities such as manipulating shapes, handling practical problems etc. The other major group factor is *v.ed.*

knee-jerk reflex, or patellar reflex, the sudden kicking movement following a sharp tap just below the kneecap of a relaxed leg. A weak or over-brisk reflex is one indication of possible damage to the *nervous system*.

Knox Cube Test, or cube imitation test, performance test of immediate *memory span* which requires the child to repeat a pattern of taps on a set of wooden cubes. The test has been used in research into the the causes of *dyslexia* and is held to be of some use in predicting later *reading comprehension*.

kwashiorkor, form of malnutrition most commonly caused by dietary deficiency and found chiefly in tropical and sub-tropical regions. It is primarily a children's disease which sets in after weaning and is associated with severe *learning difficulties*.

kyphoscoliosis, *deformity* of the spine in which there is both *kyphosis* and *scoliosis*, i.e. humpback and lateral curvature.

kyphosis (humpback), curvature of the spine in which the vertebrae project outwards forming a hump, often associated with *spina bifida*.

L

labelling, practice of categorizing individuals, e.g. as mentally handicapped, spoilt, spastic, mischief-makers, etc. and by extension attributing to them all the characteristics of that group, regardless of evidence. Many sociologists believe that labelling can cause *stigma* and lead to inappropriate education; moreover the label may influence a child's behaviour to fit the category. The effect of labelling was one of the reasons leading to the *Warnock Report* recommending the abolition of statutory *categories of handicap*, a recommendation implemented in the *Education Act, 1981*.

labyrinth, *inner ear*, containing the organs of balance and hearing.

labyrinthine righting reflex, one of many *reflexes* present in young infants enabling the child to lift the head up when in the prone position (at about 1–2 months) and when in the supine position later. Its presence or absence is noted in examinations of motor development in infancy.

Ladybird Keyword Scheme, reading scheme which makes heavy use of *keywords*.

lallation, repetition of simple sounds, such as da-da-da-da, which in young children may continue for hours. This stage in speech is based on the *ear-voice reflex* and is important in the assessment of *language development*.

lalling, *speech defect* in which difficult-to-pronounce consonants, e.g. 'r' are given an easier-to-pronounce sound; e.g. 'l' or 'w' 'pretty red rose' is pronounced as 'plitty led lose' or 'robin' as 'wobin'. Lalling occurs in all young children when first learning to talk, but usually disappears by the age of five years or so. Compare *lisping*.

LAMP project, Low Academic Motivation Project, science course sponsored by the Association for Science Education and designed for secondary school pupils who lack the motivation or ability to profit from the usual science curriculum.

language, system of words, symbols and gestures and the various ways in which they are combined, which enables an individual to interpret experiences and communicate with others. (But there are many other ways of defining language.) As communication is of vital importance in the development and education of all children, special education emphasizes acquiring adequate language skills. This is not only to help with achievement in school subjects, but also to meet the less obvious but just as important aims of gaining competence in social situations and in expressing emotions. See *expressive language, receptive language*.

language bifurcation, inadequate learning of both *languages* in a child who is *bilingual*.

language code, term used by Basil Bernstein to denote the type of *language* used by particular groups of people. He identified a 'restricted code' (which he had earlier called 'public language') consisting of short, simple utterances, often ambiguous and heavily dependent on their context, and an 'elaborated code' (which he had earlier called *'formal language'*) involving a more extensive logical and explicit language pattern. Bernstein suggested that working-class children are brought up to hear and use a restricted code, whereas middle-class children absorb both codes and thus have greater opportunities for intellectual development.

language development, growth of a child's skill in using his/her native *language*: how far this is innate or acquired is a moot point. The term is often restricted to the fundamental skills of listening, speaking, reading and writing, but is also extended to cover the growth of more specific language skills, e.g. the development of correct grammatical usages. Normal language development includes frequent repetition of sounds at 6–9 months of age; speaking a handful of recognizable words at about 15 months; using 50 or more recognisable words and forming simple sentences at about 2 years or so; asking frequent questions, listening to stories and developing more speech fluency between two and five years; recognising a small number of familiar words in print and reading simple material from about 6 years onwards — but individual children do vary very considerably in the rate at which they acquire language skills and their language development can fluctuate markedly. Writing is the last fundamental *language skill* to be acquired. See, for example, *Reynell Development Language Scales*.

language disorders, wide range of difficulties in the understanding and use of language. They can be broadly divided by cause into:
(1) organic disorders, namely those caused by physical or neurological factors as in the case of *cleft palate*, or defects of hearing;
(2) functional disorders, namely those where no observable abnormality of structure underlies the problem, as in the case of *stuttering* and some other defects of *articulation*. Particular *language* problems also occur in children with specific conditions, such as *autism*.
Note that 'language disorders' does not describe disorders of speech alone: dyslexia can be described as a language disorder, usually functional. Estimates of the prevalence of language disorders in children vary widely, depending on the criteria used. It has been suggested that about ten per cent of children show language problems sufficiently serious to worry them, their teachers and parents. In any group of children with special needs this figure is likely to be substantially higher.

language experience, activities involving the use of spoken or written *language* which help a child to develop his/her *language skills*. This experience can be greatly enriched by parents and teachers in encouraging or stimulating activities such as talk, play, singing, acting, story-telling and reading. These activities extend a child's range of vocabulary, patterns of sentence structure, powers of comprehension and language development generally, including forming a basis for reading. See, for example, *Derbyshire Language Scheme*.

language experience method, widely-used approach to learning to read. Children produce sentences describing their own experiences in their own language. Their teacher writes the sentences for the child, who is thus helped to construct a personal 'reading book', often illustrated with drawings, cut-outs, etc.

language laboratory, classroom for *language* teaching, where each pupil sits in a separate booth with its own tape-recorder and headphones and listens to pre-recorded material, comparing his/her own repetitions and responses with the original and working at his/her own pace. The teacher, at the central monitoring console, can listen to the efforts of any individual pupil and help without the rest of the class hearing, which avoids embarrassing a self-conscious pupil. A language laboratory is useful for the identification of weaknesses, the practice of speech patterns and the development of listening and comprehension skills.

Language Master, apparatus incorporating pre-recorded tapes used as an aid to *language* learning: when a card bearing a word and a picture is inserted into the machine, the word is spoken by the voice on the tape, so that the pupil sees the picture and the printed word and hears the word at the same time. Materials are available for teaching *language skills* generally or reading skills in particular to children with *special education needs*.

language skills, various abilities which enable a child to understand, use and enjoy *language*. They may be divided into the *decoding* (or receptive) skills, e.g. listening and reading, and the *encoding* (or expressive) skills, e.g. speaking and writing. They normally develop in the following order, though with some overlapping: listening, speaking, reading and writing.

language therapist, see *speech therapist*.

Language Through Reading, reading scheme for five- to nine-year olds with severe specific speech and language disorders. The scheme is designed to be compatible with the *LARSP* programme and was produced at the *John Horniman school*. (See Appendix A).

language unit, special provision for children with *language disorders*, including *speech difficulties*. Most are attached to ordinary or special schools, catering usually for pupils of primary school age.

large print, (or large type) books, reading material printed in letters about twice the size of normal print, for pupils with *visual handicaps* in particular. Materials in larger print than usual are also of great benefit to all children at the initial and very early stages of learning to read.

LARSP, *L*anguage *A*ssessment, *R*emediation and *S*creening *P*rocedure, method of analysing language disorders, in particular disorders of grammar, in order to suggest suitable programmes for treatment. It is widely used by *speech therapists* and has also been adapted for use by teachers.

larynx, organ of voice situated at the entrance to the windpipe at the front of the neck. It is enclosed by cartilages operated by a series of muscles which provide the complex movements essential for the production of speech. Disorders of the larynx can affect speech.

latch key children, children who return home from school to an empty house, usually because their parents are at work. Such children may suffer more from neglect or problems of adjustment than children who are supervised on their return home from school. Many single parent families are in this situation and in some areas a voluntary organisation, The National Out-of-School Alliance (see Appendix A) has set up schemes to provide after-school activities for this group of children.

late developer, individual who achieves higher standards later in life than appeared likely earlier.

latency period, stage in *Freudian theory of psycho-sexual development* describing the period of a child's development between about 6 years of age to *adolescence*: active sexuality was assumed to be held in suspension.

laterality, preference for using the right or left side of the body. The development of laterality and *directionality* enable the child to acquire an awareness of his/her body which is essential for *co-ordinated* activities. Children who appear to be slow in gaining a sense of laterality may be given specific training to encourage its development, though not everyone advocates this. See *cross laterality, directionality, dominance*.

Laurence-Moon-Biedl syndrome, hereditary condition, occuring in both girls and boys, in families usually previously unaware of it. There is *obesity*, some *mental retardation*, usually extra fingers and a steadily progressing retinal deterioration leading to severe *visual handicap*.

Laws, see under specific Act, e.g. *Education Act, 1981, Children's Act, 1970*, etc.

Lawther Report 1980, 'Lead and Health' report of the D.H.S.S. Working Party on lead in the environment. A large proportion of the report is concerned with the damaging effects of lead on the behaviour, *intelligence* and *attainment* of children. The report was criticised for using a concept of 'safe' blood-lead levels in children and generally underestimating the size of the problem of lead pollution. In the same year a review of contemporary lead pollution entitled 'Lead or Health' was published by the Conservation Society. It concluded that many U.K. children (in common with those in many other countries) are now suffering from an epidemic of low-grade *lead poisoning*.

LEA, see *local education authority*.

lead poisoning, toxic condition caused by the ingestion or inhalation of lead from petrol exhaust fumes, industrial emissions, lead rich soil in old lead mining areas, lead paint and cosmetics, lead-glazed pottery and polluted tap water. The body has no natural means of eliminating lead so small amounts are stored in the bone. Excessive levels of lead interfere with normal cell function and in severe cases may cause convulsions, coma and other serious symptoms. The foetus is most at risk since it readily absorbs lead from its mother and there is little evidence as to what level of maternal lead may be regarded as safe for the unborn child. Low level lead poisoning does not produce overt symptoms of illness but may be the cause of *intelligence* deficits, ranging from a few IQ points to serious *mental retardation* and/or *behavioural disorders*, such as *hyperactivity*. See *Lawther Report*.

learning difficulty, term used to describe a wide range of problems in acquiring new skills, most particularly in school. The term is used in the *Education Act 1981* to describe children with *special educational needs* — (children who do not learn as easily as most other children in the same age group whether through the presence of a physical disability or not). This followed an earlier proposal in the *Warnock Report* to introduce the term, largely to replace the *'educationally sub-normal'* category of handicap. The intention behind the change was to emphasize educational needs, not handicaps. Three levels of *learning difficulty* are recognized; mild, moderate and severe. A learning difficulty used to be seen as a child-centred problem. It is now more commonly recognized as a mismatch between the demands of the school and the skills of the child, i.e. it implicates the curriculum.

learning difficulty, mild, low *attainment* at school, usually managed by the school staff itself. A 'mainstream with support' *curriculum* is usually appropriate.

learning difficulty, moderate, noticeably lower *attainment* than mild learning difficulties, often associated with adverse social and environmental conditions, and usually needing advice from outside specialists over the appropriate programmes to be followed at school. A 'modified' *curriculum* best describes these programmes.

learning difficulty, severe, generally very acute problems in learning, not only resulting in very low *attainment* at school but often characterized by slow development of speech and *social skills* so enabling children with severe learning difficulties to be identified in the pre-school stage. Severe learning difficulties are often associated with organic or neurological damage. Many such children need to continue to learn until well beyond minimum school leaving age. Careful *assessment* by a team of specialists is usually needed in order to suggest the most suitable programmes to be followed both in and out of school. A developmental *curriculum* is usually needed.

learning difficulty, specific, difficulty in learning in one specific area, while learning successfully otherwise. Thus dyslexia has been described as a specific reading difficulty. See *Tizard Report*.

learning disabled, U.S. term for individuals who for a variety of reasons fail to learn under normal circumstances.

learning disability:
(1) in the U.S. an umbrella term usually intended to describe children with disorders in *language development* and communication skills generally, but excluding children whose learning problems are primarily due to hearing, vision or motor impairment, emotional difficulties, cultural disadvantage or general mental retardation. It thus includes such conditions as *dyslexia, minimal brain damage, perceptual disorders*, etc;
(2) sometimes, also in the U.S., used more broadly to include any child who is not achieving satisfactorily, irrespective of the presence of intellectual retardation, emotional difficulties, etc.

learning plateau, period of consolidation in the acquisition of a skill, when additional teaching or practice does not produce measurable improvement.

Learning Potential Assessment Device (LPAD), way of examining children's thinking, by assessing how they learn and solve problems. It was constructed by R. Feuerstein and based on a theory of 'cognitive modifiability', with considerable application to understanding *learning difficulties*. The LPAD can be contrasted with orthodox intelligence tests: in essence it is said that the former emphasizes *how* a child learns, the latter *what* he has learnt. The LPAD is not intended to produce a 'single', *norm-referenced* score (as an *IQ*, for example) but information on thinking processes that can be linked to methods of remedying weakness through Instrumental Enrichment.

learning theory, explanation of the process and development of learning. Psychologists from different schools have formulated theories which in their different ways have influenced educational practice generally. They also help us to see how learning and behaviour difficulties might arise and might be helped. Thus ideas from Piaget have been widely used in helping children with *learning difficulties* acquire deeper understandings and ideas from Skinner have been widely used in designing programs aimed at changing behaviour.

least restrictive environment, U.S. concept which was expressed by the courts in the early 1970s and included in the provisions of *Public Law 94–142*. It states that handicapped children shall be educated in that environment which is most appropriate to their individual needs and which places the least restrictions upon their capabilities. This means that the children shall have as normal an education as possible including the opportunity of being educated in the ordinary school where this is 'least restrictive' for the child's overall development. The concept is central to the U.S. approach to *mainstreaming,* which has influenced parallel developments in the U.K. See *Integration.*

left-eyedness, natural *dominance* of the left over the right eye, present in about a third of the population. See *cross laterality.*

left-footedness, preferred use of the left foot. See *dominance (2).*

left-handedness, preferred use of the left hand. Fewer girls than boys are left-handed and the incidence in the general population is approximately one in ten, though higher in children with *learning difficulties.* Ball-point pens avoid the need for specially-cut nibs, which were used to avoid scratching. It was once thought advisable for teachers to attempt to retrain left-handed children to write with their right hand in order to avoid smudging as the writing hand moves across the page. Today, however, attitudes to left-handedness are more tolerant and guidance over writing position, etc., helps to ease this difficulty.

left hemisphere, the *cerebral hemisphere* which controls movements on the right side of the body. It usually contains the areas that control speech. See *Broca's, Wernicke's area,* brain illustration (p. 28).

left-right progression, left-to-right movement of the eyes in reading. When children begin to read they must learn to direct their eyes from left to right along the line of print. Some children have difficulty with the left-to-right sequence and may need help in developing their sense of *directionality* in order to read fluently.

Legg-Calve-Perthes disease, see *Perthes disease.*

Leiter International Performance Scale (LIPS), *performance test* of intellectual development developed from research with retarded children. Since instructions, either verbal or mime, have almost been eliminated, the test can be used with children with various handicaps. The items include such tasks as matching colours, forms and pictures, copying block designs, completing pictures and finding similarities. The age range originally covered was from two to eighteen years. The Grace Arthur revision was designed for children between the ages of four and eight and a later revision by Allen and Collins was designed for use with children suffering from *cerebral palsy.*

leukaemia, sometimes called cancer of the blood, serious disease of the blood-forming tissues and organs, marked by an abnormal number of white cells in the blood and the progressive deterioration of the bone-marrow and other tissues. Treatment brings about periods of remission and modern developments are leading to a number of apparently genuine cures.

Lewis Counselling Inventory, schedule for identifying the problems of pupils in the third year of secondary school, aged 13 – 14 years. It consists of 40 statements covering problems in the areas of health, social confidence, instability and relationships with teachers, family and peers. Pupils can agree or disagree with each statement. The schedule can be administered to groups or individually, and includes a lie scale.

Lewis Report 1968, report of an enquiry into 'The Education of Deaf Children' by a committee under the chairmanship of Professor M. M. Lewis. It made a number of recommendations including suggestions for a range of research investigations aimed at improving teaching methods.

lexical encoding, key process in reading, when the pattern of print seen (visual code) is interpreted as a recognized and understood word or group of words (lexical code). Some children with serious reading difficulties find this step, the move from print to meaning, a most difficult one to make.

libido, in Freudian theory, the energy of the sexual impulse. Later *psychoanalysts* extended the meaning to embrace the instinctive drive which they saw as the life-force in all human beings.

lie scale, set of items in a psychological test, usually a *personality test*, which help to detect whether the test is being answered truthfully. They sometimes consist of rephrasings, or equivalent forms of earlier items, which provide a check on the validity of the answers.

life skills, those skills needed to function in society as an independent adult. They include personal skills such as hygiene and body care, domestic skills such as cookery and household management, as well as the ability to understand and deal with society's institutions. For a young person with special needs, training in life skills involves learning those skills which are needed to overcome any existing handicap as well as those which may be required for dealing with situations which lie in the future.

life-space interview, technique developed by F. Redl and used by specially trained teachers and *therapists* to help emotionally disturbed children. When the child is involved in an emotional flare-up the teacher talks the child through the crisis as it occurs. The aim is to piece together the events that caused the crisis so that the child will gain some insight into the nature of the problem and be able to adapt to a more socially acceptable pattern within the existing setting.

Likert scale, type of *attitude scale* in which the subject has to indicate to what extent he/she endorses each statement, e.g.
I always look forward to an English lesson.
Agree strongly   Agree   No view   Disagree   Disagree strongly
Likert scales usually offer five or seven possible answers, forming a scale with a neutral point.

linear programme, simple form of *programmed instruction* in which the material to be learnt is presented in a series of small sequential steps. In a linear programme every pupil moves through the same set of steps, whereas in branching programmes pupils follow different routes, depending on how well they grasp the material.

Lincoln-Oseretsky Motor Development Scale, see *Oseretsky Test of Motor Proficiency*.

linguistic method, approach used in the teaching of reading, closely connected to the *phonic method* and based on the frequency of word and language patterns used by children, derived from language studies. The child is introduced to word patterns which illustrate regular relationships between letters (*graphemes*) and their sound values (*phonemes*), e.g. 'Dan can pat the cat'. The most common spelling patterns are learnt in this way. The use of pictures is discouraged since it is argued that this distracts the child's attention.

link course, course of study planned and conducted jointly by two institutions, usually a secondary school and a college of further education. Senior pupils may divide their time between classes held at either institution. Some *special schools* participate in link courses which the *Warnock Report* described as a means of 'introducing pupils to the possibilities of further education and widening their horizons' and hence recommended an increase in their number. This principle of collaboration between two institutions has been extended at school level in recent years through the development of 'link schemes'. Pupils, staff, resources, or any combination of the three, are shared in joint arrangements between an ordinary and *special school*.

lipreading, U.S. speechreading, skill taught to the deaf and seriously *hearing impaired* to enable them to understand oral language by watching and interpreting the speaker's lip-movements, facial muscles and body gestures. The analytic method teaches recognition of speech sounds in isolation, then in words, phrases, sentences and passages: the synthetic method reverses this procedure. (Note that lip-reading is sometimes restricted to gaining meaning from lip-movements only, and in this sense is contrasted with speech-reading.)

lisping, mispronouncing the sibilant letters, s and z, e.g. 'thun' for 'sun' or 'thebra' for 'zebra', a characteristic of the speech of many young children. A lisp which continues beyond the early years may be the result of an emotional disturbance or may have a physical cause, such as irregular teeth, shortened soft palate or poor co-ordination of the muscles governing speech. *Speech therapy* usually helps. See *dyslalia*, compare *lalling*.

List D, published by the Scottish Education Department, giving brief details of the residential schools to which children may be sent as a result of court orders or if they are in the care of Scottish local authorities.

listening, ability to concentrate attention on sounds in general and on speech in particular, a central factor in children's acquisition of *language* and their educational and social development. Children who are poor listeners are at an immediate disadvantage in school since at primary level approximately 60% of classroom time is spent in listening, with an increase to approximately 90% at secondary level. Conditions associated with listening problems include *hyperactivity*, *hearing impairment*, hearing a different language or dialect at school from home and when listening has not been stimulated at home through stories, conversation, etc. Early identification of poor listeners is important so that they can be helped to develop their listening skills.

listening comprehension test, scale designed to measure a child's understanding of the spoken word, usually part of a test battery.

listening vocabulary, comprehension vocabulary, words recognized and understood when heard. Compare *oral vocabulary*, *reading vocabulary*.

literacy:
(1) in the U.K., the ability to read and write at the level of an average nine or ten-year-old (organic literacy). Reading and writing standards below this level but above those of seven-year-olds are sometimes described as 'semiliteracy';
(2) the ability to read and write as well as is expected by the culture to which that person belongs (*functional* or relative *literacy*).

Little's disease, former name for *cerebral palsy*, so called because it was first fully described by an English surgeon, W. J. Little.

Local Education Authority (LEA), local government body responsible for the provision of all state education apart from Universities in its area in England and Wales. Among many other duties the Authorities are required to make provision for children with *special educational needs* and, since the *Education Act 1981*, to integrate them into ordinary schools subject to the Act's provisions. Through their committees, education officers and advisers, the Authorities operate with considerable freedom, but are subject to Government directives and regulations via the *Department of Education and Science.*

localization of sound, ability to determine whence a sound comes; for this to be efficient, both ears must function normally. Most children learn to localize sounds in early infancy and so to associate them with other experiences. For children with severe *hearing impairment*, localization of sound presents problems and as a result they may rely heavily on visual cues.

logic blocks, blocks of different size, shape and colour used for teaching concepts by classifying into sets according to common characteristics, e.g. a set of round, blue blocks.

London Doll-Play Technique, *personality test* for young children. The children choose roles for members of a doll family to play, so giving insights into their views of the roles and relationships within their own families. See *family relations, tests of.*

longitudinal study, investigation of the development of an individual or individuals through regular observations over a period of time, e.g. the *National Child Development Study* monitored the development of 16,000 children at intervals from birth to maturity. A longitudinal study is usually expensive to mount but gives valuable information on rates of individual development that the other main approach, the cross-sectional study, cannot give. See also *Child Health and Education Survey, National Survey of Health and Development of Children.*

look-and-say method, (look-say method), or whole word method, teaching reading through encouraging the learner to recognize a word or group of words by shape. It is widely used in the early stages of learning to read and is the basis of the introductory stages of many well-known reading schemes. But teachers of reading rarely rely on a single approach and this method is usually judiciously used alongside others, e.g. *phonic method.*

loop induction system, wire loop surrounding a room which transmits sound electromagnetically to *hearing aids.*

lordosis, unusually pronounced forward curvature of the spine.

low-birth-weight, weight at birth less than 2,500 grams, regardless of length of pregnancy. Low-birth-weight may occur for many reasons, e.g. diet during pregnancy, insufficient nourishment of the foetus for other reasons, drug addiction, etc. Although most low-birth-weight babies develop normally, there is a slight risk of developmental problems.

Lowenfield Mosaic Test, *personality test* in which the child makes a design from a selection of coloured pieces. The test rests on the belief that different personality disorders, such as *schizophrenia, psychopathic personality*, etc., produce characteristically different designs.

LPAD, see *Learning Potential Assessment Device*.

LVA, Low Vision Aid, e.g. a magnifier used by children with impaired vision.

M

macrocephaly, very rare *congenital* condition characterized by the enlargement of the head in relation to the body, resulting in some degree of mental and physical *retardation*.

mainstream-with-support curriculum, see *curriculum*.

mainstreaming, U.S. term for the *integration* of children with special needs into the ordinary education system. Like integration, there are different kinds of mainstreaming.

Makaton, communication system based on a simplified version of *British Sign Language* and often used with children with severe learning difficulties, not necessarily deaf. The original Makaton vocabulary was based on studies of vocabulary development, including the vocabulary of adults with mental handicap. It was devised by *Margaret Walker, Kathy* Johnson and *Tony* Cornforth, and has since been revised.

Make a Picture Story (MAPS), test of personality, consisting of a series of small stage-like backdrops of different scenes, e.g. home, school and outdoors, which the child populates with a choice of paper doll characters to create a story. The story is interpreted by the *psychologist* to explore the child's feelings and interpersonal relationships. Although MAPS is thus widely used as a *projective technique*, it was originally developed as a measure of a child's imaginative and creative abilities.

maladjustment, development in ways that have a damaging effect on the individual, or on those who interact with him/her. The *Underwood Report* attempted to classify the varieties of maladjustment, which was one of the official categories of handicap until the *Education Act, 1981*. Many find it an unsatisfactory term, partly because of the problems associated with all categories of handicap, but additionally in this case because it covers such a wide range of behaviour as to have little meaning. *E.b.d.* is now usually preferred, though no term is without problems in trying to describe elusive human reactions.

malleus, one of three bones in the *middle ear*, resembling a tiny hammer. It transmits sound vibrations from the ear-drum to the *incus* and is thus an important link in the hearing mechanism. See *ear* illustration (p. 66).

Manchester Scales of Social Adaptation, measures of social development in children aged six to fifteen years, based on the Vineland Social Maturity Scale and constructed by E. A. Lunzer. The 88 item test contains two main scales:
(1) social perspective, assessing general social perspective; knowledge of sport; knowledge of current affairs; cultural or aesthetic knowledge; science knowledge.
(2) self-direction, assessing leisure and play activities; self-help; exercise of responsibility in the home; freedom of movement; exercise of financial responsibility.

manual alphabet, the representation of the letters by the finger and hand positions used in *finger spelling*.

maple syrup urine disease, very rare hereditary disorder somewhat similar to *phenylketonuria*, which untreated can result in severe *learning difficulties* and neurological disorders. If diagnosed early enough, it can be treated by strict *diet* with moderately good results.

mastery learning, assumption that the mastery of any skill, knowledge or topic is theoretically possible for most learners, provided that they learn at their own pace, and are given suitable teaching. This includes careful setting of objectives, divided into stages, and defining criteria to be achieved before moving from stage to stage.

mastoid bone, portion of the temporal bone behind the ear; bone conduction *hearing aids* are shaped to fit behind the ear against the mastoid bone.

matched groups, groups of identical or nearly identical composition, used in educational research, for example in experiments to compare the effectiveness of different methods of teaching reading to children with *learning difficulties*. When groups are exposed to different conditions — in the example, the teaching methods — the effects of these conditions may be more reliably determined. It is important that the groups are matched on those characteristics which may affect the results of the experiments. See *control group*, *matching procedures*.

matching procedures, technique for producing *matched groups*. These may involve matching children individually; alternatively, random samples of children may be drawn from the population. In this latter case the groups can be expected to have similar *average* characteristics (e.g. average age, *IQ*, *social class*) but individuals in one group would not necessarily have 'equivalent' partners in other groups. See *control group*.

maternal deprivation, see *deprivation, maternal*.

maternal rubella, see *German measles*.

matrices IQ test see *Raven's Progressive Matrices*.

m.b.d., see minimal brain damage.

McCann Report 1975, 'The Secondary Education of Physically Handicapped Children in Scotland', report of a committee appointed by the Secretary of State for Scotland. Though recognizing the continuing need for some *special schools* it advocated more *integration (1)* and suggested ways to encourage this.

mean, or arithmetic mean, see *average (1)*.

measles, acute highly contagious viral disease involving the respiratory tract and characterized by a spreading rash that occurs primarily in young children who have not been *immunised*. It is transmitted by direct contact with droplets spread from the nose, throat and mouth of infected persons. In rare cases the high temperature associated with the disease can lead to intellectual damage and *special educational needs*. It should not be confused with German measles or *rubella*.

median, middle point in a statistical distribution such that 50% of the cases in the distribution are above it, and 50% of the cases are below. Thus if the heights of a class of 21 children are measured and ranked, the median height is that of the 11th child.

medical model, traditional problem-solving approach to the diagnosis and treatment of illness as practised by most physicians in the western world. Much educational and psychological work with handicapped children has followed this pattern, seeking to diagnose a cause for a *learning difficulty*, for example, and then treating it. The cause is located within the child. There is a growing body of opinion which believes that more appropriate models can be found, in particular those that view learning difficulties as the result of social interactions and relationships, rather than a 'problem' in the child.

medical records, written source of a child's *medical history*. The primary medical record is that kept by the family practitioner with whom the child is registered. A secondary medical record is kept by the local authority clinic staff who have the responsibility for looking after the health of the whole community. A third set of medical records will be kept by the hospital consultants with whom a child may have been associated at some time during his development. In accordance with the *Education Act 1981* parents are entitled to see reports relating to a child for whom a *'statement' of special educational needs* has been made but this does not mean that parents themselves have direct access to any of the three medical records described. Most of those concerned with handicapped children and young people look for as full an exchange of information as possible, but access to medical records is not mandatory.

medical social worker, previously known as almoner, person who specializes in helping patients and their relatives with the social and family problems arising from illness or disability. The social work service in hospitals became the responsibility of the local authority *social services* departments in 1974 when the NHS was re-organized.

megavitamin therapy, controversial treatment programme for some forms of learning *difficulties* and *behaviour disorders*, using large doses of certain water soluble vitamins, often in conjunction with psychiatric treatments. It was devised by Linus Pauling.

Melville Report 1973, 'The Training of Staff for Centres for the Mentally Handicapped', report of a committee appointed by the Secretary of State for Scotland. It recommended that no child should be regarded as ineducable; thus *junior occupation centres* in Scotland should become schools, staffed by teachers. It also recommended that teachers should be employed in *adult training centres* to provide continuing education and training in *social skills*, a recommendation which was later endorsed by the *Warnock Report*. See *Education (Mentally handicapped Children) (Scotland) Act, 1974, mental handicap, Scott Report*.

memory span, the number of items that can be recalled immediately after their presentation, usually visually or orally. Memory span for digits or for words, for example is used as an item in several *intelligence tests*. See *Knox Cube Test*.

meninges, three membranes that surround the brain and the spinal cord, viz. the dura mater, arachnoid and pia mater.

meningitis, inflammation of the *meninges* which can lead to a number of conditions requiring special education, e.g. *learning difficulties, hearing impairment*, etc.

meningocele, sac-like object containing *cerebrospinal fluid* that protrudes through a defect in the spine. It is present at birth and may be associated with minor degrees of disorder of the *central nervous system*. It may be possible to remove it without any noticeable consequences.

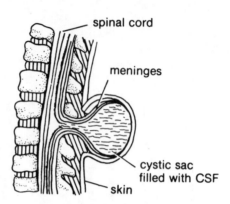

Meningocele

mental age, measure of *intelligence:* thus a 10-year-old child whose performance on an intelligence test was the same as that of the average 7-year-old's would be said to have a mental age of 7 years. This method of measuring intelligence obscures qualitative differences in thinking between the 7- and 10-year-old. Hence intelligence tests in use today usually use a *deviation quotient* as a measure of IQ. See *deviation IQ.*

mental handicap, performance in any important cognitive skill that is substantially below *average* for the child's *chronological age:* used in particular for limited scores on *intelligence tests.* In Scotland, *mental handicap* was one of the *categories of handicap*, roughly equivalent to *educationally subnormal.* In the rest of the U.K. the term is used in the Health Service. For the Education service, severe *learning difficulties* is now appropriate. See *mental impairment.*

mental handicap hospitals, previously subnormality hospitals, are for individuals with limited intellectual development who are unable to manage in the community. Some are specially for children. The number of admissions is dropping due to the policy of integration into the community.

Mental Health Act, 1983, currently governs the reception, care and treatment of patients who are mentally disordered and compulsorily detained. It also governs the process of informal admission to hospital. The Act substantially amends the provisions of the previous Act — the 1959 Mental Health Act — by strengthening the rights of the compulsorily-detained patient in relation to admission to hospital, to inpatient care and treatment and to discharge from hospital.

Mental Health Officer, former name for *approved social worker*.

mental illness, one of the four legal categories of mental disorder specified in the *Mental Health Act, 1983*. Unlike the others, this category is not defined in the Act, but broadly refers to people who have been mentally healthy, but who have suffered a breakdown, perhaps a neurosis or a psychosis. See *mental impairment, psychopathic disorder, severe mental impairment*.

mentally deficient, outmoded term used for children then thought to be too deficient in *intelligence* to profit from normal teaching in school, or for adults, then thought to be incapable of normal employment.

mental impairment, loosely used in the sense of mental handicap, but also one of the four legal categories of mental disorder used in the *Mental Health Act, 1983*. In this Act, mental impairment is defined as a state of arrested or incomplete development of mind (not amounting to severe impairment) which includes significant impairment of intelligence and social functioning and is associated with abnormally aggressive or seriously irresponsible conduct on the part of the person concerned. See *mental illness*, psychopathic disorder, *severe mental impairment*.

mental retardation, limited general intellectual functioning, used particularly in the U.S., to describe the condition of a child with an *IQ* of 70 or less and with impaired *adaptive behaviour*. There are various groupings — mild, moderate, severe, etc.

Merrill-Palmer Scale of Mental Tests, traditional series of verbal and performance tasks designed to measure the intellectual development of children from 18 months to 5 years. Several of the items are essentially speed tests, the level at which the test is passed often depending upon the time required to complete the items. Results can be expressed as a *mental age* or an *intelligence quotient*.

MESU, see *Microelectronics Education Support Unit*.

metabolic disorder, condition which mainly results from enzyme deficiencies. If not treated some can cause progressive intellectual damage but early diagnosis and treatment can prevent this. For example, recent advances in the treatment of children with *phenylketonuria* using a modified *diet* have prevented *severe retardation* though such children tend to show a lowered *IQ*. See *galactosaemia, cretinism*.

microcephaly, *congenital abnormality* characterized by an exceptionally small head and underdeveloped brain; usually associated with severe learning difficulties. In some cases the condition is hereditary, but in others environmental factors are responsible, e.g. *rubella* in early pregnancy.

Microelectronics Education Support Unit (MESU), government-funded organisation intended to promote the use of new technology as a teaching aid. It supports four *SEMERCs* and the *ACE centre*. Its work for children with special needs in Scotland is coordinated by the Scottish Council for Educational Technology and in England and Wales by the Council for Educational Technology. (All addresses in Appendix A).

middle ear, part of the ear which lies between the external and *inner ear*. The middle ear transmits vibrations from the eardrum, across three small bones, to the *oval window*. Infection in the middle ear, *otitis media*, is one of the main causes of *hearing impairment*. See *ear* illustration (p. 66).

milieu therapy, treatment in which all parts of a child's environment — home, school, social activities, etc., are involved in helping to effect the *behaviour* change sought. It can be contrasted with therapy that is specific to a situation, e.g. a *behaviour modification* programme applied in the home only.

Mill Hill Vocabulary Scales, test prepared by J. C. Raven and used particularly with older children and adults, who are required to explain words of increasing difficulty. The score is said to be an estimate of verbal *intelligence*. The scales are designed for use with *Raven's Progressive Matrices* tests. See *Crichton Vocabulary Scale*.

Milwaukee Project, influential U.S. *compensatory education* project, designed to investigate whether intensive enriched early experiences can overcome *cultural-familial retardation*. The project was established by R. Heber in a deprived area of Milwaukee from the mid 1960's onwards and involved intensive work with very young children and their parents. Results indicated that children receiving early enrichment showed substantial gains on *intelligence tests* in comparison with *control groups*, but these results are controversial.

mime, acting by gesture and movement, i.e. without speech, sometimes included in programmes for children with *special educational needs* as a therapeutic activity. It provides opportunities (particularly for those with disturbed backgrounds) to 'relive' their earlier experiences, e.g. acting out family traumas.

minimal brain damage (m.b.d.), indications of damage to the *central nervous system* leading to learning or behavioural disorders. No single indication may be significant, but taken together a pattern of *soft neurological signs* may enable minimal brain damage to be diagnosed. The term has been criticized since it carries connotations of permanence, which may be misleading.

minimal cerebral dysfunction, alternative term for *minimal brain damage*.

mirror, one-way, see *one-way vision screen*.

mirror method, technique for observing *eye-movement* in which an observer, sitting next to a reader and holding a small mirror at an angle near the text being read, can estimate the number of *fixations* by the reader as the eye moves in irregular jumps along the line of print. The technique is occasionally used in the diagnosis and treatment of some reading difficulties; better equipment is available for more accurate measurement of eye-movement if this is needed.

mirror writing, writing which is the reflection of normal writing and which can be read by holding it to a mirror. Single letters formed in this way are called *'reversals'*. It commonly occurs when children learn to write: in older children it may indicate *learning difficulties* and is held to be one sign of *dyslexia*.

miscue analysis, technique for examining a child's approach to reading through studying the errors which norm-referenced reading tests usually fail to investigate. Miscues are usually classified into reversals, omissions, etc; the pattern of miscues indicates both the strengths and weaknesses of the reader and thus provides information for planned individual reading programmes.

mixed dominance, see *dominance (2)*.

MLU, Mean Length of Utterance, a measure of *language development*. The length of utterance is essentially the number of words a young child produces at a time. The average length is calculated from time to time to show how utterances lengthen as a child develops.

mobile arm support, pivoted forearm support on ball-bearing hinges mounted on the back of a wheelchair, used to restore mobility to a flaccid arm, for desk work, feeding, etc.

mobility allowance, weekly cash benefit paid to persons aged 5–65 who are unable or virtually unable to walk and are likely to remain so for at least a year. It is intended to help with extra transport costs but it may be spent otherwise, it is tax free and does not affect other benefits or pensions. The allowance may be paid whether the *person* is living at home, *special school*, hospital or any other institution. There is a flat rate allowance for everyone and rules which govern qualification are published by the *DHSS*.

modality, any of the sensory systems for receiving, processing and responding to sensation, e.g. vision, touch, etc.

modelling, learning by imitating someone else; this is the basis of a technique sometimes employed in *behaviour therapy*, e.g. watching someone else approach and cope with feared objects may help to eliminate *phobias*.

modified curriculum, see *curriculum*.

mongolism, see *Down's syndrome*.

monoplegia, paralysis of one limb only.

monosomy the presence of one *chromosome* only, instead of the usual pair. Contrast *trisomy*; see *Turner's Syndrome*.

monozygotic twins, twins from a single fertilized egg which has separated into two in an early division of the embryo; such twins are genetically identical. See *dizygotic twins*.

Montessori Method, educational system developed by Maria Montessori, an Italian physician and educator, 1870–1952, which emphasizes self-education through practical skills, sensory experience, physical activity and learning material graded in complexity to suit the child's developing *intelligence*. Although designed for all children, many Montessorian ideas have been incorporated in teaching methods for children with *learning difficulties*.

Moon, writing system for the blind, similar to *Braille*, but requiring less finger sensitivity.

Mooney Problem Check List, U.S. personality inventory designed by Mooney to help older pupils, students and adults express their personal problems. It lists a large number of possible concerns, arranged by area, e.g. problems at school, personal problems, etc. It is used in the U.K. for *counselling* and guidance.

Morquio's syndrome, condition that results in abnormal bone and muscle development in childhood. *Dwarfism*, hunchback, enlarged breastbone and knock knees may occur.

mosaicism, presence in a single individual of two or more kinds of cell differing in *genetic* constitution. Some children with *Down's syndrome* suffer from mosaicism, for the number of *chromosomes* in the cells may differ, some cells possessing the normal number of chromosomes, others not.

mosaic test, see *Lowenfeld Mosaic Test*.

motor ability, skill in organizing and efficiency in executing muscle actions. It is important since it is necessary for successful *learning*; e.g. holding a biro involves some motor ability, so does kicking a ball; so do the more complex skills demanded by some practical subjects.

motor aphasia, see *expressive aphasia*.

motor apraxia, see apraxia.

motor defect, impairment of movement and posture; if this is due to brain injury it is sometimes, but not necessarily, accompanied by other defects, e.g. *learning difficulties*, *speech defects* and/or sensory impairments.

motor disability, commonly used as effect of *motor defect*.

motor impersistence, inability to sustain a voluntary act when told to, e.g. protruding the tongue, keeping the mouth open. Motor impersistence is related to *distractibility*, and short attention span.

motor therapy, programme of exercises for children with *motor co-ordination* difficulties. See *clumsy child syndrome*.

mouthstick (for telephoning), device made of a 7 inch length of nylon, which has one end flattened and grooved to allow the user to get a secure grip with the teeth.

movigenic theory, approach to *learning* based on ideas proposed by R. H. Barsch; the study of the origin and development of movement patterns leading to learning efficiency. The movigenic theory is the basis for a 'movigenic curriculum', a planned programme of activity, said to be of value to those children with *learning difficulties* for whom the usual school *curriculum* is unsuitable.

m.s.d., see *multisensory deprivation*.

mucopolysaccharidoses (MPS), group of *genetic disorders* characterized by deformed bones, especially of the face, retarded mental and physical development and decreased life expectancy.

multidisciplinary team, team which meets with parents to assess and follow-up the development of children with more serious *special educational needs*. Membership varies according to the child's needs, but usually includes a medical consultant, (*paediatrician* or *child psychiatrist*), educational psychologist and social worker; other disciplines, such as a teacher or *therapist*, etc., can also be involved.

multi-handicapped children, children with several handicaps. Since few children with special needs suffer from a single handicap — a child with *hearing loss* is also likely to have speech problems, for example — the term was usually restricted to children whose additional handicaps were serious and not necessarily inter-dependent — children who were both deaf and blind, for example. In the U.K., the introduction of the term '*special educational needs*' may make the term redundant.

Multiple Intelligence (M.I.), view that there is no single intelligence, e.g. musical intelligence, linguistic intelligence, etc. Contrast with '*g*'.

multiple sclerosis, gradually progressive disease of the *central nervous system*. It primarily affects older adolescents and young adults and hence does not usually appear until after the end of compulsory education. The onset is usually slow and prognosis varies since it may get better or worse unpredictably: the cause is unknown and there is no known cure. The symptoms include visual disturbance, muscular weakness, dizziness, speech difficulties, problems in walking, tremors, etc.

multi-sensory approach, teaching method which involves as many different senses as possible. See *VAKT method*.

multi-sensory deprivation (m.s.d.), the condition of *deaf-blind* children, who are unable to use either vision or hearing to receive adequate information, leading to complex problems of perception and communication.

muscle tone, normal slight contraction of muscles, also known as tonus or tonicity, which is vital for normal growth and motor skill acquisition. Poor muscle tone is characteristic of some children with physical handicaps, e.g. some children with *cerebral palsy*.

muscular dystrophy, group of genetically transmitted diseases, characterized by gradual degeneration of the muscles. See *Duchenne muscular dystrophy*.

music therapy, the use of music in the treatment of children with special needs, either through listening to music or composing/improvising or both. It is argued that music offers a means of engaging children with whom normal communication through language can be difficult, e.g. *autistic* children, that it creates awareness of sound differences in *hearing impaired* children and that it can relieve tension in children with *emotional disorders*.

mutation, alteration in *genetic* material resulting in a change of inherited characteristics so that the character of the offspring is different from that of its parents. When mutation occurs the change is transmitted to future generations.

mutism, elective, the silence of a child who is able to speak but does so only in certain situations, e.g. a child who speaks normally at home and with friends, but does not speak at all at school; in most children this is a transient condition but in others it may be more serious and require help from the *school psychological service*, for example.

myasthenia gravis, weakness and chronic fatigue of muscles, especially in the face and throat, as a result of a defect in the conduction of nerve impulses.

myelomeningocele, one of the more severe forms of *spina bifida* in which nervous tissue and membranes protrude from the back in a sac-like bulge. Contrast with *meningocele*, in which nervous tissue is not included in the bulge.

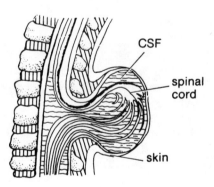

Myelomeningocele

myopia, or short sight; condition in which, when the eye is relaxed the light rays come to focus in front of the *retina* instead of directly upon it, i.e. distance vision is poor.

N

Named Person, role proposed by the *Warnock Report*, for an individual to serve as a point of contact between the authorities dealing with children with special needs and their parents. This person should give parents guidance on available services and provide the services with necessary information about the child. It was suggested that a *health visitor* would be a suitable Named Person during a child's early years but that later a different professional would be more appropriate. The *Education Act, 1981*, requires *LEAs* to provide the name of an officer from whom parents can obtain further information when a child's *special educational needs* are assessed.

National Child Development Study, *longitudinal study* of child development in which teachers, health specialists and *psychologists* monitored the development of 17,000 children born in the U.K. in the same week in March 1958 and followed them up when they were aged 7, 11 and 16 years. A subgroup was followed up at 20 years of age. The study suggested that one child in five will need some form of special educational provision at some time or other. See *Child Health and Education Survey*.

National Foundation for Educational Research in England and Wales (NFER), as well as demonstrating a strong commitment to special education through projects and publications, the NFER, through its Test Agency, is the main U.K. supplier of educational and psychological tests used in assessing special needs. See Appendix A.

National Survey of Health and Development of Children, *longitudinal study* of child development, monitoring several thousand children born in the U.K. in the same week in March 1946. See *Child Health and Education Survey*.

nature-nurture controversy, debate about the relative effect of *heredity* and environment on the development of psychological characteristics in general and *intelligence* in particular.

Neale Analysis of Reading Ability, test of reading achievement prepared by M. Neale. It is used to assess reading accuracy, comprehension and rate of reading for children aged 6–12 years by requiring them to read a set of illustrated paragraphs. It also enables reading errors to be categorized, so giving leads for remedial work. The test has been adapted by Lorimer for use with blind children aged 7½ – 13½ years; this test is in *braille* and the pictures are replaced by oral instructions.

near sighted, see *myopia*.

Nebraska Test of Learning Aptitude, scale developed by Hiskey for assessing the learning ability of hearing impaired children and standardised both on deaf and partially-hearing children. The individual test, which is administered in mime, includes eleven non-verbal sub-tests suitable for ages 4–10 years. It is also used with hearing children who have communication difficulties.

negative self-concept, feelings of inadequacy and inferiority accompanying the way a child thinks about himself/herself.

negativism, negative attitude or behaviour when a child often does the opposite of what is requested.

negative reinforcement, increasing the likelihood of desired behaviour by terminating an unpleasant experience. Thus a disruptive child may be placed in a *time-out* situation. When the child's behaviour has quietened (i.e. desired behaviour appears), terminating the time-out (unpleasant experience) increases the likelihood of quiet behaviour recurring. A technique used in *behaviour modification*. Using negative reinforcement in order to change behaviour is distinguished from using punishment, which behaviour therapists hold to be less effective. Contrast *positive reinforcement*.

neo-natal mortality, number of infant deaths per thousand births, occuring within 28 days of birth.

neonate, newly born. The term is used to describe the first four weeks of an infant's life, a time of rapid development, intense *learning* activity and considerable vulnerability.

nerve deafness, see *sensorineural hearing loss*.

neural tube defects, group of *congenital abnormalities*, characterized by defects in the spinal column or skull, mainly because the neural tube, which gives rise to the brain, spinal cord and other tissues of the *central nervous system*, fails to close before birth. These defects are usually accompanied by severe physical and mental disorders, as in *spina bifida*. The major neural tube defects can now be detected before birth.

neurological hard signs, see *hard neurological signs*.

neurological soft signs, see *soft neurological signs*.

neurologist, medical practitioner with additional specialized training in the *diagnosis* and treatment of diseases of the nervous system.

neuromuscular impairments, muscle weakness, paralysis, lack of co-ordination, etc., in which the nerves which control the muscles are affected, rather than the muscles themselves, although muscle deterioration may result. See *muscular dystrophy, multiple sclerosis, cerebral palsy*.

neurosis, psychological disorder, often resulting from inner conflict, with a variety of symptoms including anxiety, mannerisms, *phobias*, obsessions and hysterical behaviour and for which, usually, no organic basis can be found. Contrast *psychosis*.

neurotic behaviour, worry and anxiety, not as serious as a neurosis, but shown in children by behaviour such as excessive timidity, fears, food fads, etc. One of the two main categories of children's behaviour measured by the *Children's Behaviour Questionnaire*. Compare *antisocial behaviour*.

Newsom Report 1963, 'Half our Future', report of the Central Advisory Council for Education, under the chairmanship of Sir John Newsom, and concerned with the education of less able pupils in secondary schools in England and Wales. Its recommendations included raising the school leaving age to 16, more appropriate curricula and examinations, a new building programme, new teaching methods and extra payments for teachers working in difficult areas.

NFER, see National Foundation for Educational Research in England and Wales.

Niemann-Pick disease, inherited *metabolic disorder* of infancy. There is progressive mental and physical deterioration.

nine points, see *Creak's 9 points*.

nocturnal enuresis, see *enuresis*.

nominal aphasia, or anomia, or dysnomia, abnormal difficulty in recalling the names of objects.

non-directive counselling, *counselling* in which the counsellor refrains from giving advice to *clients*, but reflects their feelings and attitudes in order to help them formulate their own solutions to their problems.

non-directive play therapy, therapeutic approach to play which places the responsibility for its direction on the child. The child takes the lead while the *therapist* only joins in when the child indicates.

non-language test, psychological test requiring no written or spoken *language*, from child or examiner and which is thus particularly suitable for children who have hearing or speech problems, or who are illiterate, or for whom a test in their first language is not available. See *non-verbal list*.

non-maintained special schools, non-profit-making schools which have to meet conditions for approval as *special schools* laid down in the *Handicapped Pupils and Special Schools Regulation, 1979*; in return they may receive government grants, thus being part of the national system of *special education*. They also receive financial support from charities or trusts but the majority are financed through the fees paid by *local education authorities* who place pupils in the school. The *Warnock Report* recommended closer links between the schools and local authorities, with more visits from *Her Majesty's Inspectorate* and a governing body for each school, which should include a representative of the local education authority. Many of these special schools concentrate on educating children with particular disabilities such as *blindness* or *deafness*.

Non-Readers Intelligence Test, an orally-presented verbal test designed by D. Young for children aged 6½–14 years in normal schools where it is used in screening for children with learning difficulties. It is claimed to be useful in assessment work with older children in special schools.

non-verbal communication, information gained from non-verbal signals such as facial expression, eye contact, posture and gesture, physical contact, etc. While non-verbal communication is evident in many everyday situations, the sign and symbol systems that are used by those who are seriously hearing-impared (e.g. *British Sign Language*) are examples of highly-structured non-verbal (sometimes called non-vocal) communication systems.

non-verbal test, *intelligence* or other psychological test which requires no reading or speech on the part of the child but sets problems via pictures, designs, patterns, etc., e.g. *Raven's Progressive Matrices*. A non-verbal test is sometimes thought to be equivalent to a *non-language test*, but many non-verbal tests do require the examiner to give oral instructions.

norm:
(1) *average* or typical score against which individual scores can be compared;
(2) set of accepted rules, values, behaviour, to which members of a social group conform.

norm-referenced test, scale on which a score is interpreted by comparison with others, often to determine whether and by how much the score is better or worse than average. For children, the comparison is usually made with the scores obtained by others of similar age. Norm-referenced tests do not usually aim to identify how far specified skills have been mastered. Compare *criterion-referenced test*.

normal curve, or Gaussian curve, curve derived from probability theory, bell-shaped distribution of scores, i.e. most scores cluster around the *average* value: the further a score is from the average the less often it occurs. A good example of the normal curve is the distribution of height. Most people are close to average height: there are few very small or very tall individuals. Psychological and educational tests are often constructed so that the scores obtained approximate to a normal curve.

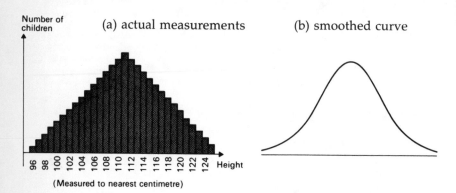

Normal curve, obtained from the heights of a group of 4-year-old children

normalization, belief that persons with handicaps should enjoy the same privileges, rights and opportunities as persons without handicaps. This implies that children with special needs should have access to the same education system as their fellows, i.e. integration is normalization applied to education.

norms of development, stages of a child's mental or physical development which are accepted as normal at particular *chronological ages*, e.g. most children walk between 1 year and 18 months of age.

number concept, way in which a child understands and uses the quantities represented by numerals. A good grasp of number concepts implies that basic ideas such as the meaning of 'greater than', 'less than', etc. are understood, as well as the values of numerals.

nursery nurses, individuals who work in *day nurseries*, *nursery schools* and residential homes, with responsibilities for the care and well-being of young children. The Certificate of the National Nursery Examination Board, the recognized qualification, gives nursery nurses a good basic knowledge of child development but the *Warnock Report* recommended training for an advanced certificate to give them a deeper knowledge of children with *special educational needs*.

nursery school, school offering a range of social, educational and play activities for children under five years old (pre-primary age) and which may be provided by the local authority, or a voluntary agency. Local authority nursery schools are required to employ qualified staff. In some instances, *units* for children with *special educational needs* have been set up in nursery schools.

nurture groups, small groups, usually of primary school pupils, who have been socially and emotionally deprived. The nurture groups aim to provide the normal relationships and experiences of early childhood that these children have missed. See *compensatory education*.

nystagmus, involuntary oscillating movements of the eyes.

O

object cathexis, in psychoanalytic theory, diversion of love from its normal aim; e.g. a child may invest a toy or object with a strong love bond and attachment.

Object Relations Technique, *projective technique* developed by Phillipson, and based on psychoanalytic principles. It provides *psychologists* with an insight into personality, particularly attitudes to interpersonal relations, through describing pictures which represent a solitary situation, two or three person relationships and group relationship situations. It is used with 14-year-olds upwards for counselling and in treatment.

objective test, test administered and scored according to set procedures. The aim is to provide results that are consistent, no matter who gives or scores the test.

observation and assessment centre, centre attended part-time or full-time by children with special needs so that their educational and social needs can be investigated by careful and prolonged observation, perhaps over several months. Recommendations for suitable longer-term placement are then made. A centre is usually staffed by a child development team, often consisting of teachers, educational psychologists and social workers. It may be housed in its own premises or in rooms set aside in a school building.

obsessive behaviour, conduct that results from a persistent idea, in spite of efforts to banish it, e.g. continually washing hands, or checking to see if the door is locked. A variety of *neurotic behaviour*.

occipital lobe, part of the brain concerned primarily with vision and perception. Visual stimuli are registered and interpreted in this area; damage either at birth or through illness may contribute to *learning difficulties*. See *brain* illustration (p. 28).

occupational classification, system of classifying parents' occupations often used in research into the link between occupation and aspects of *special educational needs*, e.g. the incidence of moderate *learning difficulties* varies with occupational classification whereas the incidence of severe learning difficulties bears little relationship to it. See *socio–economic status*.

occupational therapist, non-medical specialist employed in hospitals or occasionally in schools for children with special needs who uses handicrafts and creative hobbies in their mental or physical *rehabilitation*.

occupational therapy, *rehabilitation* programme, prescribed by a doctor and directed by an *occupational therapist*. The programme employs activities for improving musclar control and promoting physical and mental well-being, leading towards independence.

ocular dominance, consistent use of one eye in preference to the other in situations such as sighting, where *fixation* is involved.

ocular motor control system, structure which focuses and adjusts the eyes. It controls the eye movements in reading and thus plays an important part in learning. Some authorities believe disorders of this system to be one of the causes of *dyslexia*.

ocular preference, choosing to use one eye in preference to the other, though both eyes are functioning efficiently, e.g. closing one eye to look through a camera view-finder: often used in the same sense as *ocular dominance*.

Oedipus complex, condition in Freudian theory in which a boy's feelings for his parents, which characterize the *Oedipal phase*, are not resolved: they remain and colour his relationship with adults, leading to emotional disorders in later childhood and beyond. See *Electra complex*.

Oedipal phase, the unconscious sexual attachment of a son to his mother, usually disguised in various ways. It is assumed that the son will be jealous of the father, who can have intimacies with the mother that are denied to the son. Aggression to the father as well as fear of retaliation may be shown. The Oedipal phase is an element in the *Freudian theory of psychosexual development*.

oligophrenia, *mental retardation*; term used especially in French and German research on the subject, usually in a medical context. It is also found in Russian educational/psychological literature.

one-parent family, family where any parent, whether divorced, separated, widowed, unmarried, a prisoner's spouse or one whose partner is seriously disabled or in hospital is bringing up a child or children single-handed.

one-way vision screen, usually a specially-silvered mirror but sometimes wire mesh or lightweight cloth, brightly lit on the child's side but dark on the observer's side. It is sometimes used in observing child behaviour, for diagnostic purposes, since it enables the child to be observed unseen. For ethical reasons, permission from the child or parent should first be obtained.

ontogeny, development of the individual from conception onwards.

open-plan school, school where traditional classrooms have been replaced by a few large open rooms with teaching areas and learning bays which lend themselves to flexible and informal learning and teaching situations. Open plan schools often feature the *integrated day*, as well as *vertical grouping* and *team teaching*. Their advantages have to be set against the discipline and control problems which sometimes occur.

Open University, founded in 1969, originally to enable students of 21 years and over to study at a distance for degrees; unlike other universities entry is not based on formal qualifications, but on a first-come first-served arrangement. Teaching uses a mixture of correspondence texts, television, radio broadcasts and personal tuition. Credits are awarded on continual *assessment* and examination results. The *university* offers courses on *handicap* and on *special educational needs*. It also offers strong support services for handicapped adults (who can be enrolled at 18 years of age).

operant conditioning, use of controlled *reinforcement schedules* to encourage desired behaviour; the main principle of *behaviour modification*. It is widely used in special education, perhaps most frequently in modifying the behaviour of children with *learning difficulties* or *emotional and behavioural disorders*. See *token economy*.

opthalmic surgeon, surgeon with additional specialized training in surgery of the eyes.

ophthalmograph, instrument for recording the movements of both eyes during reading.

ophthalmologist, medical practitioner with additional specialized training in working with the eyes, who is qualified to conduct diagnosis, prescribe drugs, perform surgery, measure refraction and prescribe glasses.

opportunity groups, playgroups specially set up for young handicapped children, although non-handicapped children may also attend. Parents can discuss normal play development with playleaders and can sometimes meet professionals, such as *educational psychologists*, and *social workers*, etc., in order to discuss their child's development.

optacon, device for converting print into *tactile* images for the visually impaired. 144 pins are vibrated in different ways to produce patterns that can be 'read' by the reader's index finger.

optic atrophy, degeneration of the *optic nerve* leading to varying degrees of loss of vision, ranging from total *blindness* to very minor effects.

optic nerve, nerve which conveys sight impulses from the *retina* to the brain. See *eye* illustration (p. 76).

optometrist, non-medical specialist in eye function. In particular an optometrist measures the *refraction* of the eye, and prescibes glasses and may also carry out vision training.

ORACLE project, Observational Research And Classroom Learning Evaluation, studied what took place in primary classrooms. One finding was that although most of a teacher's time was spent in interacting with pupils, individual pupils interacted with a teacher for a very small proportion of their time. But pupils with special needs received higher levels of attention than others.

oral comprehension vocabulary, store of words that are understood, even if not used. Contrast with *reading vocabulary*, for example. Oral comprehension vocabulary is often measured as part of an *intelligence test*, e.g. the *Stanford Binet Intelligence Test and the* Wechsler Intelligence Test for Children both measure it. The child is asked to explain the meaning of a set of words of gradually increasing difficulty, spoken by the examiner. Notwithstanding the wide use of these vocabulary tests as quick measures of language development, speed may well be their main virtue. A quality as rich and complex as language demands much more thorough assesment. (Note that oral refers to the method of testing, i.e. the examiner provides the words orally.)

oral method, or oralism, system of teaching hearing-impaired children, in which communication is carried out through spoken language, *lipreading*, listening and writing, without the use of *sign language* or *finger spelling*. The use of the child's hearing is emphasized. See *signing*.

oral stage, earliest stage in *Freudian theory of Psychosexual development*, lasting from birth to about the second year of age, in which gratification is centred on the mouth and its functions, e.g. sucking and biting.

oral vocabulary, words a child has learned to use in speech. Teachers of reading devote a great deal of effort in the early stages to helping children enlarge and enrich their oral vocabularies, so that the child can regard reading as something more than merely pronouncing words; attempts to use words correctly in speech help in grasping their meaning.

oralism, see *oral method*.

organic aetiology, refers to any condition caused by *organic damage*. When organic damage cannot be identified, the condition is said to be functional. See *functional hearing loss*.

organic damage, injury to a body organ; in special education this often refers to injury to intact brain cells which either destroys them or permanently disorganizes their functioning. Some learning difficulties and behaviour disorders are clearly linked with organic damage and are contrasted with those linked with growing up in unfavourable circumstances. It is sometimes difficult to separate the two causes and for this reason careful neurological and psychological assessment is needed.

orienting reflex, automatically responding to a stimulus, such as a sound, by turning towards it. This reflex, which is present in very young children, is used in detecting hearing impairment and distractibility.

orthopaedic disorder, damage to bones, joints and muscles.

orthopaedic surgeon, surgeon with additional specialized training in surgery for correcting physical deformities associated with muscles, bones and joints. Orthopaedic surgeons work closely with *physiotherapists*, *occupational therapists* and *remedial gymnasts*.

orthoptics, treatment of defective vision through exercises: thus a child with a *squint* is given exercises to align the axes of vision of the eyes.

orthoptist, person who practices *orthoptics*, usually working with *ophthalmologists* in the investigation, diagnosis and treatment of *squint* and other visual defects.

Orton Society, U.S. society for helping children with *dyslexia* and associated *language* problems. Founded by the neurologist S. T. Orton.

Oseretsky Test of Motor Proficiency, test for measuring *sensori-motor development*, e.g. *eye-hand co-ordination*, finger dexterity and large motor skills. It originated in Russia but was later translated into English and revised and published in the U.S. as the Lincoln-Oseretsky Motor Development Scale. A more recent revision and development is the Bruininks-Oseretsky Test of Motor Proficiency, which measures such skills as running speed, balance, co-ordination, visual-motor control, etc., and provides separate measures of fine motor skills and gross motor skills. The scale is used in the assessment of children with learning difficulties, for whom separate norms are provided.

osteogenesis imperfecta, alternative name for *fragilitas ossium*.

otitis media, inflammation or infection of the *middle ear* which may be accompanied by pain, fever, interference with hearing and giddiness. It is the most common cause of mild hearing impairment (conductive loss) in young children, often undetected, and so leading to learning difficulties. These are largely preventable, for if treated quickly it is curable.

otolaryngologist, medical practitioner with additional specialized training in diseases of the ear, nose and throat.

otologist, medical practioner with additional specialized training in the functioning of the ear; sometimes called an aurist.

otosclerosis, hereditary disease of the bony capsule that surrounds the *inner ear*, which starts in young people, occurring twice as often in girls. It can be helped by surgery.

outer ear, the first of the three main divisions of the total ear; the protruding part is the *auricle*, which intercepts sound waves and directs them to the external *auditory canal*. This is subject to malformations, injury, hardening of wax, or blocking due to a foreign body, any of which can affect hearing. To prevent serious damage to the delicate tissues, only a doctor should be permitted to remove anything from the ear. See *ear* illustration (p. 66).

outreach, providing expertise away from base. For example, staffs of some further education colleges offer courses for young people with special needs in settings such as hospitals, employment rehabilitation centres, etc. The term is also used to describe staffs of special schools and units offering a service to ordinary schools.

oval window, opening from the *middle ear* into the *inner ear* containing the base of the *stapes*. See *ear* illustration (p. 66).

over-achiever, pupil who achieves at a level above that expected from prior performance and test results.

over-learning, learning that results from more practise than is necessary for immediate recall. It also describes over-practising the performance of a skill after a period of disuse, e.g. the use of limbs after being bedridden.

oxycephaly, see acrocephaly.

oxygen deprivation at birth, insufficient supply of oxygen to the baby during the birth, often leading to damage to the brain cells, which in turn may lead to learning and behaviour difficulties. The degree of severity depends on the extent of *deprivation*.

P

paediatrician, medical practitioner with additional specialized training in the health, disorders and diseases of children. The paediatrician is often the first to inform the parents that their child is handicapped.

on

sleep

Paget-Gorman signs. See entry on p.150.

Paget-Gorman sign system, one of the sign systems used by children who are deaf or show serious language delay. It is an elaborate communication system, e.g. the names of animals have a similar basic sign but slight differences in detail. One of its advantages is that it is said to correspond well with the grammatical structure of spoken English. See photo on p. 149.

page-turner, wand, attached to a head-band, for turning pages. Magnets on the wand contact metal clips on pages, or a suction cup may be attached. Either way, the wearer can turn the page with a right-to-left head movement.

paired reading:
(1) originally a method of teaching reading in which a child is paired with a fluent reader; both read aloud together;
(2) development of (1) in which the fluent reader is a parent, hence *parent* assisted *instruction in reading*.
In both cases the fluent reader is expected to follow agreed procedures for correcting errors, helping the transition to reading alone, etc. The method is widely used with children with reading difficulties.

PAIRS, *Parent Assisted Instruction in Reading and Spelling*, development of *paired reading*.

palmar-crease, one of the identifying signs on the palm of the hand. There is a characteristic palmar crease in *Down's syndrome*.

paranoia, *chronic* mental disorder, in which the affected individual has delusions of persecution and sometimes hallucinations; one of several forms of *psychosis*.

paraplegia, paralysis of the lower limbs. There are two forms. In spastic paraplegia the disorder is due to brain dysfunction and the legs, which are stiff with increased *muscle tone* (spastic) , are unable to move. In flaccid paraplegia the muscles are weak and floppy, either through injury to the spine or through *spina bifida*.

partially hearing pupils, were defined by the Handicapped Pupils and Special Schools Regulations, 1959, (as amended) as those 'with impaired hearing whose development of speech and language, even if retarded, is following a normal pattern and who require special arrangements or facilities for their education, though not necessarily all those methods used for deaf pupils'. This category of handicap was abolished by the *Education Act, 1981*, and replaced by *special educational need*.

parietal lobe, part of the brain which helps to control *perceptions* of pain, position, temperature and touch.

partially hearing unit, centre or *unit* usually in an ordinary school, equipped and staffed to provide education and advice for children with hearing impairment. The extent to which individual pupils integrate with the school varies widely. This type of provision has grown substantially in recent years.

partially sighted pupils, pupils having imperfect sight, legally defined as being between 3/60 and 6/60 vision after correction, but with allowances for other conditions. It is commonly caused by severe conditions such as short-sightedness (*myopia*) and *astigmatism*. Partial sight as a category of handicap was replaced by special educational need in the *Education Act, 1981*. See *Vernon Report*, *Snellen ratio*.

patellar reflex, see *knee-jerk reflex*.

Pathway Employment Service, specialist employment service for people with a mental handicap started by the *Royal Society for Mentally Handicapped Children and Adults* (see Appendix A). It introduces the mentally handicapped person to an employer, sorts out possible difficulties, pays wages for a trial period of six to twelve weeks and gets a 'foster worker' to keep a friendly eye on progress.

Paul Sandifer Day Centre, pre-school *unit* for multiply-*handicapped* children, based at Great Ormond Street Hospital, London. The object of the unit is to involve the whole family in the treatment and management of the handicapped child so that help can be continued at home.

Peabody Language Development Kit, one of the early structured language kits, consisting of 180 lessons and equipment for them, aimed at improving the language skills of pre-school children, particularly those living in unfavourable surroundings, and older children with *learning difficulties*. Through this emphasis on language, the kit is claimed to help a young child's prospects of making good progress in the school system. The kit originated in the U.S. but has had considerable use in the U.K. See illustration (p. 152).

peer relationships, relationships between members of a group, e.g. between children and their class-mates.

peer tutoring, one child acting as another's teacher, usually when the class teacher has set out the learning task clearly. As well as the academic benefit to the child being taught, it offers social benefits (enhanced self-esteem) to the child acting as tutor.

pencil-tracking test, test of *psychomotor* development in which the child uses the preferred hand to draw a continuous pencil line within a figure-

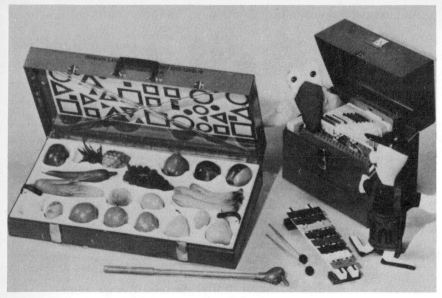

Peabody Language Development Kit

of-eight track. It is used particularly to assess *eye-hand co-ordination* and small-muscle control.

percentile, method of indicating the relative position of a score in a distribution; the 35th percentile is the point below which fall 35% of all scores.

perception, interpreting information gained through the senses. Thus a child sees four straight lines. but may perceive a square (visual perception), or hear some notes and perceive a tune (auditory perception). *Perceptual disorders* are important to identify, for they are significant causes of *learning difficulties*.

perceptive hearing loss, older term for *sensorineural deafness*.

perceptual defence, not perceiving what one does not wish to perceive, in order to protect the personality. Thus a child who does not wish to acknowledge criticism may fail to 'hear' it.

perceptual disorder, inability to recognize objects or situations correctly, even though the senses involved are intact. In the case of vision, for example, perceptual disorder may lead to poor performance in activities such as drawing, writing and recognizing forms, shapes or sizes.

perceptual-motor ability, perceptuo-motor ability, ability to co-ordinate perceptual and motor skills. Thus the ability to manipulate jigsaw pieces, for example, is heavily dependent on perceptual-motor ability, since it relies on visual, *tactile* and *kinaesthetic* perceptions being successfully integrated with hand and finger movements.

Performance IQ, intelligence quotient based on a *performance test* of *intelligence*.

performance test, test requiring observation and action rather than spoken or written answers, e.g. arranging pictures in a logical sequence, manipulating blocks, etc. It can be a helpful measure in the *assessment* of children with learning difficulties. Whereas a *non-verbal test* might require paper and pencil, a performance test rarely does.

perinatal disorders, disorders which occur in a baby shortly before, during or immediately after birth.

peripatetic teacher, teacher who travels from school to school. Peripatetic teachers with special skills are used extensively for teaching children with *special educational needs*, usually when a single school does not justify the services of a full-time teacher for the purpose.

Perkin's brailler, most commonly used typing machine for producing *braille*. It has six keys and a spacer bar for the production of letters; synthetic speech and print may be added to the machine by using a micro-computer and interface.

perseveration, continuing to respond or behave in a certain way when it is no longer appropriate, e.g. repetition of a word several times or an inability to stop one activity and transfer to another.

personal construct theory, model for understanding how we perceive and make sense of things, developed by G. A. Kelly. Each person has a unique (but neither totally independent nor unchanging) set of principles or constructs, used in characterizing the world around us. Thus one mother might characterize (or construe) her children in terms of whether they learn well or not, whether they are healthy or not, etc. Another may construe her children in terms of whether they are healthy or not, whether they are lovable or not, etc. Techniques based on personal construct theory are used by psychologists and others — for example in helping to understand how parents and children interact.

personality test, any test which assesses psychological characteristics other than abilities and attainments, e.g. tests which explore relationships, measure interests, assess temperament, etc. They can be *objective tests*, but most personality tests used in clinical work with children's emotional and behaviour disorders are *projective techniques*, e.g. *Children's Apperception Test*, or checklists, e.g. *Children's Behaviour Questionnaire*.

Perthes' disease, also known as Legg-Calve-Perthes' disease, coxa plana, pseudocoxalgia, a bone disease causing deformity of the head of the femur. The condition is most frequently seen in boys between the ages of 4 and 6, causing pain, limping and restricted movement. If untreated all hip movement may become limited, but with bed rest and relief of strain by means of crutches, hip splints or traction, recovery is complete and the bone regions return to normal.

petit-mal, mild form of *epilepsy* characterized by a sudden, momentary loss of consciousness, in which all voluntary motor activity ceases.

Peto method, see *conductive education*.

phallic stage, phase in *Freudian theory of psychosexual development* when toilet training is usually complete and the young child shows sexual curiosity. It usually covers the period between three and five years of age, approximately, and is followed by the latency period.

phenylketonuria (PKU), *metabolic disorder* which if untreated causes intellectual damage and hence leads to *learning difficulties*. P K U is inherited. It can be detected early in life and controlled by special diet.

phobia, persistent abnormal dread or fear. Freud divided phobias into two groups:
(1) common phobias, i.e. an exaggerated fear of all those things most people dislike or fear to some extent, e.g. solitude, death, snakes etc.
(2) specific phobias, i.e. fear of circumstances that would normally inspire no fear, e.g. fear of open spaces, or *agoraphobia*. Some phobias can seriously interrupt children's activities and education, e.g. *school phobia*. Behaviour therapy and psychotherapy are often used to help deal with it.

phoneme, distinct speech sound. Spoken English is said to use more than 40 different phonemes. Children who have difficulty in distinguishing similar phonemes, e.g. the sounds of 'b' and 'p', will not find language acquisition easy, confusing similar-sounding words, e.g. 'bat' and 'pat'. Contrast *grapheme*; see *grapheme-phoneme relationship*.

phonic error, reading error which results from trying to apply phonic rules to words which are phonically irregular, e.g. yacht.

phonic method, or phonics, approach to the teaching of reading and spelling that stresses regular symbol-sound relationships, thus enabling children to read words not previously met. Contrast *look-and-say method*.

phonic readiness, stage in early reading when pupils have gained a reading vocabulary of roughly 70–100 words and are able to read simple material fluently and with understanding. It is claimed that they are then ready to follow the *phonic* method of learning to read.

phonics, see *phonic method*.

photonic wand, head-worn light pen, used by pupils who find a computer keyboard difficult to manage. Small head movements allow choices to be made from a computer's visual display unit, enabling programmes to be run.

physically handicapped, children not necessarily with defective sight or vision, but suffering from a crippling defect or disease such as *cerebral palsy, spina bifida, heart disease,* etc. This category of handicapped pupil has now been replaced by the idea of *special educational needs*. See *Education Act, 1981*.

physiotherapist, qualified member of the Chartered Society of *Physiotherapy* who treats physical *disabilities*, usually in collaboration with a doctor and/or medical rehabilitation team. The physiotherapist's role includes planning treatment programmes and giving advice on management; e.g. for *spina-bifida* babies, the physiotherapist provides exercise programmes to help movement, information about equipment and services appropriate for different stages of growth and advice on handling baby. Physiotherapists work mainly within hospitals, *special schools* and *units*; a few work within the community, making home visits.

physiotherapy, treatment of physical *disabilities* by methods such as massage, exercise, manipulation, *hydrotherapy*, light, heat, etc., rather than by *drugs*; it is also used to restore normal function when this has been damaged following an illness.

picture vocabulary test, measures either *oral vocabulary*, in which case the child has to identify (by naming correctly) a series of pictures, or, more usually, *oral comprehension vocabulary*, in which case the child has to choose from a set of pictures the one which most closely represents the word spoken by the examiner. Since the only response required is pointing, picture vocabulary tests are particularly useful in assessing the development of children with speech impairments. See *English Picture Vocabulary Test*.

pilot study, preliminary study undertaken before a major project. It may be intended as a feasibility study, or to practise the proposed methods or try out alternatives, whilst there is still an opportunity to make modifications: a trial run.

place of safety order, order, issued by a magistrate or a juvenile court to protect immediately children in an emergency by taking them into a place of safety for a period of up to 28 days. They may go into a *community home* provided by a local authority or a controlled community home, any police station or any hospital, surgery, or other suitable place where the occupier is willing temporarily to receive them.

play therapy, *psychotherapy* with young children, who can express feelings and fantasies more readily through play than in talk. Play itself is an important activity for children, since it helps their development and is also naturally therapeutic. But play therapy is a specialized technique for treating some of the problems of early childhood, derived from psychoanalytic principles and used in *child guidance clinics*.

Plowden Report 1967, report of the Central Advisory Council (England) on 'Children and their Primary Schools'. It called for the establishment for *educational priority areas (EPAs)* into which extra resources are put as a means of positive discrimination in favour of deprived children; a chapter was devoted to handicapped children in ordinary schools, which made a limited number of recommendations including a call for early identification and a full-scale inquiry into their education.

poliomyelitis, or infantile paralysis, infectious disease caused by a virus. The symptoms are fever, headache, vomiting, stiff neck and varying degrees of paralysis. Poliomyelitis can be prevented by *immunization*.

Portage Project, systematic programme of home teaching, that uses the parents of pre-school handicapped children as teachers. The parents collaborate closely with a trained visitor, usually an experienced teacher who helps to plan weekly activities based on regular *assessment* and evaluation of the child's progress. The project originated in Portage, Wisconsin, and a British network has now developed. See *National Portage Association* in Appendix A.

Porteus Problem Check List, set of 28 common adolescent worries, grouped into nine areas or subscales. It is used in *counselling* in order to identify adolescent problems.

positive discrimination, see *discrimination (3)*.

positive reinforcement, increasing the likelihood of desired behaviour recurring by providing an appropriate reward, e.g. praise, money, etc., as a consequence. It is a technique used in *behaviour modification*. Contrast *negative reinforcement*.

Possum, (Latin for 'I can'), electronic keyboard which translates simple muscular responses, e.g. pressing a button, moving a foot lever, into controlling the environment, e.g. typing, using the telephone, etc. It can also be used to select letters which build up words on a T.V. monitor. The Possum system was developed for use by people with severe physical handicaps.

pragmatics, branch of linguistics which stresses the importance of the context in which *language* patterns develop. It is argued that language-impaired children may benefit from a programme of language exercises emphasising language routines occurring in familiar situations.

precision teaching, system which specifies clear objectives for each pupil, records daily progress by short tests or probes, and points to the need to change techniques when targets are not being met. It is primarily a teaching method which sets great store on carefully monitoring a child's performance.

prematurity, birth before the appropriate time, i.e. before 37 weeks of gestation. The lower the birth weight of premature babies the greater the risk of handicapping conditions.

pre-reading activities, planned experiences that prepare a child for systematic reading instruction. They develop skills such as *listening* to stories, *auditory* and *visual discrimination* and aim to foster a keen interest in reading.

presbyopia, loss of elasticity of the lens of the eye.

pre-school education, education provided for children from two years of age in *nursery schools* and classes and run by the *LEA*. It is distinguished from experiences provided in playgroups and *opportunity groups* which are usually organized by parents, and day nurseries, which are run by the social services department. The *Warnock Report* recommended that education should be available for all young children with special needs as 'early education is the key to their individual development and the prevention or mitigation of later disturbances'. The *Education Act, 1981* empowers *local education authorities* to assess, with the consent of the parents, the *special educational needs* of 'children less than 2 years old'. Notwithstanding the formal meaning of pre-school education, provision for this age-group can be made through *opportunity groups*, parent support, etc. See *Portage project*.

prevalence, see *incidence*.

probation officer, officer of the court; *social worker* attached to the court, including *juvenile courts*. As well as guiding, assisting and befriending offenders on probation, probation officers assist the court by preparing social enquiry reports. Apart from working with juvenile delinquents and adult offenders, they also have functions in relation to matrimonial proceedings, in supervising those discharged from penal institutions, in recruiting and training suitable voluntary workers to befriend ex-prisoners and in running schemes connected with court orders for community service.

problem families, families which appear to be so overwhelmed by difficulties, such as debt, poor housing, mental and physical ill-health, etc., that they are unable to make constructive use of the normal services, e.g. the children may be poor attenders at school, the mother may fail to keep hospital appointments, the rent may be in arrears or the father may be in and out of prison. *Family Service Units* were pioneers in using intensive *casework* methods to help such families; local authority social service departments may employ special *social workers* to help them, in particular to prevent a situation deteriorating until the children have to be taken into care.

product-moment correlation coefficient, perhaps the most useful index of the *correlation* between two sets of measures. See *correlation coefficient*.

profound retardation, used in the U.S. for a level of intellectual functioning so impaired that a profoundly retarded child requires constant supervision throughout life. The American Association for Mental Deficiency uses the term to describe an intellectual level of about 20 IQ points or lower on an individual *intelligence test* (technically, a score lower than five standard deviations below the mean).

programmed instruction, structured teaching method which takes the child through a series of carefully graded steps, usually in the form of statements or questions, which require the child to respond in a predetermined way. The material is usually presented in book form, or via a *teaching machine* or via a computer. The child is enabled to learn independently, a step at a time, and at his/her own rate. See *computer-assisted instruction, linear programme*.

Programmed Reading Kit, scheme for teaching reading, devised by D. H. Stott, which has been widely used in *remedial education*.

Progress Assessment Charts (PAC), method of assessing the development of mentally handicapped individuals, devised by H. Gunzburg. The charts cover 120 skills, graded according to difficulty, and are divided into four areas: self-help, communication, socialization and occupation.

projection, in psychological terms, a *defence mechanism* to protect oneself from unacceptable feelings by accusing others of them. For example, someone who feels aggressive but cannot admit to this may project the feelings on to others, suggesting that they are aggressive.

Progressive Matrices, see *Raven's Progressive Matrices*.

projective technique, method of studying personality characteristics based on the theory of *psychoanalysis*. For example, a child might be asked to describe the feelings of characters in a picture. The techniques work on the principle of *projection*, i.e. it is assumed that feelings that are consistently ascribed to the characters may reflect those feelings that the child is finding hard to accept. Other tasks might involve drawing situations, completing unfinished sentences, telling stories, etc. These techniques are used by some *psychiatrists* and *psychologists* working with children's *emotional* disorders. They demand skilful and experienced interpretation.

projection test, particular kind of *projective technique* in which standard material and instructions are usually used and where common responses may also be listed.

prosthetics, application, evaluation, treatment and prescription of artificial body parts, or prostheses.

pseudohypertrophic muscular dystrophy, see *Duchenne's muscular dystrophy*.

psychiatric disorder, behaviour, emotions or relationships which cause persistent suffering or handicap to the child or distress or distubance to the family or community. Child psychiatric disorders can be classified in various ways. One approach uses seven main categories:

(1) neurotic disorder, (see *neurosis*)
(2) *conduct disorder,*
(3) mixed conduct and neurotic disorder,
(4) developmental disorders, (see *developmental delay*)
(5) hyperkinetic syndrome, (see *hyperactivity*)
(6) child *psychosis,*
(7) *personality disorder.*

But see *classification*.

psychiatrist, medical practitioner with additional specialist training in the prevention, diagnosis and treatment of *psychiatric disorders*.

psychoanalysis, method of treating *psychiatric disorders* which emphasizes bringing unconscious thoughts and feelings into consciousness in a controlled way, using techniques such as *free association* with older children and *play therapy* with younger children. It can be contrasted with other forms of treatment, such as *behaviour therapy*. There are different schools of psychoanalysis (which is a body of theory, as well as a treatment method), most of which have developed from the pioneer work of S. Freud. (See *Freudian theory of psychosexual development*).

psychoanalyst, *psychiatrist* who practises *psychoanalysis*.

psychodrama, *group therapy* technique in which group members act out their problems and conflicts through assigned but impromptu roles; it is used in order to release tensions, to gain insight into oneself and others, and to learn desirable social behaviour.

psychogenic disorders, disorders which originate in psychological conditions, though they may come to involve physiological changes as a result.

psychologist, person with a training and qualification in psychology recognized by the appropriate professional association (in the U.K., the British Psychological Society). There are many different kinds of psychologist. *Educational psychologists* are most heavily involved in special education, though some *clinical psychologists* work with children through the health service.

psychometrics, or psychometry, branch of psychology dealing with the measure of behaviour including the development, administration and interpretation of psychological tests. Its main use in the education system is in the *assessment* of educational abilities and attainments.

psychometry, see *psychometrics*.

psychomotor skills, skills requiring *co-ordination* between mind and muscle. All movements other than *reflex* actions involve psychomotor skills, e.g. buttoning a coat, using a pen, catching a ball, driving a car, etc.

psychopathic disorder, one of the four legal categories of mental disorder, defined in the *Mental Health Act, 1983*, as a persistent disorder or disability of mind (whether or not including significant impairment of intelligence) which results in abnormally aggressive or seriously irresponsible conduct on the part of the person concerned. See *mental illness, mental impairment, severe mental impairment*.

psychopathic personality, ill-defined term for an individual who consistently behaves antisocially and is impulsive, irresponsible and pleasure-seeking. A psychopathic personality lacks conscience, showing little guilt or remorse, and finding it difficult to give affection.

psychopharmacological agent, drug or other active substance sometimes used in the treatment of emotional and behavioural disorders.

psychosis, serious mental disorder, characterized by such features as distorted *perception*, defective memory and impaired language; in contrast to a *neurosis* the sufferer may not be in touch with reality and may not recognize that he/she is ill. *Schizophrenia* and *manic depression* are well-known psychoses in adults: in children, psychoses are rare. See *autism*.

psychotherapist, person who practises *psychotherapy*.

psychotherapy, treatment of *emotional* and *behaviour disorders*; also used only for methods derived from psychoanalytic theory and stressing the importance of relationships. See, for example, *family group therapy*, or the *play therapy* practised by followers of psychoanalysts such as Anna Freud or Melanie Klein.

psychotic, person suffering from *psychosis* (noun):relating to psychosis (adjective).

Public Law 94–142, U.S. federal legislation which in 1975 guaranteed free public education to all children, whatever their degree of disability. Education had to be provided in the *least restrictive environment*, which has increased the integration, or *mainstreaming*, of handicapped children, and an *Individualized Education Program* had to be provided for each child.

Pudenz valve, see *shunt*.

Pultibec system, method of rating the severity of a child's handicap under eight main headings, *P*hysical capacity; *U*pper limbs, *L*ocomotion; *T*oilet; *I*ntelligence; *B*ehaviour; vision (*E*yes); *C*ommunication. The A (PULT) side of the profile is mainly concerned with physical motor/capacities; the B (IBEC) side with *behaviour/communication skills*.

pupil-teacher ratio, the *average* number of pupils per teacher, a statistic that can be calculated for a single school, or for a *local education authority*, or for a phase of education nationally, such as primary education. The pupil-teacher ratio in segregated *special education* is substantially lower and more flexible than in ordinary education, rarely rising above twelve but varying considerably according to the pupils' special needs.

pure-tone audiometer, instrument used in *pure-tone audiometry*. It produces pure tones — i.e. there are no overtones, and so it helps to provide a more accurate picture of hearing.

pure-tone audiometry, method of assessing hearing for tones at particular *frequencies*. At each frequency the tone is produced at different loudness levels, usually steps of five *decibels*. The child has to indicate when a sound is heard. The results are drawn as an *audiogram*. See *audiogram* illustration; compare *speech audiometry*.

Q

QBRS, *Qualitative Behaviour Record Sheet*, used by teachers of children with severe learning difficulties to monitor a child's progress in mastering such skills as washing hands, identifying coins, etc.

Q-technique, or Q-sort, *personality test* in which the subject sorts out a number of descriptive statements which he/she believes to be self-descriptive, thus revealing personality characteristics.

quad canes, four lightweight aluminium canes with a central support, providing stability for the unsteady walker.

quadriplegia, weakness or paralysis affecting all four limbs. See *cerebral palsy*.

questionnaire, series of suitably selected and carefully designed questions devised to survey opinions, assess personality traits or gain information on some specific topics.

Quirk Report 1972, 'Speech Therapy Services', review of the training and work of *speech therapists*, which included recommendations to expand *speech therapy* services and establish a professional organization. The levels of staffing recommended are being approached very slowly.

Queen Elizabeth's Foundation for the Disabled (QEF), voluntary organization operating four *units* which provide *assessment*, *further education*, *vocational training*, *sheltered workshops*, holidays and convalescence for disabled men and women and young people. (See *Queen Elizabeth's Training College for the Disabled* in Appendix A).

R

r, symbol used for a form of *correlation coefficient*.

Ralphs Report 1973, report of a Local Government Training Board working party, chaired by Sir Lincoln Ralphs, on 'The Role and Training of Educational Welfare Officers' (EWOs). It recommended that EWOs should have the salary, status and training of *social workers* but retain their administrative links with the educational sector. It emphasized the value of social work in an educational setting.

Rampton Report 1981, interim report of the Committee of Inquiry, chaired by Sir Anthony Rampton, on the educational needs and attainments of children from ethnic minority groups. One of the reasons for establishing the Committee was the concern of parents and others at the preponderance of pupils of West Indian origins in special schools and classes for children with *learning difficulties* and *behaviour disorders*. It argued that major determinants of the underachievement of West Indian children were difficult social conditions which led to poor pre-school care, parental attitudes, as well as 'unintentional racism', negative attitudes and low expectations on the part of some teachers. By comparison, Asian children did as well as or better than white children. The committee recommended aiming at creating a multi-cultural education system in which the cultures of ethnic minority children would be valued and racial bias reduced. See *Swann Report*.

random sampling, method of *sampling* in which all members of the population being studied have an equal chance of being chosen for the sample; therefore findings from the smaller, more manageable sample can be applied to the larger population, with a known estimate of error.

rank-order correlation coefficient, variety of *correlation coefficient* which uses a measure of the correspondence between two sets of ranks as an index of their correlation.

rapport, harmonious personal relationship, creating an atmosphere of mutual confidence. Rapport between child and tester is essential for valid psychological and educational assessment: rapport between child and teacher is essential for effective learning.

rating scale, method of assessment which depends on personal judgement. A rater makes an assessment by checking one of several descriptions of the quality being assessed. Thus a rating scale might offer three possible descriptions of aggressive behaviour:
(1) very aggressive, often attacks other children;
(2) retaliates when attacked, otherwise peaceful;
(3) never shows aggression, withdraws if attacked;
The rater is required to check the most appropriate description of a child's behaviour. Sometimes a scale of numbers is used instead of verbal descriptions.

Rating scales are used for various purposes, e.g. in case studies of individual children, in screening for children with special needs and in research.

ratio reinforcement, technique used in *behaviour modification*; the reward offered is related to the number of correct responses. Thus a child can be rewarded for every tenth correct answer, an example of fixed-ratio reinforcement. As the required behaviour — correct answering, indicating learning — becomes established, the ratio can be extended or 'stretched', perhaps to a reward for every 20 correct answers. Reinforcement in which the ratio is varied is known as variable-ratio reinforcement. Ratio reinforcement is an example of a *reinforcement schedule*. See *interval reinforcement*.

rationalization, as used in *psychoanalysis*, finding an excuse, e.g. maintaining that a goal which cannot be achieved is undesirable anyway, or that poor behaviour is justified by plausible but untrue motives. This kind of explanation protects the individual from having to acknowledge personal failings and is an example of a *'defence mechanism'*.

Raven's Progressive Matrices, *intelligence tests* developed by J. C. Raven between 1938 – 1958. The standard form consists of sixty designs arranged in groups of twelve. Each design has a piece missing; the missing piece has to be chosen from a number of possibilities. There is a version using coloured patterns which is suitable for 5 – 11-year-olds, the elderly, those who cannot understand or speak English and for mentally retarded children and adults. The matrices are said to assess reasoning skills not involving speech but requiring visual discrimination and the capacity to see logical relationships.

raw score, actual score or mark obtained on a test before it is changed or transformed into an equivalent, more meaningful measurement. Thus a raw score of 33 points on a reading test might be transformed into a *reading age* of 7.9 years, say.

readability, comprehensibility and interest of reading material. It is usually assessed by measuring qualities such as legibility, style, length of words and sentences, etc. Readability measures are used to match reading material to a child's reading level, but the reader's motivation, abilities and interests also affect the readability of text.

readability formulae, methods of calculating difficulty levels of reading matter, used in assessing the suitability of texts for children. Earlier formulae used simple techniques such as counting *average* sentence length, but more sophisticated methods have now been developed. See *cloze procedure, Fog index, SMOG index*.

reading age, reading performance measured against the *average* reading standards of children of different ages. Thus an advanced 6-year-old may have a reading performance similar to the average reading performance of children aged 8½ years, in which case his/her reading age would be 8 years 6 months.

reading comprehension, one of the major reading skills, which can be contrasted with others, such as accuracy of *word recognition*. It is usually assessed by asking questions on sentences or passages that a child has read in order to gauge understanding, but the use is sometimes extended to include the ability to criticize as well as to interpret.

reading laboratory:
(1) special classroom or library which contains reading tests, schemes and materials, often with particular emphasis on *remedial reading*;
(2) commercially prepared graded reading schemes designed for individual reading at the child's own rate.

reading pacer, equipment for improving speed of reading. There are various kinds of apparatus, but essentially all follow the principle of preventing the reader following the text at his own (slow) pace: the apparatus reveals text at a set rate which the reader has to follow lest text moves out of sight before it is read. As speed of reading improves, the rate at which text is revealed can be increased until a satisfactory reading speed is reached.

reading readiness, stage at which a child is sufficiently mature physically, emotionally and intellectually, to begin formal reading instruction. Some authorities used to suggest that children were not usually ready to read until they were at least six years of age and that earlier teaching might not help and might actually hinder later progress. But it is now recognized that this is an oversimplification and there is a tremendous variation in the age at which children can begin to profit from reading teaching.

reading readiness test, test for assessing some of the skills a child needs in order to profit from formal reading instruction. The skills usually covered in these tests include *visual discrimination*, *auditory discrimination*, *motor ability*, comprehension vocabulary and general information. They help to predict a child's later reading attainment, but other factors, such as parental encouragement, for example, also play a part. See *Thackray Reading Readiness Profiles*.

reading scheme, series of graded books and other material designed to help children learn to read. Many teachers use a wide range of schemes, selecting the most suitable one for the needs of the individual child. See *graded reader*.

reading vocabulary, usually, the words recognized and understood in *silent reading*: sometimes, the words pronounced correctly, whether understood or not. Compare *oral comprehension vocabulary*, but distinguish carefully from *vocabulary of reading*.

reality therapy, rests on the belief that behaviour disorders stem from a person's faulty perceptions of the world and that treatment consists of helping the person adjust these perceptions, often by the judicious use of a series of 'contracts' with the therapist. In the contract, the individual accepts responsibility for changing his/her behaviour, in small ways at first but more radically later. Reality therapy was originated by W. Glasser. It is sometimes described as an example of cognitive therapy, rooted neither in the behaviourist nor the psychoanalyst tradition.

rebus, picture or symbol which represents a word or phrase. Many road signs are examples of rebuses. Some children with reading difficulties respond to *reading schemes* which use rebuses, rather than letters and words, in their initial stages, e.g. the Peabody Rebus Reading Program.

reception centre, place for the temporary reception and observation of children coming into the care of local authorities, so that long term arrangements are can then be made, e.g. finding a foster home.

receptive aphasia, or sensory aphasia, loss or impairment of the ability to understand speech. See *aphasia*, contrast *expressive aphasia*.

receptive language, usually reading and listening: that part of communication which involves receiving and understanding information from others. Difficulties in this are known as receptive language disorders, e.g. *receptive aphasia* is a serious receptive language disorder. Tests which assess abilities that are important for good receptive language skills, e.g. *auditory discrimination*, *word recognition*, etc., are sometimes collectively known as receptive language tests. Contrast *expressive language*.

recessive gene, *gene* whose characteristics appear only if paired with another on the *chromosomes*. So for a child to be affected by a disease carried on a recessive gene, such as *cystic fibrosis* or *phenylketonuria*, both parents must be *carriers (2)*. Contrast *dominant gene*.

recidivism, repeated relapses into *delinquency* or crime, despite treatment or punishment.

reciprocal inhibition, '*counter-conditioning*' an unwanted reaction, such as fear, by pairing its source (conditioned stimulus) with a source of pleasure. Thus the sight of a spider, to which a fear response has been conditioned, is paired with relaxing music and reassuring words, in order to diminish and eventually remove the fear. This approach is sometimes used in *behaviour therapy*.

Record of Need, in Scottish legislation, the equivalent of a *Statement of Special Educational Needs*.

Reed Test, screening test for the early detection of high-frequency *hearing losses*. The child is required to point to the picture of an object named by the tester for each item. There is a choice of four pictures, representing objects whose names differ in high-frequency consonants only, e.g. bus, duck, jug, and cup. The number of errors is an indication of difficulty in discriminating high-frequency sounds, usually due to high-frequency hearing loss.

reflex, involuntary muscular or neurological response to a sensory stimulus, as an eyeblink is an involuntary response to a puff of air. See *Babinski reflex, knee-jerk reflex*.

refraction, bending of light rays, as when light rays are bent by the lens of the eye to produce a clear image. Errors in refraction, which result in poor *visual acuity* and other defects of vision, can be put right by corrective lenses.

Register of Disabled Persons, list of disabled and handicapped persons, kept by the Employment Services Division of the Manpower Services Commission under the *Disabled Persons (Employment) Acts, 1944, 1958*, for the purpose of helping disabled persons find employment.

regression:
  (1) reversion to *behaviour* typical of an earlier stage of mental or emotional development, as when an older child throws a temper tantrum;
  (2) backward movement in symptoms or conditions as when a sick child who has been improving takes a turn for the worse;
  (3) relationship between sets of scores, often expressed as an equation, the regression equation. This enables the most probable scores on one set, e.g. reading performance, to be predicted, knowing scores on the others, e.g. *intelligence* and *language development*;
  (4) *eye-movement* in which the eye returns to rescan material already read.

regression to the mean, particular feature of *regression (3)*, namely the tendency for predicted scores to be closer to the *mean*, when this is the most probable value, than might have been expected from other scores. Thus a child whose *intelligence test* score is very low would be expected to have a reading score which is closer to, though still below, *average*. A specific illustration occurs in *genetics*, where there is a tendency for characteristics of children, e.g. *intelligence*, to be nearer to the population mean than those of their parents.

rehabilitation, process of education or training which helps recovery from or adjustment to mental or physical handicap.

reinforcement, changing the likelihood of behaviour occurring by using a reinforcer, an important principle in behavioural psychology. Note the difference between *positive reinforcement* (a pleasant consequence, such as being awarded a star) and *negative reinforcement* (stopping an unpleasant experience, such as ending isolation, or time-out). A planned programme of reinforcement is known as a reinforcement schedule. See *interval reinforcement, ratio reinforcement, operant conditioning*.

reinforcer, that which results in changing the probability of behaviour recurring, such as giving a child a star for good behaviour, particularly if the stars can be exchanged for a desired reward.

rejection, consciously or unconsciously excluding or denying affection to a person. Children can be rejected by their parents, siblings, teachers, or peers.

reliability, extent to which a test or *assessment* procedure gives consistent results when used at different times or by different administrators. It is usually expressed as a *correlation coefficient* between results obtained on the same children at different times or by different testers. Thus the closer a quoted reliability approaches +1.00 the better it is. As a rule of thumb, reliabilities above +0.90 are usually regarded as satisfactory for measures of *intelligence* or *attainment*: for *personality tests*, lower reliabilities are usually acceptable, but the values do need skilled interpretation in the light of the standardization of the test.

remand homes, now known as *community homes*.

remedial education, or remedial teaching, special teaching (now often called support teaching) in any area of school work for children who are not progressing as well as expected. Remedial reading is probably the most frequent help offered. Remedial teachers operate in various ways: the child can attend a full-time remedial class, or attend part-time at a withdrawal class or, increasingly, receive support in the ordinary classroom, often through the remedial teacher and class teacher combining in a *team-teaching* approach. This last method is gaining in popularity and 'support teaching' is often a preferred term. Occasionally remedial teaching takes place in remedial centres, *school psychological service* offices or *child guidance clinics*. It draws on a wide variety of special techniques and teaching materials. In secondary schools in particular, where there may be a number of remedial teachers on the staff, a remedial department may be established, with an appointed Head. Again, terminology is changing as functions alter and remedial departments are being retitled support departments, special education departments, etc.

remedial service, non-school-based organization, usually provided by an *LEA*, for delivering *remedial education*, e.g. through *peripatetic teachers*, remedial centres, etc. Many remedial services have now developed into advisory services for special needs. See *special services*.

remedial teacher, or support teacher, see *remedial education*.

remedial treatment, programme of *physiotherapy* and exercises given to a child with a physical *disability*.

remission, partial or complete disappearance of the symptoms of a disease, either as a result of treatment or spontaneously.

Remploy, public, non-profit making company which organizes employment for handicapped people. There are several full-time paid directors and other part-time, unpaid directors who have industrial experience and are interested in the problems of disabled workers. Remploy runs about eighty factories, providing work for thousands of severely disabled people. It offers a consultancy service to workshops for the blind run by charities and local authorities. Some factories arrange work for disabled workers in their own homes. Workers must be on the *Register of Disabled Persons*. For Remploy address, see Appendix A.

Repertory Grid Technique, method based on *personal construct theory* exploring attitudes, feelings, concepts, and thought processes generally.

repression, as used in *psychoanalysis*, *defence mechanism* to protect oneself from unacceptable feelings, by refusing to allow them into consciousness.

Research Centre for the Education of the Visually Handicapped, established at the University of Birmingham Faculty of Education. As well as working with visually handicapped adults the Centre conducts enquiries into the *integration* of visually handicapped pupils in ordinary education, the use of microcomputers in their education, the introduction of *Braille* to young visually handicapped children and many other topics.

residential school, any boarding school, but in particular a boarding school catering for children with special needs that cannot be managed in the local school, or children whose home circumstances necessitate education away from home. Some residential schools specialize in educating children with particular special needs, e.g. sensory defects such as blindness. Residential schools may be provided by LEAs, voluntary bodies or privately, but all must be approved by the Department of Education and Science.

residual hearing, any usable hearing possessed by a hearing-impaired child.

residual vision, any usable sight possessed by a child whose vision is impaired.

resonance, vibration of air in a cavity, e.g. resonance in the mouth, nose and throat; it is important for the production of clear speech.

resource centre, place where learning materials are housed. The centre may be used as a work place, or a source from which materials such as films, tapes, books, specimens and models may be borrowed. Larger resource centres carry permanent staff. A resource centre for special needs consists of specialized staff and the facilities required for providing and organizing the support for educating children — often with severe disabilities — in ordinary schools. Such a centre is seen as an important component of a whole-school approach to special needs. Some special schools have changed their role and function as resource centres for ordinary schools in their area.

resource room, U.S. term for a specially equipped room within a school where a specialist teacher works with children with *learning difficulties*. Similar to a remedial classroom. It may also function as a source of materials and equipment, as a base for support staff and a venue for case conferences.

resource teacher, U.S. term for a specialist teacher who works with children with *learning difficulties*, sometimes advising other teachers, providing materials and methods for helping such children in the ordinary classroom. The resource teacher may work from a *resource room*: similar to *remedial teacher* or support teacher.

retardation:
(1) in the U.K., educational performance which is substantially below intellectual performance. Thus a child with a *mental age* of 10 years and a *reading age* of 7 years could be described as showing 3 years retardation in reading. Note the difference between retardation and *backwardness*, where *chronological age*, not mental age, is the criterion;
(2) in the U.S., condition of a child whose intellectual functioning is significantly below average.

retina, sense organ for sight, an extension of the *optic nerve* inside the eyeball in a thin layer of cells which are sensitive to light and colour. It receives images of external objects and sends the resulting impulses along the optic nerve to the vision centres in the brain. See *eye* illustration (p. 76); see *Irlen lens*.

retinitis pigmentosa, *chronic*, progressive and degenerative disease of the retina. It starts as night blindness and sight gradually deteriorates.

retinoblastoma, *congenital* hereditary condition caused by a malignant tumour originating from the *retina*. It occurs in children and treatment may involve the removal of the eye and as much of the *optic nerve* as possible.

retinopathy of prematurity, see *retrolental fibroplasia*.

retrolental fibroplasia, or retinopathy of prematurity, retinal overgrowth which limits vision, caused by over-exposure of premature infants to oxygen whilst in an incubator. It is a rare condition now because of the better-controlled use of oxygen.

reversal, error, usually in reading or writing, in which a single symbol is reversed, e.g. writing 'b' for 'd', or the sequence of several symbols is reversed, e.g. reading 'rat' for 'tar'.

Reynell Developmental Language Scales, provide a measure of *expressive language* (speech) and verbal comprehension (aspects of *receptive language*). They are often used with young children, for they cover the age-range 1 – 7 years. There are separate instructions for children with hearing loss and physical disabilities.

Reynell-Zinkin Developmental Scales, six tests of language and other skills for use with visually handicapped children up to six years of age, and which are used in order to help to plan a suitable educational programme, which parents can introduce.

Rh factor, or Rhesus factor, inherited characteristic of blood. If there is incompatibility between the Rh factors of the mother and the unborn child, the child can be damaged and, if it survives, there may be *mental* or *physical handicap*. In most cases the situation only occurs if the mother is Rh negative and the child is Rh positive and even then the affected child can usually be treated successfully by blood transfusion. Nowadays, with proper antenatal care, the situation can be anticipated and almost entirely avoided by giving the mother appropriate injections.

Rhesus factor, see *Rh factor*.

rheumatic fever, disease which usually starts following an infection of the upper respiratory tract. It occurs most often in school-age children but is now very rare in the U.K. It may affect the heart and joints. Rheumatic *chorea* is an uncommon variation characterized by involuntary twitching movements which appear over a period of many months. Teachers should consult with doctors and parents to find out which activities are permissible for a child who has had rheumatic fever or chorea.

rheumatoid arthritis, see *Still's disease*

Right and Left tests, tests to check a child's understanding of 'right' and 'left' from various stand points. Poorly oriented children may have difficulty in reading and in letter formation, for example. The tests consist of pointing to different parts of the child's body and that of the examiner, who notes the child's speed and accuracy. See *directionality*.

risk registers, see *'at risk registers'*.

rituals, unusual behaviour resulting from neurotic compulsions, e.g. a child may need to button and unbutton his coat many times before going outside: an example of *obsessive behaviour*.

role-playing, way of learning principles of inter-personal relationships by taking a part in a playlet or scene. It is used in training for professions such as *counselling*, social work, etc. and can be used in *psychotherapy*. See *psychodrama*.

room management, procedure used, for example with children with severe *learning difficulties*, and involving several adults. One may teach a new skill, another may help the children practice it while a third deals with distractions and any reorganization needed. One purpose is to increase and focus the engagement of children with staff.

Rorschach Inkblots Test, *projective technique* developed by H. Rorschach consisting of ten cards with symmetrical ink-blots on them. The individual is given the cards in sequence and asked to say what each inkblot represents. The answers are interpreted to reveal various aspects of personality. Lengthy and detailed training is said to be needed in order to give the test and interpret the answers effectively. The validity of the test has been criticized but some psychologists and psychiatrists, particularly psychoanalysts, believe that it has value in diagnosing psychiatric disorders.

Rosenzweig Picture Frustration Test, *projective technique* which is available in several forms, including one for children ages 4 – 13 and one for adolescents. Each form consists of a series of cartoons showing two main characters. The situations depicted are mildly frustrating and the subject has to write the frustrated person's response to the situation in the caption box. Each reply is classified according to the kind of reaction shown and how aggressive feelings are managed.

Rowntree Family Fund, see Family Fund.

rubella, or German measles, disease caused by a virus infection; when contracted by a woman in early pregnancy there is a strong likelihood that the child will show one or more severe handicaps, e.g. severe *learning difficulties*, heart defects, *cerebral palsy*, impaired hearing and vision.

Rudolph Steiner Schools, see *Camphill Schools*.

Ruth Griffiths Scale, see *Griffiths Scale of Infant Development*.

Rutter Scales, see *Children's Behaviour Questionnaire*.

S

's', symbol used for *standard deviation*.

's' (specific factor), specific ability, first described by Spearman as a factor specific to performance on tests of particular abilities. According to Spearman, a child's performance on a reading test would thus depend on his/her *g*, or general intelligence, but also on his/her *s* for reading. This two-factor theory of the structure of ability has been overtaken by later models, though the underlying notion has a simplicity which may account for its persistence in some quarters. See *group factor*, contrast *g*.

saccadic eye movements, saccades, quick jumping *eye-movements* as *fixation* is shifted from place to place, e.g. in moving along a line of print. The characteristics of saccadic eye movements are sometimes said to be helpful in diagnosing reading difficulties.

sampling, selecting a small group or sample to represent a larger group or population. The sample is used in educational experiments, test construction, etc. when working with a complete population is impractical, or too expensive. There are different ways of drawing a sample: it is important to be able to state the error involved in generalizing the findings for a sample to the population. See *random sampling*.

sanctuary unit, class or *unit* with a low *teacher/pupil ratio* and more resources than normal. Its emphasis is on the treatment and management of pupils with emotional and behavioural disorders, in particular disruptive pupils. It may be staffed by specialist teachers; units are small, with rarely more than three staff. Similar to *behavioural unit*.

Sander's dysfluent words, words which are prolonged or broken when uttered, interrupted by an interjection or repeated in whole or part. Sander's Dysfluent Word Index is the number of dysfluent words per hundred words read or spoken. It is used in measuring *stuttering*.

satiation, state which results from presenting a *reinforcer* too often or in too great a quantity. Satiation is deliberately produced in some *aversion therapy*, by allowing or insisting that an individual continues to produce the initially rewarding undesired behaviour to such an extent that eventually he/she tires of it.

schizoid, resembling *schizophrenia*: a schizoid personality is a very withdrawn personality.

schizophrenia, the most common *psychosis*; a serious psychological condition in which the sufferer loses touch with reality and may show confused, disorganized thinking. At one time it was believed that schizophrenia often started in *adolescence*, but authorities now recognize childhood schizophrenia as a relatively rare condition, usually requiring special education. *Autism* has been classed as a form of childhood schizophrenia but this is a matter of debate.

Schonell Graded Word Reading Test, individual *word recognition* test produced by F. J. Schonell. It consists of a card on which are printed a hundred words in order of reading difficulty. The number of words correctly pronounced is converted into a *reading age*. It is one of the commonest quick reading tests in use in British schools. An updated version has been produced by E. Goodacre. See *graded word reading test*.

Schonell Graded Word Spelling Test, consists of a hundred words, dictated by the teacher, to be written by the child. The words are arranged in order of spelling difficulty. The number of words correctly spelt is converted into a spelling age. There are two parallel tests.

school attendance officers, see *education welfare officers*.

school counsellors, see *counselling*.

School Curriculum Development Council, one of the two bodies which in Spring 1983 replaced the Schools Council. Its membership is nominated by the Secretary of State for Education and Science. It has continued to support a number of projects concerned with the *curriculum* for children with special needs.

school health service, organization which provides health care for pupils, supplying the services of medical staff to ordinary and *special schools*, making arrangements for medical examinations and *immunisation*, for dental care, eyesight and *hearing tests*, for advice to parents and teachers on handicapping conditions and health education, and for health counselling services. It was established in 1906, but in 1974 responsibility for the service was transferred from the local education authorities to the health service.

school medical examination, every child normally has a medical examination on school entry and again at about the ages of 8, 11, and 14 years. For children with special needs, more frequent medical examinations are usually made as part of regular assessments which parents are invited to attend. Additional medical examinations can be arranged at the request of parents, teachers or the school nurse, at other times.

school phobia, pattern of intense negative reactions to school which, can lead to *school refusal*. It tends to appear more frequently in early *adolescence*, often after transfer from primary to secondary school, and may include physical symptoms such as sickness, stomach pains, etc. as well as feelings of fear. It is managed by *behaviour therapy, psychotherapy*, transfer to adjustment *units*, etc. School phobia is usually found in conscientious, law-abiding children, who, at a conscious level, want to attend school. See *school refusal; truancy*.

school psychological service, organization provided by the *local education authority* and staffed mainly by *educational psychologists*. It is largely concerned with the educational well-being of individual children with special needs and the *assessment* and management of their development, using mainly a *case-work* or a consultancy model. This involves close collaboration with the range of educational, medical, social and other services concerned. But the main focus of the work is the child, his/her teachers and the family. The LEA also looks to it for a psychological contribution to policies which affect the education of all children.

school refusal, *school phobia* so intense that children are unable to attend school. It is distinguished from *truancy* in which children avoid school and enjoy being absent.

school social worker, trained *social worker*, based in the school(s), who offers a *casework* service for families and children with referrals from headteachers and from parents themselves. A school social worker may also do group work with deprived and/or delinquent children. Part of the role is to increase teachers' awareness of children's social problems.

Schools Council, body with membership representative of the teaching profession, the local education authorities and the Department of Education and Science, responsible for *curriculum* development in schools in England and Wales, and for advice on public examinations. It was established in 1964 and abolished in 1983 by the respective Secretaries of State for Education and Science. In its later years in particular it funded a number of influential projects concerned with the curriculum for children with special needs; their findings were published. It has been replaced by two bodies, one concerned with examinations, called the Secondary

Examinations Council and the other with curriculum development, called the *School Curriculum Development Council*.

scoliosis, lateral curvature of the spine; a not uncommon abnormality of childhood, particularly in girls, with various causes. Early treatment including exercises, corrective surgery, braces and casts may prevent the curvature from getting worse.

Scott Report 1962, report of a sub-committee of the Minister of Health's Standing Mental Health Advisory Committee, set up in 1959 to consider the training and supply of staff working with the mentally handicapped and numbers required. It made a number of recommendations aimed at improving the training and status of teachers of mentally handicapped children. The report was a significant step on the way to the full incorporation of provision for mentally handicapped children within the education service. See *Education Act, 1970*.

screening, identifying or selecting a small number of children from a larger group, usually to allow a more detailed *assessment* to be made; e.g. *audiometric screening* is used to detect children who may have *hearing loss*.

secondary handicap, handicap resulting from an individual's major handicap, e.g. deaf children may be additionally handicapped by lack of normal social relations with their peers.

Seebohm Report 1968, Report of the Committee on Local Authority and Allied Personal Social Services. The report advocated a more positive approach to community care, recommending that local social services should be reorganized into comprehensive social service departments, to avoid administrative confusion and inefficiency, and to provide a 'family' social service. As a result, the Local Authority Social Services Act 1970, established social services departments.

segregation, separating one group of people from the rest of the population on an arbitrary criterion such as race, gender, etc. In special education, the provision of separate facilities for children with special needs in classes, *units* or schools where they are grouped with others who have a similar handicap. See *discrimination (2)*.

seizure, sudden violent involuntary contraction of a group of muscles. See *epilepsy*.

self-concept, or self image, how a person thinks or feels about him/herself. This is influenced by the views of others who are significant in the person's life. A teacher of children with special needs, who displays a positive, encouraging attitude will foster a healthy self-concept.

self-fulfilling prophecy, the belief that a child's performance reflects what others expect: a child whose teacher has low expectations of him/her will perform poorly at school; conversely, if good work is expected it will be produced. The self-fulfilling prophecy is held to be one possible reason for a child's low *attainment*.

self-image, see *self-concept*.

self-injury behaviour, s.i.b., for example, hair-pulling, head-banging, skin-tearing — behaviour in which an individual harms him/herself. S.i.b. is not common, but is probably most often seen in some children with very severe learning difficulties or some autistic children. It can be difficult to remove and seems to be self-reinforcing for some children.

self-stimulation, compensating for *sensory deprivation (1)* by means such as rocking, or head movements: characteristic of some children with *multisensory deprivation* in particular.

S E M E R Cs, Special Education Micro Electronic Resource Centres, resource centres for teachers and others who wish to use microelectronics to help in teaching children with special needs either through the use of specially designed *computer-aided instruction* and *computer-assisted learning* programmes or through the use of electronically-controlled aids. They offer information, contribute to teacher education and training and circulate newsletters. They were originally funded by the *Department of Education and Science's* Microelectronic Education Programme, but are now supported by its successor, the *Microelectronics Education Support Unit*. See Appendix A.

semicircular canals, three tubes in the *inner ear* which are filled with fluid and act as the sense organs for balance. See *ear* illustration (p. 66).

semiliteracy, see *literacy*.

SENIOS, Special Educational Needs In the Ordinary School. See *whole school approach*.

SENNAC(Special Educational Needs National Advisory Council), aims to coordinate the activities of the various organizations concerned with children with special educational needs. It was formed in 1982, replacing the Joint Council for the Education of Handicapped Children, and is funded by its eight constitutent organizations, each of whom nominates two members. See Appendix A.

sensorimotor skill, see *perceptual-motor abilities*.

sensorineural hearing loss, *hearing loss* caused by disease or damage to the *inner ear* and/or *auditory nerve* often affecting high frequency sound in particular. Contrast *conductive hearing loss*.

sensory aphasia, see *receptive aphasia*.

sensory apraxia, see *apraxia*.

sensory deprivation:
(1) less sensory stimulation than is usual. It is believed that sensory deprivation in early childhood, e.g. when infants have to remain in hospital wards for long periods, can retard growth of *intelligence*. This is one reason why interesting and varied activities are an important part of a young child's experience, wherever he/she may be;
(2) psychological experiment in which an individual receives no stimulation through the senses for a given period of time. The effects help in the study of *perception* and other phenomena;.
(3) effect of *hearing impairment, visual disability*, etc.

sensory integration, liaison between the separate senses on which depends the individual's organization of experience. Many children with *specific learning difficulties* appear to lack the ability fully to integrate information from their senses, as may some children with *cerebral palsy*. Some 'clumsy' children may not easily integrate information from their eyes with *kinaesthesis*.

sequela, (pl. sequelae), any abnormal condition that follows and is the result of an injury, treatment or disease, e.g. paralysis following *poliomyelitis*, or a scar after a laceration.

sequencing skills, skills involved in relating items in the right order, such as learning to count or to give the days of the week correctly. They are particular examples of *language development* skills.

s.e.s., see *socio-economic status*.

setting, grouping pupils for certain subjects, e.g. reading, mathematics, according to their attainment in that subject. Setting offers a compromise between mixed-ability classes and *streaming*.

severe mental impairment, one of the four legal categories of mental disorder specified in the *Mental Health Act, 1983*, and defined as a state of arrested or incomplete development of mind which includes severe impairment of intelligence and social functioning and is associated with abnormally aggressive or seriously irresponsible conduct on the part of the person concerned. See *mental illness, mental impairment, psychopathic disorder*.

sex education, teaching about the anatomy and physiology of sex, giving basic medical information about contraception and sexually transmitted diseases, pregnancy, birth and infant care, and discussing emotional and moral issues in interpersonal relationships. Most schools offer some formal or informal sex education to their pupils. Careful and sensitive guidance on sexual matters is needed for young people with physical or mental handicap who can worry more about their attractiveness to the opposite sex, or may in some instances have unrealistic ambitions about having children and a normal family life.

sex-linked defects, group of inherited conditions determined by the sex *chromosomes*, e.g. *colour blindness*, *haemophilia*, *muscular dystrophy*. Once a sex-linked condition is identified in an affected child it is possible to predict with varying degrees of accuracy the likelihood of the same condition occurring in further children, in other branches of the family and in the next generation. See *genetic counselling*.

shaping, example of *operant conditioning*: in order to produce a new pattern of behaviour, reinforcement is given only for behaviour which comes progressively closer to the behaviour that is wanted. *Forward chaining* is a more formalized version of shaping. This technique is applied to teaching by providing easy tasks which can be successively approximated to the task to be taught. Thus children can be taught to thread a fine needle by reinforcing the threading of needles with eyes reducing in size from very large to fine.

sheltered workshop, place of work for the more seriously disabled which is protected from the pressures of ordinary employment. Workers are paid a wage, although their output may not cover the full costs. Sheltered workshops are provided by local authorities or voluntary agencies. The main employer is central government through its special company 'Remploy'.

shunt, surgically implanted valve used to control *hydrocephalus*. It reduces and then maintains the pressure of *cerebrospinal fluid* on the brain. The excess cerebrospinal fluid is usually shunted to the heart or abdomen thus draining directly or indirectly into the bloodstream. The two most commonly used systems are the Spitz-Holter uni-directional valve and the Pudenz valve.

s.i.b., see *self-injurious behaviour*.

sibling, sister or brother, a child of the same parents. Siblings of a child with special needs can be exposed to general anxiety in the home, differences in discipline and limitations on their activities, through attention being focused on their handicapped sibling. Hospital admissions for a handicapped brother or sister can give rise to extra tension. Siblings of children with special needs are said sometimes to show troubled behaviour for these reasons, but there is little evidence to support this view.

sickle-cell anaemia, inherited condition, largely limited to members of the black community. The red blood cells assume a sickle shape and do not function properly in carrying oxygen. It results in lethargy, joint pains, etc., and can be associated with a wide variety of disorders, including learning difficulties.

sight word, word instantly recognized and read, not requiring analysis.

sigmatism, difficulty with the 's' sound.

sign language, any agreed system for communicating by *gestures* and manual signs. See *Ameslan, British Sign Language, finger spelling, Makaton, Paget-Gorman Sign System, signed (exact) English*.

signed (exact) English, manual method of communication used by deaf children. It closely follows standard English grammar and hence is more compatible with spoken and written English than *Ameslan* or *British sign language*. Used with speech, it has been called the simultaneous system.

significant living without work, the problem facing young people with disabilities so serious that employment in the normal sense is not possible. It raises the question of how else to provide for the sense of purpose and opportunity for special intercourse that work offers. Recognizing this problem has implications for the school *curriculum*, which usually places preparation for employment as one of its main aims.

signing using a *sign language*. Whether children with serious *hearing impairment* should be taught to sign, or whether they should be taught to communicate through speech, learned by the *oral method*, has been a long and at times fierce debate among their teachers. See *total communication*.

simultaneous oral spelling, (*S.O.S.*), naming of letters aloud as they are written. It is used to help link sound and letter.

sinistral, left-sided, a left-handed person.

sinistrality, preferred use of the left side of the body. See *laterality*, compare *dextrality*.

Sixteen Personality Factor Test (16 P.F.), group test of adult personality designed by R. B. Cattell and based on his theory of the structure of personality. It measures sixteen primary personality factors e.g. practical v. imaginative, reserved v. warmhearted, etc., and is used in *counselling*, vocational guidance, and other settings.

skeletal age, method of expressing the *maturity* of children's bone structure. Thus a 12-year-old child whose bone structure has developed to the level of an average 8-year-old would be said to have a skeletal age of 8 years.

Skinnerian Learning Theory, behaviourist *learning theory* based mainly on *operant conditioning* principles, derived from analysing observable *behaviour* and developed by F. B. Skinner. *Programmed instruction, teaching machines* and *behaviour modification* are some of the applications of particular relevance to the education of children with special needs.

sleeper effect, effect which appears after an interval of time; delayed effect. The term is used to describe some of the results of the *Head Start Programme*. Thus the *Westinghouse* investigators found these to be negligible at first; years later, when the 'Head Start' children were in High School the incidence of *delinquency, special class* membership, etc. was found to be significantly lower for them than for others.

slow learner, old term for a child with *learning difficulties*.

small-for-dates babies, babies who are small for their gestational age. This is often taken as being more than two *standard deviations* below the *mean* birthweight for the length of gestation.

SMOG index, Simple Measure Of Gobbledygook, one of the methods of assessing the *readability* of printed material. Take 30 sentences, 10 at the start, 10 from the middle and 10 at the end of the passage. Total the words with three or more syllables, and find the nearest perfect square, P. Then $\sqrt{P} + 3.0$ is the index of the grade level for which the reading material is suitable. To convert to a *reading age*, add 5. Thus if the 30 sentences contained a total of 22 words with three or more syllables, the nearest perfect square to 22 is 25, i.e. 5^2. $5 + 3.0 = 8$. This is the appropriate grade level. The reading age equivalent is $8 + 5 = 13$ yrs. See *cloze procedure, Fog index*.

SNAP, Special Needs Action Programme, structured approach to supporting children with special needs in the ordinary school, developed in Coventry. The programme aims to encourage the identification of pupils with special needs, to help teachers develop suitable curricula and to organize support services for these purposes. It provides handbooks for developing courses to be followed by school-based coordinators, who in turn involve their own colleagues in the programme. SNAP was designed for primary schools but has since been developed for secondary schools.

Snellen chart, test of vision. It consists of a number of lines of letters, in descending size of type face from top (large size) to bottom (small size).

The size of the type face on each line is appropriate to the distance at which a person with normal visual acuity can read it correctly. Thus the '12' line can normally be read at 12 metres; the '6' line only at 6 metres. See *Snellen ratio*.

Snellen ratio, a fraction which indicates visual acuity. The numerator is usually 6, the distance in metres at which the child usually stands from the *Snellen chart*, the denominator is the smallest line of print the child can read. A child who can read correctly as far as the 6-metre line has 6/6 vision, i.e. normal vision. A child who can read correctly as far as the 12-metre line only has 6/12 vision. A child who can read correctly as far as the 18-metre line only has 6/18 vision, and so on. See *twenty-twenty vision*.

Snowdon Report, 1976, 'Integrating the Disabled', report of a committee chaired by Lord Snowdon, which recommended the planned introduction of a system of integrated education for all *handicapped* children and adults at all levels of education. It also recommended integration in employment and improvement of housing, transport and mobility facilities for handicapped people. Its recommendations on education were overtaken by the report of the *Warnock Committee*.

social competence, ability to function adequately in society, exercising personal independence and social responsibility: a central aim of educating all children, including those with *learning difficulties*. See *adaptive behaviour, Manchester Scales of Social Adaptation, Vineland Scale of Social Maturity*.

social education,
(1) education in social skills such as personal relationships, hygiene, etc.; a significant part of a *developmental curriculum* for children with severe *learning difficulties*;
(2) educating children for a greater understanding of their community and their environment. Schools often have links with community organizations for this purpose.

social maturity, extent to which children have developed *social competence*.

social quotient (SQ), index of an individual's social maturity calculated by dividing social age (SA), as measured by a test of *social competence*, by *chronological age* (CA) and multiplying by 100. Some tests convert performance to a *deviation quotient*.

social skills, skills needed to achieve *social competence*, e.g. co-operation, independence, personal hygiene, mobility, etc. Some children with special needs may not have had the experiences needed for these skills to develop adequately and may need specific teaching in them. This may be particularly important for successful integration into normal schooling. See *social education*.

social worker, member of a profession concerned to help people cope with disabilities and associated emotional, economic and social handicaps, including children with special needs and their families. Most, but not all, social workers are employed by local authorities, within Social Service Departments. They co-ordinate the services which are available, working in private homes, day and residential centres, hospitals and schools. Some social workers now work mainly with children who have a particular disablity. Social workers may undergo professional training leading to a Certificate of Qualification in Social Work (CQSW) or Certificate in Social Service (CSS), both of which are validated by the Central Council for Education and Training in Social Work (CCETSW). New developments are proposed for the 1990s. See *Seebohm Report*.

socio-economic status (s.e.s.), individual's standing in society, as determined by occupation in the first instance. Five occupational categories are commonly used: professional; intermediate; skilled; semi-skilled; unskilled. The 'skilled' class is often subdivided into 'manual' and 'non-manual' groups. The incidence of children with special needs varies with s.e.s., children growing up in unskilled homes being more likely to have special educational needs than children growing up in professional homes. But some genetic defects giving rise to special educational needs are not associated with social class.

sociodrama, kind of *psychodrama*.

sociogram, diagram illustrating the patterns of relationships within a group, revealed by *sociometry*. See illustration (p. 184).

sociomatrix, table illustrating the pattern of relationships within a group, revealed by *sociometry*. It is particularly helpful for showing the existence of sub-groups.

sociometric status, numerical index of the social approval which members of a group give to one another, as revealed by *sociometry*. There is a positive relationship between sociometric status and school achievement, children with high sociometric status being more likely to be high achievers and vice versa.

sociometry, technique initiated by J. L. Moreno, for measuring social relationships by investigating the expressed choices of group members for each other. At its simplest, pupils in a class can be asked with whom they would most like to work on a project and the choices made shown as a *sociogram* or *sociomatrix*. It has been used in studies of *group dynamics*, leadership, friendship, etc. and also for the identification of *maladjustment*, in particular by identifying children who have difficulty in making normal relationships. See *isolate*.

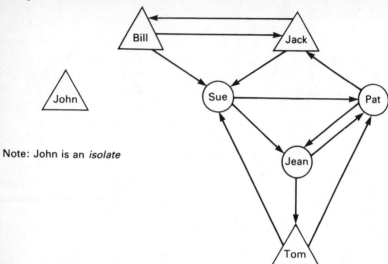

Sociogram for project work, two choices per pupil

soft neurological sign, neurological sign whose significance is unclear, i.e. it does not indicate major neurological damage but may suggest minor neurological abnormality, e.g. mild speech impairment, poor *fine motor skills*.

soft palate, soft, muscular, movable back part of the roof of the mouth.

soiling, absence of bowel control, which can be due to organic damage, e.g. with *paraplegics*, or a sign of psychological problems. See *encopresis*.

solvent abuse, use of solvents to produce temporarily a pleasurable mental state, e.g. glue sniffing, when the solvent used in the preparation of the glue causes the intoxication. *Addiction* can result. See *drug abuse*.

s.o.s., see *simultaneous oral spelling*.

sound blending, combining the sounds of individual letters or *graphemes* to pronounce a syllable or a whole word. It is an important skill in learning to read and one which some children have difficulty in mastering.

Southgate Reading Tests, two *group tests* designed by V. Southgate and intended to enable teachers to make rapid assessments of reading skills without hearing each child read aloud. Test 1 is a *word recognition* test for 6 to 8-year-olds and older retarded readers. Test 2, which involves sentence reading, extends to a *reading age* of 9 years.

Spache readability formula, method of estimating the difficulty of reading materials, which was developed by G. Spache. It is based on the average number of words in a sentence. The greater the number, the more difficult the reading material.

spasm, involuntary contraction of a muscle or organ. Spasms are common in some children with cerebral palsy.

spasticity, increased muscle tone in one or more limbs, leading to resistance to stretching. It is associated with one particular form of *cerebral palsy*.

spatial ability, ability to perceive the relationship between objects occupying space. It is measured in many *intelligence tests*, sometimes by requiring patterns to be copied correctly. Some children with brain injuries show damaged spatial abilities. See *Benton Visual Retention Test*.

special care units, rooms, usually within a *special school*, where children who are profoundly retarded and *physically handicapped* can receive extra attention. In practice these rooms are sometimes also used to accommodate especially disruptive pupils.

special care school, Northern Ireland provision for children who in England and Wales would usually be regarded as having severe learning difficulties. The special care schools were the responsibility of the health and social services authorities and the children were described as 'unsuitable for education in school' until 1987. These arrangements were then changed and the schools transferred to the education authorities, bringing Northern Ireland into line with the rest of the U.K.

special classes, classes containing a small number of children with special needs whose problems are not so extreme that they need to be educated in *special schools*. The classes are usually staffed by specially trained teachers and non-teaching assistants are often provided. The special classes are usually attached to or are part of an ordinary school, offering many opportunities for *integration* into normal school activities.

special education, education intended for children with special needs, i.e. children who, for various reasons, cannot take full advantage of the curriculum as it is normally provided. These are usually children who are physically *handicapped*, who have *learning difficulties* or show *emotional and behavioural disorders*. The *Education Act 1944* ruled that special education must be provide by local authorities, who can send children to special day or boarding schools, organize tuition in hospital, arrange classes which may be full or part-time within ordinary schools, or withdraw children from ordinary classes to provide individual help. The *Education Act 1981* modified and extended these obligations emphazising that as far as possible all children should be educated in ordinary schools. Whereas special education used to be broadly considered as separate education, it is now more usually interpreted as techniques for enabling all children to have access to as normal a curriculum as possible.

special education advisory and support service, see *special services*.

special educational needs, basis for providing education for children who find difficulty in profiting from normal education. It replaced the previous principle, *category of handicap*, following the *Education Act, 1981*. The new principle represents a move away from a medical orientation, which has been welcomed, but it has been criticized for a lack of logical soundness. Thus section 1 of the Act states that a child has special educational needs if he has a *learning difficulty* which requires special education provision to be made to meet those needs. Learning difficulty is defined for this purpose as a learning difficulty (whether due to a physical or mental disability or for any other reason) which is significantly greater than that experienced by the majority of children of the same age. The legalities of the Act were not able to delimit the somewhat amorphous — though useful — principle of special educational needs any further, except to exclude those learning difficulties which may arise because the language of teaching is not the same as the language at home. This point has relevance for children from some ethnic minorities, for children from some bilingual areas, e.g. Wales, and some immigrants, (it does not affect an LEA's responsibilities for providing suitable education for these children under other legislation; it does mean that they do not fall for consideration under the 1981 Act).

Special Olympics, sports activities, first organized in the U.S. in 1968 by the Joseph P. Kennedy Jr. Foundation, to give mentally retarded young people and children over the age of eight the opportunity of participating in a variety of sports from local to international level. It is not a complete physical education scheme but aims to encourage the development of physical education for the mentally retarded, prepare them for sports competitions, supplement existing programmes and provide training for coaches.

special school, residential or day school for children with special needs. In the U.K. most are maintained by the *local education authorities*. The *pupil-teacher ratio* is low and extra services are provided, e.g. by *speech therapists, physiotherapists*, etc. According to the *Warnock Report*, many of these schools should be phased out and the children integrated into normal schooling, though it was recognized that some children with severe and complex handicaps would continue to need special schools. Special schools, whether maintained or non-maintained, must be approved by the appropriate Secretary of State. See *residential school*.

special services, *local education authority* advisory service which provides support for children with special needs and their teachers. It is usually staffed by advisers and/or advisory teachers, some of whom cover particular kinds of special needs, e.g. those of the hearing impaired, or children with *learning difficulties*, etc. It is sometimes called the special education advisory and support service, but there are many other titles used.

specific learning difficulty (s.l.d), problem with one area of the *curriculum* for a child who manages the rest normally. Note the distinction between s.l.d. and *learning difficulties* mild, moderate and severe, where most of the curriculum is usually involved. The most common example is *specific reading difficulty*.

specific learning disability, defined by the U.S. Office of Education as a 'disorder in one or more of the basic psychological processes involved in understanding or in using language, spoken or written.' The disorders include such conditions as 'perceptual handicaps, brain injury, minimal brain dysfunction, dyslexia and developmental aphasia.' Thus it covers a mixed group of conditions and is really equivalent to *learning disability (1)*.

specific reading difficulty, inability to learn to read as well as would be expected from achievements in other areas. Some experts use this term instead of *dyslexia*: others believe that dyslexia has characteristics which enable it to be distinguished from specific reading difficulty.

speech audiometry, method of assessing hearing, using speech as the stimulus. This gives an estimate of the quality of hearing in 'real-life' situations rather than the more precise but less realistic measurements obtained through a *pure-tone audiometer*. In practice, both techniques are used in conjunction, often with other methods as well.

speech difficulty, any kind of speech which interferes with normal oral communication or gives rise to problems of adjustment for the speaker. Speech difficulties often occur in association with other handicaps: hence the demand for *speech therapists* in many branches of *special education*. Pupils with speech difficulties may have special educational needs for this reason alone, however. The most common difficulties in schoolchildren are problems with articulation, but others, e.g. stuttering, or voice production problems may also cause concern. Many technical terms exist, e.g. alalia, dyslalia, anarthria, dysarthria (articulation problems for various reasons) aphonia, dysphonia (loss of voice). See also *aphasia, cleft palate, stuttering*.

speech disability, see *speech difficulty*.

speech disorder, see *speech difficulty*.

speech reading, see *lipreading*.

speech therapist, specialist in the diagnosis and treatment of *speech* and *language disorders*, who usually works in schools, hospitals and clinics. Though speech therapists are based in the Health Service, the demand for them to work with children and teachers in schools continues to increase.

speech therapy, the diagnosis and treatment of *speech* and *language disorders*; it can also help to co-ordinate throat muscles and thus alleviate the swallowing and eating problems which some children suffer. Children are normally referred for speech therapy by a doctor.

speed reading, group of techniques used for improving rate of reading. It is particularly helpful for tasks which require skimming large quantities of print to extract the essentials. See *reading pacer*.

spina bifida, group of *congenital defects* in which the arches of one or more of the spinal verterbrae have not fused together so that the spine is split in two. The spinal cord or its surrounding membranes may protrude through this gap. The severity of the handicap depends on the position of the defect and the number of vertebrae involved. Whenever possible, surgery is performed at an early age. Spina bifida is frequently associated with *hydrocephalus* and intellectual development can be affected, resulting in *learning difficulties*. The incidence varies from area to area; the U.K. incidence has been estimated as 2 to 3 per 1,000 births; the Celtic parts of the U.K. are most affected and in some of the South Wales valleys it is particularly high, with implications for *special education*. See *encephalocele*.

spina bifida cystica, spina bifida accompanied by *meningocele* or *myelomeningocele*. In meningocele, the vertebrae are split but the spinal cord itself is normal. The baby is born with a small swelling in the back where the defect occurs. This can be corrected by surgery. There is often some weakness of legs, bladder or bowel, but usually no damage to nerves or paralysis. Myelomeningocele is more common. The spinal cord itself is damaged and the child suffers from some paralysis of legs, bladder or bowel. See *meningocele* and *myelomeningocele* illustrations.

spina bifida occulta, spina bifida in which the vertebrae are split at some point, but the underlying structures are normal. The defect may be unnoticed and seldom results in any malfunction.

Spitz-Holter valve, see *shunt*.

spontaneous remission, clearing of a *chronic* condition without active treatment.

squint, or strabismus, condition where the gaze of an individual's eyes cross because of weakness in the muscles of one or both eyes. Both eyes do not focus on the same object. The squint may be convergent, (the eyes turn inwards), divergent (they turn outwards), or alternate.

S.Q.3.R., method of improving study skills, first introduced by F. Robinson. The material is surveyed, then a clear purpose for reading is established through questioning. This is followed by reading to answer the question, reciting the answer and reviewing the assignment.

S.R.A. Reading Laboratories, sets of reading material which cover the whole reading range from initial reading skills up to adult level. They are sometimes used for *remedial reading*.

stammering, speech characterized by spasmodic involuntary blocking, or hesitation at sounds and words, i.e. the speaker finds difficulty in starting words. It was originally contrasted with stuttering, but both terms are often used to describe speech which is not fluent.

standard deviation, one measure of the 'spread' of data; the extent to which a set of scores deviates from the mean, or average score. The square root of the variance.

standard error (of measurement), index of the range of scores from which a single score is drawn. No score on a standardized test is unassailably 'correct' — a child's repeat score is unlikely to be identical with the original — so which is 'right'? The standard error of measurement (s.e.m.) is an estimate of the range from which a child's score is drawn and so gives a truer though less precise picture of performance than a single score. The range of score which is often used for this purpose is one s.e.m. Thus if a child obtains a score of 90 on a reading test which has an s.e.m. of 5 points, the child's performance is often interpreted as falling in the 85 to 95 range, i.e. 90 ± one s.e.m.

standard English braille, contracted system of the original form of *braille*.

standard progressive matrices, see *Raven's Progressive Matrices*.

Standard Test of Reading Skills, tests for children up to 9 years of age, constructed by Daniels and Diack, who analyse reading development into stages, or 'standards'. Each stage is described and *diagnostic tests* provided for children showing difficulties at it. There are twelve separate tests; the last two can also be *group tests*. The tests are widely used with older children with reading difficulties in secondary schools.

standardized scores, test scores which have been adjusted so that they can be compared with scores from a different test. Thus a child's mark on a leniently marked test of reading, with a maximum of 100, can be more meaningfully compared with his/her mark on a severely marked test with a maximum of 40, if both marks are changed into standardized scores.

standardized test, test which meets various criteria, in particular a test which has been tried out on a representative sample, which provides data on its validity and reliability, which has set procedures for administration and scoring, and which provides a table for converting raw scores into *standardized scores*.

Stanford-Binet Intelligence Scale, (Form L-M), 1960, age range 2 years upwards. This is an individual *intelligence test* produced in 1960 and incorporating the most relevant items from the 1937 *Terman-Merrill* Test. The child has to follow oral directions and the verbal content of the tests is high at the upper age levels. *Fine motor skills* are required for bead stringing, paper/pencil manipulation and other such tasks, and adequate vision is required for small detailed pictures. More than most tests, a child's performance demands interpretation, by a skilled examiner. There are adaptations of the Terman-Merrill scales for the handicapped, e.g. *Williams Intelligence Test for Children with Defective Vision*. The scale has been widely used by educational psychologists for assessing the development of children with special needs.

stapes, one of the three bones in the *middle ear*, resembling a small stirrup. It transmits sound vibrations from the *incus* to the *inner ear*. See *ear* illustration (p. 66).

Statement (of special educational needs), description of a child's educational needs made by a local education authority under the *Education Act, 1981*, for children whose special needs cannot be met informally, using normal resources, i.e. the minority of children with more serious special needs. (In practice this seems to be taken as about 2% of the school population and a smaller proportion of the preschool population). The procedures for providing a statement are controlled by the Act and include a requirement to review statements annually. Parents receive a draft of the statement and can make representations. See *individualized Education Program*.

status epilepticus, continuing grand mal seizures, which if prolonged may lead to brain damage and if not stopped will result in death.

sterilization, removal of the ability to father or bear children. It raises serious social and moral problems, partly because it is usually an irreversible operation generally performed for non-medical reasons. The issues can be particularly difficult in relation to some handicapped young persons, who need skilled help to take a decision. See *genetic counselling, sex education*.

Stern apparatus, coloured wooden blocks representing various numbers which are used by young children to develop mathematical concepts. The blocks fit into cases which illustrate the numerical properties of the blocks. One type of *structural apparatus*.

Stewart Report 1968, report of the Committee on Young School Leavers, set up to provide evidence about attitudes at home and in schools to the way schools prepared their pupils for adult life. It considered the influence of home background on early or late school leaving, teacher morale and support and the usefulness of the curriculum.

stigma, sociological term, perhaps best illustrated in special education as the feeling of inferiority said to mark children who were placed in particular *categories of handicap*, e.g. the *educationally subnormal*, especially those who attended *special schools*. This was one of the reasons for the *Education Act 1981* abolishing categories of handicap. See *labelling*.

Still's disease, form of rheumatoid arthritis which usually affects all the joints of young children. The spleen and lymph glands are enlarged and there is irregular fever. The pain and suffering may cause periods of paralysis and skeletal development may be affected.

Stott Adjustment Pointers, quick guides to the presence and severity of emotional and behavioural disorders in children.

Stott Programmed Reading Kit, designed by D. H. Stott, to teach children *phonic skills* through a variety of group and individual games which are mainly self-correcting. Widely used in *remedial education* of children with reading difficulties.

strabismus, see *squint*.

Strauss syndrome, essentially, unco-ordinated behaviour, learning problems and lack of concentration. A. A. Strauss believed that these symptoms indicated some brain damage. The term is sometimes used in relation to children who have no diagnosed brain injury but demonstrate hyperactive behaviour.

streaming, placing children of the same year-group in classes, according to an estimate of their general ability. Some educators believe that this leads to more efficient teaching at all levels. Others think it acts as a *self-fulfilling prophecy*, particularly among the lower streams where it contributes towards *learning difficulties* and general dissatisfaction. See *setting*.

strephosymbolia, obsolescent term coined by S. T. Orton to describe *reversals* (e.g. 'd' for 'b') in reading and writing. Literally, 'twisted symbols'.

structural apparatus, equipment which helps a pupil work with mathematical ideas, e.g. *Stern apparatus, Cuisenaire apparatus* — even fingers.

stuttering, speech characterized by marked repetition of some sounds or words, i.e. the speaker finds difficulty in stopping a sound. It was originally contrasted with stammering, but both terms are now used to describe speech which is not fluent.

Stycar Tests, screening tests of the hearing, language and vision of young children, designed by M. S. Sheridan. They can be used with children between the ages of six months to eight years; depending on the test.

subcultural mental deficiency, see *cultural-familial retardation*.

subdural haematoma, bleeding in the membranes covering the brain.

sublimation, Freudian concept involving the diversion of energy from a basic drive such as sex, to another activity, such as artistic creativity.

subnormality, being subnormal, or significantly below *average*, usually used in relation to intellect, e.g. mentally subnormal, educationally subnormal. This term is now rarely used; *'learning difficulties'* offers a more hopeful description of the condition of children whose performance may be below average in some respects, but who can often develop satisfactorily given special help.

subnormality hospitals, see *mental handicap hospitals*.

Summerfield Report,1968, 'Psychologists in Education Services', report of a working party, under the chairmanship of A. Summerfield, set up by the Secretary of State for Education and Science to consider the field of work of educational psychologists, their qualifications and training and the numbers required. The Report arose from a developing awareness of the needs of handicapped children and increased demands for the involvement of *educational psychologists*. It recommended a ratio of one educational psychologist to 10,000 children, i.e. approximately doubling their numbers, a recommendation which has been overtaken by the Warnock Report, which advocated a minimum ratio of one educational psychologist to 5,000 children and young people in England and Wales.

superego, conscience; in Freudian theory, values and principles based mainly on the individual's early relationship with parents and parent figures, which oppose the demands of the *id*.

supervision order, order made in care proceedings by a *juvenile court* for the supervision of a young person or child. The supervisor is usually a *social worker* but may be a *probation officer*. The supervisor advises and helps the juvenile for the duration of the order.

support teacher, or remedial teacher, see *remedial education*.

support teaching, see *remedial education*.

suppression amblyopia, see *amblyopia*.

Swann Report,1985, 'Education for All', report of a committee set up to review the needs and *attainments* of children from ethnic minority groups, to consider arrangements for monitoring their educational progress and to establish the role of education in a multi-racial society. The committee produced an interim report, the *Rampton Report* in 1981. The report considered neither assimilation nor separation of ethnic groups to be a satisfactory principle. It noted major areas of concern in teaching English, which should be provided within the mainstream; in teaching the mother tongue; in teaching religious education and in training teachers. It also established clearly the existence of substantial underachievement among children from some ethnic groups, but concluded after an exhaustive survey of research, that any group differences in inherited *intelligence* could safely be ignored as explanations for these *learning difficulties*.

Swansea Project, 1967–72, *Schools' Council compensatory education* project at the University College of Swansea, which aimed to provide *screening* techniques to identify children in need of educational support at an early age; to study the emotional development and response to schooling of 4 to 8 year old school children in deprived areas; to develop teaching programmes in different media to help culturally deprived children of infant age; to study the special problems of Welsh-speaking school children. The project produced the Swansea Test of Phonic Skills for diagnosing reading difficulties towards the end of the infant school, the

Swansea Evaluation Profile, for identifying infant school entrants likely to have *learning difficulties* later and a book of suggestions for teaching *language skills* in the infant school, as well as various research reports.

sweep frequency test, *screening* test for identifying possible *hearing loss* in which a few selected *frequencies* are presented at a set loudness (normally 20 dB). A large number of tests can be administered in a relatively short time and children failing to respond have further *audiometric screening*.

Symond's Picture Story Test, *projection test* of adolescent personality, which uses twenty pictures on cards. It is based on similar principles to those underlying the *Thematic Apperception Test*, but each picture contains one or more people with whom the subject may easily identify.

synkinesis, involuntary movement accompanying a voluntary one; a *soft neurological sign*.

systematic desensitization, was developed by Wolpe and is a form of *behaviour therapy* which aims at substituting adaptive behaviour, such as relaxed calmness for maladaptive behaviour, such as anxiety. The person is gradually exposed to a series of successively more anxiety-making situations, while engaged in behaviour (such as deep relaxation) which is incompatible with anxiety. Treatment begins with the least-worrying situation. When this can be managed in the relaxed state, treatment moves to the next worrying situation, and so on.

T

TACADE, Teachers' Advisory Council on Alcohol and Drug Education, body which disseminates information, including publishing a journal.

tactile, relating to the sense of touch, capable of being felt, e.g. *braille* can be described as tactile writing.

tactile agnosia, inability to identify familiar objects by touch.

tactile discrimination, ability to separate successfully 'touches' of different strengths and positions. It is used in some neurological examinations. See *Gerstmann syndrome*.

talipes, see *club foot*.

talking book, record or tapes of reading matter, used by people with limited sight.

talking typewriter, device which helps to teach reading by enabling a pupil to hear the sound of letters and words as they are typed.

task analysis, breaking down a defined task into its component skills, which may themselves need dividing (or slicing) into subskills. Task analysis recognizes that children with learning difficulties may progress better if they are taught material with a carefully planned gradient of difficulty.

TAT, see *Thematic Apperception Test*.

Taylor Manifest Anxiety Scale, measure of anxiety used in clinical work with adolescents and designed by J. A. Taylor. The Scale consists of 50 questions requiring a 'true' or 'false' response, e.g. 'I have very few headaches'. There is a children's form.

Taylor Report 1977, 'A New Partnership in our Schools', report of the Committee of Inquiry into the management and government of maintained primary and secondary schools in England and Wales. It suggested equal representation in school government for *local education authority* appointees, members of the local community, parents and teachers; the new bodies were to help to establish the school's objectives, including the *curriculum* and they should have access to professional guidance. The Committee's terms of reference excluded *special schools* but its proposals were strongly reflected in the provisions of the *Education Act 1980*, which stated that parents and teachers should be represented on governing bodies of special schools as well as ordinary schools. The *Warnock Report* had previously endorsed the recommendations. The responsibilities of governors are currently being re-examined.

teacher aide, originally a U.S. term for a teaching auxiliary, a person normally without teaching qualifications who assists in a classroom, usually with supervisory or clerical tasks, e.g. supervising study or preparing class material. They may be paid or unpaid, and play a particularly important part in the education of children with special needs.

teaching machine, device capable of presenting *programmed instruction* at the pace of the learner's response without a teacher's assistance. It is useful with children with learning difficulties because it gives immediate feedback and can be used with programmes of suitable difficulty gradient, thus ensuring a high success rate. Nowadays teaching machines have often been replaced by classroom microcomputers.

team teaching, several teachers planning all or part of their teaching programme together, so that they can make best use of their special skills with their combined pupils. It is a particularly suitable method for *open-plan schools* as resources, equipment and space can be shared easily.

temporal lobe epilepsy, *epilepsy* whose focus is the temporal lobe; sometimes associated with *behavioural disorders* as well as *fits*.

Terman-Merrill Test, an individual test of *intelligence*; specifically the 1937 version of the Stanford revision of the Binet-Simon Scale. It was produced in two paralled forms, Form L and Form M, by *L*.Terman and *M*.Merrill. See *Stanford-Binet Intelligence Scale*.

test battery, group of educational or psychological tests given to obtain a fuller picture of performance than could be obtained from a single test.

tetraplegia, type of *cereral palsy* in which all four limbs are affected; also called *quadriplegia*.

Thackray Reading Readiness Profiles, *group test* developed by D. and L. Thackray, for four and five-year-olds. The test consists of four subtests covering *oral comprehension vocabulary*, *auditory discrimination*, *visual discrimination* and *intelligence*, a selection of the skills needed to learn to read successfully. See *reading readiness test*.

thalamus, part of the brain concerned with relaying sensory impulses to the surface of the *cerebrum* and from one part of the brain to another.

Thematic Apperception Test (TAT), projective technique developed by Murray. The adult test consists of 19 cards containing black and white pictures, often deliberately vague, to permit imaginative interpretation, and one blank card. Different cards are available for children. A story has to be told to each card and the story content is analysed to gain insight into personality structure. See *Children's Apperception Test*.See illustration (p. 197).

therapeutic education, teaching children with emotional disorders who need psychotherapeutic experiences in an educational framework. The teacher works closely with the *educational psychologist* in developing a suitable teaching programme, e.g. an aggressive child may need particularly firm discipline: a withdrawn child may respond to a programme which emphasizes creative work.

therapist, one who practices *therapy*. See, for example, *occupational therapist*; *physiotherapist*; *psychotherapist*.

theta waves, one of four types of electrical waves which are recorded from the brain on an *electroencephalogram*. They are slow frequency brain waves which are normal in young children but may indicate abnormality in adults.

A Thematic Appreciation Test card

Thomas Report 1963, 'The Handicapped School Leaver', report of a committee chaired by E. Thomas, which noted that many handicapped children left school with an unsatisfactory standard of education. The report recommended that local authorities should review their provision of faculties for advanced and technical education for handicapped children. It urged *local education authorities* to consider the establishment of residential courses of general education as a preliminary to *vocational training*.

Thomas Report 1985, 'Improving Primary Education', report of a committee set up by the *Inner London Education Authority* and chaired by N. Thomas. Among other recommendations it advocated that children's reading difficulties should be investigated by the age of eight at the latest, that in assessment work more emphasis should be placed on the use of diagnostic tests and that parents and other volunteers should be encouraged to help with reading difficulties.

threshold of hearing, see *hearing threshold.*

throat microphone, used when an individual has a weak voice. It is held in place against the individual's larynx by a tight band. The microphone is only sensitive to mechanical vibrations from the larynx, not to surrounding noises.

thyroid, gland which produces the hormone thyroxin which helps to regulate the metabolic rate and is essential for normal body growth. Poor thyroid function in infancy and childhood can lead to mental retardation. See *cretinism.*

tic, habitual, brief, localized spasm. Tics of the facial muscles are quite common.

time-out, placing a child where unwanted behaviour cannot be given *reinforcement.* It is often used for managing disruptive behaviour in class by placing a child for a period of time-out in a separate, often empty room (time-out room). The return of quiet behaviour is reinforced by allowing the child to return to the society of the class. See *negative reinforcement.*

tinnitus, constantly hearing noises, such as ringing or buzzing. Tinnitus is often, but not always associated with deafness. It can affect children as well as adults.

Tizard Report,1972, 'Children with Specific Reading Difficulties': report of the *Advisory Committee on Handicapped Children*, chaired by J. Tizard. The main issue was the existence or not of a *dyslexia* syndrome. The report concluded that dyslexia was best seen as a kind of reading backwardness, preferring the term '*specific reading difficulties*' to 'dyslexia'. It recommended regular *screening* and progress monitoring, the development of skilled remedial teaching in all schools and the development of *remedial education* centres.

t.o., traditional orthography, i.e. normal English spelling, not the regularized spelling found in the *initial teaching alphabet.*

token economy, environment in which most behaviour is managed by *token reinforcement.* It has been instituted in some hospital wards, in schools and individual classrooms.

token reinforcement, *behaviour therapy* in which tokens, e.g. plastic discs, are given as a reward for appropriate behaviour. The tokens can be exchanged for desired objects or privileges. Thus pupils could be given tokens for praiseworthy work. The tokens could be exchanged for sweets, or extra play. The 'rates of exchange' are laid down in advance and the tokens should be convenient to handle, the privileges genuinely rewarding and the system clearly understood and implemented fairly. There has been some debate over the ethics of managing behaviour in this way, perhaps most particularly when it has been extended into a full-scale *token economy*.

tongue-tied:
(1) having limited tongue movement because of a short membrane on the underside of the tongue;
(2) being too shy to speak.

tonic, referring to tone in a muscle, as in *tonic neck reflex*.

tonic neck reflex, when a very young baby is held by the back it normally extends the arm and leg on the side to which the head is turned and flexes the limbs on the opposite side. This asymmetrical response pattern usually disappears by the time a baby is three or four months of age, as the baby develops. Medical examinations may use the characteristics of this reflex as one indication of the integrity of the *central nervous system*.

toxic metals, metals which, if taken into the body, cause poisoning, leading in some cases to *learning difficulties* or *emotional and behavioural disorders*. See *lead poisoning*.

toxins, poisons.

toy library, centre for lending toys to children, particularly those with disabilities or *learning difficulties*. The National *Toy Libraries Association* (Appendix A) provides a wide range of information on how to set up and run a toy library and acts as a link between toy libraries, manufacturers, teachers, *psychologists* and others.

tracking, U.S. system of school organization which is similar to *streaming*.

training centre, see *adult training centre, junior training centre*.

tranquillizer, *drug* that quietens and calms without decreasing consciousness. Some tranquillizers are used in the treatment of psychological disorders such as *schizophrenia*, and others are used to treat anxiety, irritability and tension.

Transactional Analysis (TA), a method of *counselling* and *psychotherapy*, developed by E. Berne. It is essentially a technique for analysing the transactions or exchanges that take place between people. It emphasizes that people can take command of and control their own behaviour, once, with the help of the therapist, they begin to understand what is really taking place in their own transactions. To this end, TA provides a model of personality structure and descriptions of some of the games or strategies of transactions that people use.

transference:
(1) shifting symptoms from one part of the body to another;
(2) in *psychiatry*, transferring feelings and attitudes associated with childhood events and people to current relationships and situations;
(3) in *psychoanalysis*, the tendency to transfer attitudes and emotions felt for one person, e.g. a parent, to the *psychoanalyst*.

translocation, rearrangement of *genetic* material within the same *chromosome* or the attachment of one *chromosome* to another. Normal individuals can act as *carriers* for this translocation. A small number of children with Down's syndrome owe their condition to a translocation, not a *trisomy*.

transposition, change in sequence of two or more words, letters or sounds, in writing, reading or speech. It is one of the various categories used in analysing errors in children's language.

Trethowan Report 1975, 'The Role of Psychologists in the Health Services', findings of a committee set up to consider the work of *clinical psychologists* in the newly reorganized health service. The report suggested that the best way to achieve an integrated child psychology service was via co-operation between individual *psychologists* working in the education and health service.

triple X syndrome, condition in which an extra X (female) *chromosome* is present, usually accompanied by some degree of *mental retardation*.

triplegia, type of *cerebral palsy* in which three limbs are affected.

trisomy, the presence of three chromosomes instead of the usual pair. Contrast *monosomy*. See *Down's syndrome*.

TROG, Test of Reception of Grammar, assesses how well children aged 4–13 years understand grammatical structures and contrasts, such as plural forms, passive voice, etc. As with picture vocabulary tests the child has only to point to a picture which best represents what the examiner says. One of the purposes of TROG is to reveal which grammatical structures need developing in order to improve language skills.

truancy, unlawful absence from school, usually without the parents knowing. Persistent truancy may be seen as a *behaviour disorder*. Truancy reaches a peak in the secondary school years and is more prevalent in boys than girls. It is a deliberate avoidance of school, and is distinguished from *school phobia*.

tunnel vision, condition in which the visual field is so reduced that it is like looking through a tunnel.

Turner's syndrome, inherited condition characterized by the absence of one X (female) chromosome, which results in some *learning difficulty*, retarded physical growth and sexual development. It is an example of *monosomy*.

twenty-twenty vision, normal vision; material normally read at 20 feet can be read at that distance by the person being tested. It is the non-metric equivalent of a *Snellen ratio* of 6/6: twenty feet is roughly six metres.

tympanic membrane, see *eardrum*.

two-factor theory of intelligence, theory of *intelligence* put forward by Spearman who maintained that all intellectual activities share a single common ability, called the general factor '*g*'. In addition there are numerous specific abilities or '*s*' factors, each being specific to a single activity.

U

unconditioned response, unlearned automatic reaction, e.g. blinking when an object suddenly approaches the eye: commonly referred to as a *reflex*.

underachiever, pupil whose level of educational attainment is significantly lower than would be expected on other grounds, such as performance on *intelligence tests*. See *achievment*.

underprivileged, child whose experiences have been restricted by poor or adverse social and economic circumstances, often leading to intellectual handicap. See *cultural deprivation, compensatory education*.

Underwood Report 1955, report of a committee chaired by J. H. Underwood which reviewed the provision for maladjusted children and made recommendations that formed the basis for the organization and future development of a comprehensive *child guidance* service. It listed eleven different symptom groups indicating *maladjustment*.

Unesco, United Nations Educational, Scientific and Cultural Organization, founded to promote international culture and educational co-operation. Its programme covers several areas of activity which include education in general and special education in particular, and it publishes several free 'Guides for Special Education'. The organization provides the means of co-ordinating and exchanging information concerning new developments in special education throughout the world. The U.K. has recently withdrawn from membership. See Appendix A for address of the special education programme.

unilateral, condition which affects one side of the body only; e.g. unilateral *hearing loss,* loss of hearing in one ear only.

unit, separate department within a school or other educational institution, offering specialized services and facilities — e.g. a unit for *partially hearing* children; a remedial unit. The unit is one method of organizing the special provision for and the partial *integration* of handicapped children into ordinary schools.

university, independent and self-governing institution of higher education, which provides advanced teaching and research facilities with the authority to confer first and higher degrees. Many universities have made special provision for disabled students, e.g. adapted residential accommodation and special teaching. Disabled students also qualify for an increased grant to cover expenses arising as a result of their handicap. See *Open University, National Bureau for Handicapped Students* in Appendix A.

unsuitable for school, term originating in the *Mental Health Act 1959,* and replacing the concept 'ineducable' which had meant the exclusion of mentally handicapped children from education. In the *Education (Handicapped Children) Act 1970,* the term 'unsuitable for school' was abandoned as the education service became responsible for the schooling of all children, including the mentally handicapped.

uraniscolalia, abnormal speech resulting from a *cleft palate.*

Usher's syndrome, condition in which *congenital hearing loss* is associated with vision which, from the late teens onwards, steadily deteriorates into blindness. It is obviously important to prepare the child for later life as a deaf-blind adult.

uvula, small cone-shaped piece of connective tissue that hangs down in the mouth at the back of the *soft palate.* If it is abnormally formed it may cause nasal speech.

V

vaccination, using the cowpox virus to give immunity against smallpox: more commonly, injecting bacteria or virus to give protection against an infectious disease.

vaccine-damaged, children who have suffered damage to the brain or nervous system as a result of *vaccination* against *measles*, whooping cough or smallpox. The risk of damage occurring is very slight, and as it is difficult to prove a connection between vaccination and brain or nervous system damage, this remains a controversial term. *The Vaccine Damage Payments Act 1979* lays down the conditions under which benefit is payable for children who have suffered severe disablement after vaccination.

Vaccine Damage Payments Act, 1979, see *vaccine-damaged*.

VAKT method/system multisensory approach to the teaching of reading, developed by Grace Fernald and used with some children with serious reading difficulties. VAKT. stands for *v*isual *a*uditory *k*inaesthetic and *t*actile. While seeing a letter or word (visual) the child is expected to say it aloud (*auditory*), while also tracing the shape (kinaesthetic) on a rough surface (*tactile*). See *Gillingham method*.

validity, extent to which an *assessment* method meets its objectives, i.e. measures what it purports to measure. Thus an interview procedure which nearly always identified the best candidates would be a highly valid assessment method for that purpose. An *intelligence test* which required children to read questions would have low validity if used with children with reading difficulties; while purporting to measure *intelligence* it would in effect be measuring reading skills.

Valium, trade name for a minor *tranquillizer* and muscle relaxant, prescribed to relieve anxiety and tension. It is also used to treat *convulsions* and to control muscle spasms, as in *cerebral palsy*.

Vanguard areas, services for the mentally handicapped, on the lines suggested by the All-Wales Working Party on services for handicapped people, were established by the Welsh Office in two Vanguard areas, one each in Gwynedd and Mid-Glamorgan.

variable-interval reinforcement, technique used in *behaviour modification*; suitable behaviour is rewarded at irregular time intervals. Thus a child may be given a star after one minute's concentration on work, another star after ten minutes, yet another after a further five. Variable interval reinforcement is said to be more effective than fixed-interval reinforcement since it keeps children 'on-their toes', as it were, but both schedules are used, depending on circumstances. Contrast *fixed-interval reinforcement*.

variance, one measure of the extent to which scores deviate from the mean in a particular set of scores; the 'spread' of data. It is obtained by squaring the deviation of each score from the mean of the set and calculating the mean of the resulting set of squared values.

v.ed., *verbal-ed*ucational ability, one of the two major groupings of abilities, or group factors, into which intellectual abilities are often divided. V.ed. represents abilities such as reading skills, number competence, writing fluency, etc. It is contrasted with the other major group factor, *k.m.*

verbal ability, proficiency in *language skills* generally, often referring particularly to the ability to solve written problems.

verbal factor, verbal-education factor, see *v.ed.*

verbal IQ, measure of *intelligence* based on tests assessing *verbal abilities* only, and which are sometimes referred to as verbal *intelligence tests* or verbal reasoning tests.

verbal-performance discrepancy, difference between scores on a verbal test and a performance test; often derived from a child's scores on a test such as the *WISC* which provides both a *verbal IQ* and a *performance IQ*. Thus if a child gained a verbal IQ of 120 and a performance IQ of 85, the verbal-performance discrepancy would be 35 points (120–85). This discrepancy is useful in the diagnosis of *learning difficulties*, including those resulting from hearing impairment and in formulating recommendations to meet *special educational needs*.

Verbal Reasoning Quotient (VRQ), one particular form of verbal intelligence quotient or *verbal IQ*, concentrating on the ability to understand and use logical relationships; one item might require the child to complete the following: dry is to wet as good is to . . .?

verbal reinforcement, *reinforcement* usually by means of the spoken word. Praising a child's *behaviour*, by using phrases such as 'well done!' is an example of verbal reinforcement, if used appropriately.

Vernon Report 1972, 'The Education of the Visually Handicapped', report of a committee of enquiry into the education of the blind and partially-sighted, chaired by M. D. Vernon. It recommended drawing up a national plan for the siting, organization and management of special schools for the visually handicapped, supporting children with visual impairment in sighted schools, pressing for early diagnosis, early education and regular reassessment of a child's progress, keeping parents better-informed, improving careers guidance, further education and vocational training. These recommendations made slow progress. See *Warnock Report*.

vertical grouping, placing children of widely different ages, e.g. 5 to 8-year-olds, in the same class. It is argued that this organization, which is usually found in primary schools, resembles family structure, enabling younger children to be helped by their older class-mates. The wide age-span emphasizes the need for individual work programmes for the children.

Vineland Social Maturity Scale, set of standarized questions, to be answered by the parent, for assessing social competence. It is used as a measure of *adaptive behaviour*, important for all children, but particularly so for many children with special needs. The original test was based on work done at the Vineland training school. A new revision, the Vineland Adaptive Behaviour Scales, is now available. See *Manchester Scales of Social Adaptation, Adaptive Behaviour Scales*.

visible speech:
(1) transformation of speech into a readable form; the sound waves of speech are transformed by an oscilloscope into a visible pattern. It is used as an aid in teaching speech to deaf children who imitate the teacher's sound patterns on the display until theirs are approximately the same;
(2) term used by Alexander Bell to describe his system of *phonetic alphabet* symbols.

visual cortex, part of the brain concerned with sight and *visual perception*. Injury near the visual cortex, while not causing serious impairment of vision, may nevertheless damage perceptual skills, e.g the ability to recognize patterns.

visual disability, any disorder affecting eyesight, ranging from mild and correctable conditions such as a *squint*, to *blindness* itself. Clumsiness, poor *eye-hand co-ordination*, squint, excessive blinking and headaches may be some of the indications of a visual disability. See *visual handicap*.

visual discrimination, ability to differentiate visually between different shapes, as in recognising individual letters. Visual discrimination activities are tasks designed to improve this ability, e.g. fitting shapes into their correct places on a form-board. Programmes designed to develop these skills are available and are said to help with some learning difficulties, perhaps most particularly reading difficulties.

visual handicap, effects of *visual disability*. Children who have adequate vision but whose *visual perception* is particularly poor are also regarded as visually handicapped.

visual memory, ability to recall something seen, an important facility for academic progress, since so much educational material is presented visually.

visual perception, ability to register what is seen, and give meaning to it. Tests of visual perception are used to diagnose difficulties that some children face in interpreting what they see. The tests usually consist of interpretation and copying of designs, patterns or figures. See *Bender Visual Motor Gestalt Test*.

visuo-motor ability, ability to co-ordinate the eyes and body muscles, e.g. judging the correct time and place for catching a ball. Many other visuo-motor skills are important for education, e.g. co-ordinating the eye and hand muscles in writing neatly. Visuo-motor disorders are sometimes found in children with *cerebral palsy* and are a characteristic of *clumsy children*.

vocabulary of reading, the words often used in teaching reading, such as page, first, line, word, etc. Children need to have grasped the meaning of these words in order to follow when teacher asks the group to 'Go to the first line on the next page', for example.

vocabulary test, test which assesses an individual's store of understood words; usually given by presenting the subject with a standard list of words to define. See *oral comprehension vocabulary, listening vocabulary, reading vocabulary*.

vocational guidance and counselling, discussions with a specially trained person who helps with the selection of an occupation, and who assists in seeking, making application for and obtaining employment. *Careers Services* often employ a person who specializes in vocational work with young people with *special needs*. A *Disablement Resettlement Officer* (DRO) fulfils similar functions for adults.

vocational training, programme designed to teach the knowledge, skills and attitudes required for proficiency in a particular job or task; especially careful planning is needed for handicapped clients, so that their strengths are maximized and realistic achievement goals set. This is available at a number of residential colleges, many of which have been established by voluntary bodies to meet the needs of people with a specific handicap, and also at *Employment Rehabilitation Centres*.

voice disorder, spoken *language* which sounds abnormal in loudness, pitch quality or duration.

vowel digraph, or diagraph, combination of two vowels resulting in one speech sound, e.g. 'ai'. Vowel digraphs are taught as part of a phonics programme in learning to read.

W

Warnock Report 1978, 'Special Educational Needs', report of the Committee of Enquiry into the Education of Handicapped Children and Young People, chaired by M. Warnock, whose recommendations have since had a significant influence on special educational policy and practice. The report argued that the scope of special education should be widened, and services based on the assumption that about one in six children at any time and up to one in five children at some time during their school career will need some form of special education; that most special education should take place in ordinary schools; that parents should be more closely involved in the practice and procedures of special education. Given these principles, the report went on to identify three priority areas, teacher education, special education in the pre-school and special education for the 16–19-year-old age grup. The first of these areas reflected the importance attached to making the whole educational community more aware of special educational needs: the second and third areas effectively extended the view of special education, which had previously been confined to the age limits of compulsory education, i.e. 5–16 years.

The report made many more recommendations, some sweeping, others more detailed. Some of the more important include the idea of *special education needs* as opposed to a mainly medical diagnosis, the consequent abolition of *categories of handicap*, the use of *learning difficulties* to point to the needs of children who had previously been described as *educationally subnormal* and those who were in *remedial education*, the continued existence of *special schools* for children with some severe and complex disabilities, the designation of a *Named person*, etc.

The *Education Act 1981*, followed the report and incorporated many of its recommendations in the law affecting special education.

Wechsler Intelligence Tests, range of *intelligence tests* developed and standardized by David Wechsler, a U.S. *clinical psychologist*. They consist of:

Wechsler Adult Intelligence Scale (WAIS), *intelligence test*, published in 1955 as the revised and renamed version of the *Wechsler Bellvue Intelligence Scale*. It is used with young people aged 16 years and over and is composed of eleven subtests grouped into a verbal and performance scale.

Verbal scale: information, comprehension, arithmetic, similarities, digit span and vocabulary;

Performance scale: digit symbol, picture completion, block design, picture arrangement and object assembly.

An individual's score is based on the number of items answered correctly. Three kinds of intelligence quotient can be calculated; a *performance IQ*, a *verbal IQ* and a *full scale IQ* which reflects the individual's scores on the verbal and performance subtests combined.

Wechsler-Bellvue Intelligence Scale, an adult *intelligence test*, prepared by D. Wechsler and published in 1939; the forerunner of the *Wechsler Adult Intelligence Scale*, (*WAIS*).

Wechsler Intelligence Scale for Children (WISC), *intelligence test*, designed by D. Wechsler in 1949, for the age range 5 to 16 years. There are twelve subtests, eleven of which parallel those in the *Wechsler Adult Intelligence Scale*. The extra subtest is a performance subtest, — 'mazes'. This test, and its revised version, has been widely used by educational psychologists in assessment work with children with special needs, since the pattern of scores on the verbal and performance subtests can be diagnostically useful.

Wechsler Intelligence Scale for Children -Revised (WISC-R), revised version of the *Wechsler Intellignece Scale for Children* but for ages 6–17 years.

Wechsler Preschool Primary Scale of Intelligence (WPPSI), designed for children between 4 and 6.5 years, thus overlapping with the *WISC* and *WISC -R intelligence tests*. It is claimed that the WPPSI gives a more sensitive assessment of development at these ages.

welfare assistant, ancillary helper in school, dealing with the general care of pupils and sometimes helping teachers with programmes and schemes of work. They are often based in schools and classrooms where children with *special educational needs* are taught.

Wepman Auditory Discrimination Test, *screening* test for children aged 5–8 years. The examiner pronounces pairs of words, sometimes identical and sometimes differing slightly, e.g. sip; ship. The child has to state whether the words are the same or different. The numbers and nature of the errors give an insight into any difficulties with *auditory discrimination* and may indicate the need for a hearing examination, *speech therapy*, etc.

Wernicke's Area, area of the brain involved in understanding language and sometimes implicated in receptive aphasia. See *brain* illustration (p. 28).

Westinghouse Study, the first major evaluation of the effects of the *Head Start Programme*. It purported to show that gains made by children participating in the programme were small and transient. It has since been criticised, particularly on the grounds of poor design, and its conclusions have been challenged. See *sleeper effect*.

whisper test, *screening* test for *hearing loss*, in which the child turns away and the examiner, at a distance of 6 metres, whispers words or digits which the child tries to repeat. Failure to repeat words correctly indicates the need for a hearing examination.

whole school approach, method of meeting *special educational needs* in the ordinary school which is often contrasted with approaches based on ideas of deficit or defect, as in the medical model. Deficit models rest on the belief that children's difficulties lie within the child and are best met by special teaching, often in a withdrawal class or special unit: the whole-school approach locates responsibility for a child's *learning difficulties* in the school and attempts to meet the needs of children by mobilizing the resources already existing in the school. Techniques such as the individualized learning demanded by mixed-ability teaching, *team teaching*, enhancing esteem by the use of profile reporting, etc., are all used to change the learning environment to help the child learn.

whole-word method, see *look-and-say method*.

Williams Intelligence Test for Children with Defective Vision, a test designed by J. Williams in which virtually all the questions require a spoken answer. It covers skills such as comprehension, vocabulary, memory for numbers, sentences and objects, and for older children, problem-solving. It is intended for blind and partially-sighted children aged 3–16 years and is adapted from the *Terman-Merrill Test*.

withdrawal class, form of *remedial education* in which children with special needs are taken out of their ordinary classes for short periods of regular intervals, e.g. a lesson every day, to receive extra help in small groups, usually from a remedial teacher.

withdrawal symptoms, physiological or psychological changes which occur when an addict fails to get a dose of a drug or alcohol within an interval of hours after the last dose (the period varying with the addict).

word association test, *projection test* in which a series of unrelated words is read to a child, who has to answer each with the first word which comes to mind. Unusual anwers give clues to a child's thought processes and to feelings, etc., which may be disturbing.

word-blindness, outdated term for *dyslexia*.

word-deafness, outdated term for *receptive aphasia*.

word recognition test, measure of ability to identify single words correctly, an important basic skill in learning to read. The child is usually required to try to pronounce the words, in which case other skills are also being tested: some word recognition tests proper may require pointing to a word pronounced by an examiner, or use other methods for testing word recognition. See *Southgate Reading Tests*.

Words in Colour, method of teaching reading designed by C. Gattegno and claimed to be helpful for some children with reading difficulties. Each of the main sounds, regardless of spelling, has been allocated a colour. The colours enable a child to attack new words successfully, for each colour consistently represents the same sound value, or *phoneme*. See *colour coding*.

work experience, work preparation in which young people are placed in simulated work conditions, or given the opportunity of seeing a number of different jobs and working conditions at first hand. It can also take the form of a planned period of supervised employment in industry, commerce or the public service. Work experience can be an integral part of the school *curriculum*, tailored to the particular needs of individual pupils, whether with special needs or not. It is often part of a preparation for work programme which involves teaching social and personal skills.

Y

Yale developmental examination, procedure for evaluating the development of pre-school children, devised by A. Gesell and his collaborators, and incorporating the *Gesell tests*.

Younghusband Report 1959, report of a working party, under the

Chairmanship of Dame Eileen Younghusband, on 'Social Workers in the Local Authority Health and Welfare Services' which drew attention to the gaps and unevenness in the provision of help for children and families with special needs. One of its main recommendations, the establishment of national arangements for the training of *social workers* was incorporated in the Health Visiting and Social Work (Training) Act, 1962, but the shortage of trained social workers, both psychiatric and general, persisted. The report pointed out that handicapped pupils leaving school and wanting to start work were the responsibility of several statutory services and that often, because of lack of co-ordination among these services, the young person did not know of or receive the full benefits available.

youth custody centre, establishment for the detention of males aged 15 –20 and females ages 17–20 years. Until May 1983 these establishments were known as Borstals. A youth custody order may be made by a Crown Court in relation to an offence punishable in an adult by imprisonment.

Youth Service or Youth and Community Service, partnership between *local education authorities* and voluntary organizations which operates youth clubs and educational, social and recreational facilities for all young people under the general guidance of the *Department of Education and Science*. Some specialize in providing facilities for handicapped young people. See *further education, Physically Handicapped and Able-Bodied* in Appendix.

Z

Z-score, a common form of *standardized score*: the number of standard deviations by which a score differs from the mean. This allows comparisons of scores measured originally in different scale units.

Appendix A

List of some useful Associations, etc.

ACE (Aids for Communication in Education) Centre, Ormerod School, Waynflete Road, Oxford OX3 8DD. Tel: 0865 63508

ADVISORY CENTRE FOR EDUCATION (ACE), 18 Victoria Park Square, Bethnal Green, London, E2 9PB. Tel: 01 980 4596

ADVISORY COMMITTEE FOR THE EDUCATION OF ROMANY AND OTHER TRAVELLERS (ACERT), Mary Ward Centre, 42 Queen Square, London, WC1. Tel: 01 831 7079

AFASIC, see Association For All Speech Impaired Children.

ANTHROPOSOPHICAL SOCIETY IN GREAT BRITAIN, Rudolph Steiner House, 35 Park Road, London NW1 6XT. Tel: 01 723 4400

ARTS FOR DISABLED PEOPLE IN WALES, Channel View, Jim Driscoll Way, The Marl, Grangetown, Cardiff CF1 7NF. Tel: 0222 377885

ASSOCIATION FOR ALL SPEECH IMPAIRED CHILDREN (AFASIC), 347 Central Markets, Smithfield, London, EC1A 9NH. Tel: 01 236 3632/ 6487

ASSOCIATION FOR BRAIN DAMAGED CHILDREN, 47 Northumberland Road, Coventry, CV1 3AP. Tel: 0203 56517

ASSOCIATION FOR RESEARCH INTO RESTRICTED GROWTH, 24 Pinchfield, Maplecross, Rickmansworth, Herts., WD3 2TP. Tel: 0923 770759

ASSOCIATION FOR SPINA BIFIDA AND HYDROCEPHALUS (ASBAH), 22 Upper Woburn Place, London, WC1. Tel: 01 388 1382

ASSOCIATION OF BLIND AND PARTIALLY SIGHTED TEACHERS AND STUDENTS (ABAPSTAS), B.M. Box 6727, London WC1V 3XX.

ASSOCIATION OF EDUCATIONAL PSYCHOLOGISTS, 3 Sunderland Rd., Durham DH1 2LH. Tel: 091 3849512

ASSOCIATION OF PARENTS OF VACCINE DAMAGED CHILDREN, 2 Church Street, Shipton-on-Stour, Warwickshire, CV36 4AP. Tel: 0608 61595

ASSOCIATION OF PROFESSIONS FOR MENTALLY HANDICAPPED PEOPLE, Greytree Lodge, Second Avenue, Greytree, Ross-on-Wye, Herefordshire HR9 7HT. Tel:0989 62630

ASSOCIATION OF SWIMMING THERAPY, 4 Oak Street, Shrewsbury, Salop. SY3 7RH. Tel: 0743 4393

ASSOCIATION OF WORKERS FOR MALADJUSTED CHILDREN, Redhill School, East Sutton, Nr Maidstone, Kent ME17 3DQ.

BARNARDO'S HEAD OFFICE, Tanner's Lane, Barkingside, Essex, IG6 1QG. Tel: 01 550 8822

BOBATH CENTRE FOR PHYSICALLY HANDICAPPED CHILDREN, 5 Netherhall Gardens, London, NW3 5RN. Tel: 01 435 3895

BREAK, 20 Hooks Hill Road, Sheringham, Norfolk. NR26 8NL. Tel: 0263 823170/823025

BREAKTHROUGH TRUST (DEAF/HEARING INTEGRATION), Charles W. Gillett Centre, Selly Oak Colleges, Birmingham, B29 6LE. Tel: 021 472 6447 (voice): 021 471 1001 (Vistel only)

BRITISH ASSOCIATION FOR SPORTING AND RECREATIONAL ACTIVITIES OF THE BLIND, 34 Yew Tree Close, West Derby, Liverpool L12 9JQ. Tel: 051 220 2516

BRITISH ASSOCIATION OF ART THERAPISTS, 13C Northwood Road, London, N6 5TL

BRITISH ASSOCIATION OF THE HARD OF HEARING (BAHOH), 7–11 Armstrong Road, London, W3 7JL. Tel: 01 743 1110/1353. Vistel: 01 743 1492

BRITISH ASSOCIATION OF TEACHERS OF THE DEAF (BATOD), 99 Hertford Road, Stevenage, Hertfordshire SG2 8SE.

BRITISH DEAF ASSOCIATION, (formerly the British Deaf and Dumb Association), 38 Victoria Place, Carlisle, Cumbria, CA1 1HU. Tel: Carlisle 0228 48844 (voice) 0228 28719 (vistel)

BRITISH DIABETIC ASSOCIATION, 10 Queen Anne Street, London, W1M 0BD. Tel: 01 323 1531

BRITISH DYSLEXIA ASSOCIATION, Church Lane, Peppard, Oxfordshire, RG9 5JN. Tel: 0734 668271/2

BRITISH EPILEPSY ASSOCIATION:
  National Office, Anstey House, 40 Hanover Square, Leeds LS3 1BE. Tel: 0532 439393
  Northern Region, 313 Chapeltown Road, Leeds LS7 3JT. Tel: 0532 621076
  Northern Ireland Region, The Old Postgraduate Medical Centre, Belfast City Hospital, Lisburn Road, Belfast BT9 7AB. Tel: 0232 248414
  Midlands Region, Room 1, Guildhall Buildings, Navigation Street, Birmingham B2 4BT. Tel: 021 643 7524
  South East Region, 92–94 Tooley Street, London SE1 9SH. Tel: 01 403 41
  Southern Region, 72a London Street, Reading RG1 4SD. Tel: 0734 58
  Epilepsy Wales, 142, Whitchurch Road, Cardiff CF4 3NA.
  628744.

BRITISH INSTITUTE FOR BRAIN INJURED CHILDREN, Knowle Hall, Knowle, Bridgwater, Somerset TA7 8PJ. Tel: 0278 684060

BRITISH INSTITUTE OF MENTAL HANDICAP, Wolverhampton Road, Kidderminster, Worcestershire DY10 3PP. Tel: 0562 850251

BRITISH RETINITIS PIGMENTOSA SOCIETY, Greens Norton Court, Greens Norton, Towcester, Northants NN12 8BS. Tel: 0327 53276

BRITISH SOCIETY FOR MUSIC THERAPY, 69, Avondale Avenue, E. Barnet Herts EN4 8NB. Tel: 01 368 8879

BRITISH SPORTS ASSOCIATION FOR THE DISABLED (BSAD), Haywood House, Barnard Crescent, Aylesbury, Bucks. HP21 9PP. Tel: 0296 27889

BRITTLE BONE SOCIETY, Unit 4, Block 20, Carlunie Road, Dunsinane Industrial Estate, Dundee DD2 3QT. Tel: 0382 817771

CAMPAIGN FOR THE ADVANCEMENT OF STATE EDUCATION (CASE), The Grove, High Street, Sawston, Cambridge CB2 4HJ. Tel: 0223 833179

CAMPAIGN FOR PEOPLE WITH MENTAL HANDICAPS, 16 Fitzroy Square, London, WP1 5HQ. Tel: 01 387 9571

CENTRE FOR STUDIES ON INTEGRATION IN EDUCATION (CSIE), 840 Brighton Road, Purley, Croydon CR2 2BH. Tel: O1 660 8552

CHEST AND HEART/STROKE ASSOCIATION, Tavistock House, North Tavistock Square, London, WC1. Tel: 01 387 3012

CHILDREN'S LEGAL CENTRE, 20 Compton Terrace, London, N1 2UN. Tel: 01 359 6251

CHILDREN'S SOCIETY (CHURCH OF ENGLAND CHILDREN'S SOCIETY), Edward Rudolf House, Margery Street, London WC1X 0JL. Tel: 01 837 4299

COLLEGE OF SPEECH THERAPISTS, Harold Poster House, 6 Lechmere Road, London. NW2 5BU. Tel: 01 459 8521/2/3

CONTACT A FAMILY, 16 Strutton Ground, London, SW1. Tel: 01 222 2695

COUNCIL FOR EDUCATIONAL TECHNOLOGY, 3 Devonshire Street, London W1N 2BA. Tel: 01 636 4186

CYSTIC FIBROSIS RESEARCH TRUST, 5 Blyth Road, Bromley, Kent. Tel: 01 464 7211

DISABILITY ALLIANCE, 25 Denmark Street, London, WC2 8NJ. Tel: 01 240 0806

DISABLED DRIVERS' ASSOCIATION, Ashwellthorpe, Norwich, NR16 1EX. Tel 050 841 449 (10 a.m. – 3 p.m.)

DISABLED GRADUATES DATA BANK, Careers Advisory Service, University of Nottingham, Nottingham NG7 2RD. Tel: 0602 506101 x 2947.

DISABLED LIVING FOUNDATION, 380/384 Harrow Road, London W9. Tel: 01 289 6111

DISABLEMENT ELECTRONIC AIDS REFERENCE SERVICE (DEARS), c/o 7 Wickham Close, West Wickham, Kent, BR4 0BQ. Tel: 01 777 7560

ENT INCOME GROUP (DIG), Attlee House, London, E1. Tel: 01

DOWN'S SYNDROME ASSOCIATION, 12/13 Clapham Common
Southside, London SW4 7AA. Tel: 01 720 0008
DYSLEXIA INSTITUTE, 133 Gresham Road, Staines, Middlesex TW18 2AJ.
Tel: 0784 59498

ELIZABETH FITZROY HOMES, Caxton House, Station Approach,
Hazelmere GU27 2PE. Tel: 0428 52001/53872

FAMILY FUND, Administered by the Joseph Rowntree Memorial Trust,
P.O. Box 50, York YO1 1UY.
FAMILY WELFARE ASSOCIATION, 501–505 Kingsland Road, London E8
4AU. Tel: 01 254 6251
FOUNDATION FOR CONDUCTIVE EDUCATION, University of
Birmingham, P.O. Box 363, Birmingham B15 2TT. Tel: 021 472 1301 until
31.12.87. Thereafter 021 414 3344.
FRIEDREICH'S ATAXIA GROUP, Burleigh Lodge, Knowle Lane,
Cranleigh, Surrey, GU6 8RD. Tel: 0483 272741
FRIENDS FOR THE YOUNG DEAF, East Court Mansion, Council Offices,
College Lane, East Grinstead, Sussex, RH19 3LT. Tel: 0342 23444

GARDNER'S TRUST FOR THE BLIND, Oldebourne House (3rd Floor),
46/47 Chancery Lane, London, WC2A 1JB. Tel: 01 242 2287
GYDE CHARITY FOR BLIND AND DEAF AND DUMB CHILDREN, 4–7
Rowcroft, Stroud, Gloucestershire, GL5 3BJ. Tel: 04536 3381/4

HAEMOPHILIA SOCIETY, 123 Westminster Bridge Road, London SE1
7HR. Tel: 01 928 2020
HANDICAPPED ADVENTURE PLAYGROUND ASSOCIATION, Fulham
Palace Playground, Bishop's Avenue , London SW6 6EA. Tel: 01 736 4443
HESTER ADRIAN RESEARCH CENTRE, University of Manchester, Oxford
Road, Manchester, M13 9PL. Tel: 061 2733 333
HOME FARM TRUST, Merchants House North, Wapping Road, Bristol BS1
4RW. Tel: 0272 273746
HYPERACTIVE CHILDREN'S SUPPORT GROUP, 71 Whyke Lane,
Chichester, Sussex. Tel: 0903 725182.

INDEPENDENT PANEL OF SPECIAL EDUCATION EXPERTS, 20
Compton Terrace, London, N1 2UN.
IN TOUCH TRUST (Mental Handicap and Rare Disorders Parent Contact
Service), 10 Norman Road, Sale, Cheshire, M33 3DF. Tel: 061 962 4441
INVALID CHILDREN'S AID NATIONWIDE (ICAN), 198 City Road, London
EC1V 2PH. Tel: 01 608 2462

JEWISH BLIND & PHYSICALLY HANDICAPPED SOCIETY, 118 Seymour
Place, London, W1. Tel: 01 262 2003

JOHN GROOMS ASSOCIATION FOR THE DISABLED, 10 Gloucester Drive, Finsbury Park, London, N4 2LP. Tel: 01 802 7272

JOHN HORNIMAN SCHOOL, (for severe specific speech and language disorders) 2 Park Road, Worthing. Tel: 0903 200317

KIDS Family Centre, 13 Pond Street, London, NW3 2NP. Tel: 01 431 0596

LADY HOARE TRUST FOR PHYSICALLY DISABLED CHILDREN, 7 North Street, Midhurst, West Sussex, GU29 9DJ. Tel: 073 081 3696

LEUKAEMIA CARE SOCIETY, P.O. Box 82, Exeter, Devon EX2 5DP. Tel: 0392 218514

LIMBLESS CHILDREN'S ASSOCIATION (REACH), c/o 6 Eddy Close, Romford, Essex.

MENCAP, (ROYAL SOCIETY FOR MENTALLY HANDICAPPED CHILDREN AND ADULTS), 123 Golden Lane, London, EC1Y 0RT. Tel: 01 253 9433

MIND (NATIONAL ASSOCIATION FOR MENTAL HEALTH), 22 Harley Street, London, WIN 2ED. Tel: 01 637 0741

MULTIPLE SCLEROSIS SOCIETY, 25 Effie Road, Fulham, London, SW6 1EE. Tel: 01 736 6267

MUSCULAR DYSTROPHY GROUP OF GREAT BRITAIN AND NORTHERN IRELAND, Nattrass House, 35 Macaulay Road, London, SW4 0QP. Tel: 01 720 8055

NATIONAL ASSOCIATION FOR DEAF/BLIND RUBELLA HANDICAPPED, see entry under SENSE.

NATIONAL ASSOCIATION FOR GIFTED CHILDREN, 1 South Audley Street, London, W1Y 5QD. Tel: 01 499 1188

NATIONAL ASSOCIATION FOR MENTAL HEALTH see MIND.

NATIONAL ASSOCIATION FOR REMEDIAL EDUCATION (NARE), 2 Lichfield Road, Stafford, ST17 4JX. Tel: 0785 46872

NATIONAL ASSOCIATION FOR THE CARE AND RESETTLEMENT OF OFFENDERS (NACRO), 169 Clapham Road, London, SW9 0PU. Tel: 01 582 6500

NATIONAL ASSOCIATION FOR THE WELFARE OF CHILDREN IN HOSPITAL, Argyle House, 29–31 Euston Road, London, NW1. Tel: 01 833 2041

NATIONAL ASSOCIATION OF CITIZEN'S ADVICE BUREAUX (NACAB), 115–123 Pentonville Road, London N1 9LZ. Tel: 01 833 2181

NATIONAL ASSOCIATION OF DISABLEMENT INFORMATION AND ADVICE LINES, Victoria Buildings, 117 High Street, Clay Cross, Chesterfield, Derbyshire, S45 9DZ. Tel: 0246 864498

NATIONAL ASSOCIATION OF INDUSTRIES FOR THE BLIND AND DISABLED INC., 43a High Street South, Dunstable, Bedfordshire LU6 3RZ. Tel: 0582 606796

NATIONAL ASSOCIATION OF SWIMMING CLUBS FOR THE HANDICAPPED, 219 Preston Drove, Brighton, Sussex, BN1 6FL. Tel: 0273 559470

NATIONAL AUTISTIC SOCIETY, 276 Willesden Lane, London NW2 5RB. Tel: 01 451 3844

NATIONAL BUREAU FOR HANDICAPPED STUDENTS (NBHS), 336 Brixton Road, London SW9. Tel: 01 274 0565

NATIONAL CENTRE FOR CUED SPEECH FOR THE DEAF, 29/30 Watling Street, Canterbury, CT1 2UD. Tel: 0277 450757

NATIONAL CHILDREN'S BUREAU, 8 Wakley Street, Islington, London EC1V 7QE. Tel: 01 278 9441

NATIONAL CONFEDERATION OF PARENT/TEACHER ASSOCIATIONS, (NCPTA), 43 Stonebridge Road, North Fleet, Gravesend, Kent, DA11 9DS. Tel: 0474 60618

NATIONAL COUNCIL FOR SPECIAL EDUCATION, 1 Wood Street, Stratford-upon-Avon, CV37 6JE. Tel: 0789 205332

NATIONAL COUNCIL FOR VOLUNTARY ORGANIZATIONS, 26 Bedford Square, London, W1CB 3HU. Tel: 01 636 4066

NATIONAL DEAF/BLIND AND RUBELLA ASSOCIATION (see SENSE), 311 Gray's Inn Road, London WC1X 8PT. Tel: 01 278 1005

NATIONAL DEAF CHILDREN'S SOCIETY, 45 Hereford Road, London, W2 5AH. Tel: 01 229 9272/4

NATIONAL FEDERATION OF THE BLIND OF THE U.K., Unity House, Smyth Street, Wakefield, West Yorks., WF1 1ER. Tel: 0924 377012

NATIONAL FEDERATION OF GATEWAY CLUBS, 117 Golden Lane, London, EC1Y 0RT. Tel: 01 253 9433

NATIONAL FOUNDATION FOR EDUCATIONAL RESEARCH IN ENGLAND AND WALES, The Mere, Upton Park, Slough, Berks SL1 2DQ. Tel: 0753 74123

NATIONAL LIBRARY FOR THE BLIND, Cromwell Road, Bredbury, Stockport SK6 2SG. Tel: 061 494 0217

NATIONAL LIBRARY FOR THE HANDICAPPED CHILD, London University Institute of Education, Dixon Gallery, 20 Bedford Way, London WC1H 0AL. Tel: 01 636 1500

NATIONAL LISTENING LIBRARY (TALKING BOOKS FOR THE HANDICAPPED), 12 Lant Street, London, SE1 1QH. Tel: 01 407 9417

NATIONAL OUT-OF-SCHOOL ALLIANCE, Oxford House, Derbyshire Street, Bethnal Green Road, London, E2 6HG. Tel: 01 739 4787

NATIONAL PORTAGE ASSOCIATION, King Alfred's College, Sparkford Road, Winchester. Tel: 0962 62281

NATIONAL SOCIETY FOR THE PREVENTION OF CRUELTY TO CHILDREN (NSPCC), 67 Saffron Hill, London EC1N 8RS. Tel: 01 242 1626

NATIONAL STAR CENTRE FOR DISABLED YOUTH, Ullenwood Manor, Cheltenham, Gloucestershire, GL53 9QU. Tel: 0242 524478

NATIONAL STUDY GROUP ON FURTHER AND HIGHER EDUCATION FOR THE HEARING IMPAIRED, Shirecliffe College of F.E., Shirecliffe Road, Sheffield. Tel: 0742 78309

NATIONAL TOY LIBRARIES ASSOCIATION, 68 Churchway, London NW1 1LT. Tel: 01 387 9592

NETWORK FOR THE HANDICAPPED, (Law and Advisory Centre for the Handicapped and their Families), 16 Princeton Street, London WC1R 4BB. Tel: 01 831 7740/8031

NORDOFF-ROBBINS MUSIC THERAPY CENTRE, 3 Leighton Place, London NW5 2QL. Tel: 01 267 6296

NORTHERN IRELAND COUNCIL ON DISABILITY, 2 Annandale Avenue, Belfast. Tel: 0232 64001

NORTHERN IRELAND COUNCIL FOR EDUCATIONAL RESEARCH, Stanmillis College, Stanmillis Road, Belfast BT9 5DY. Tel: 0232 666212

NUFFIELD HEARING AND SPEECH CENTRE, Royal National Throat, Nose and Ear Hospital, Gray's Inn Road, London WC1. Tel: 01 837 8855

PARTIALLY SIGHTED SOCIETY, Queen's Road, Doncaster, South Yorks DN1 2NX. Tel: 0302 68998

PHYSICALLY HANDICAPPED AND ABLE-BODIED, (PHAB), Tavistock House North, Tavistock Sq., London WC1H 9HX. Tel: 01 388 1963

PRESCHOOL PLAY GROUPS ASSOCIATION (PPA), 61–63 Kings Cross Road, London WC1X 9LL. Tel: 01 833 0991

QUEEN ELIZABETH'S TRAINING COLLEGE FOR THE DISABLED, Leatherhead Court, Leatherhead, Surrey, KT22 0BN. Tel: Oxshott 2204

RATHBONE SOCIETY, 1st Floor, Princess House, 105–107 Princess Street, Manchester, M1 6DD. Tel: 061 236 5358

REMPLOY, Remploy House, 415 Edgware Road, Cricklewood, London NW2 6LR. Tel: 01 452 8020

RESEARCH CENTRE FOR THE EDUCATION OF THE VISUALLY HANDICAPPED, The University of Birmingham Faculty of Education, Department of Special Education, Selly Wick House, 59 Selly Wick Road, Birmingham, B29 7JE. Tel: 021 4711303

RIDING FOR THE DISABLED ASSOCIATION, c/o British Horse Society, Avenue 'R', National Agricultural Centre, Kenilworth, Warwickshire, CV8 2LY. Tel: 0203 56107

R.N.I.B. STUDENT TAPE LIBRARY, Braille House, 338–346 Goswell Road, London EC1V 7JE. Tel: 01 837 9921

ROYAL ASSOCIATION FOR DISABILITY AND REHABILITATION (RADAR), 25 Mortimer Street, London W1N 8AB. Tel: 01 637 5400

ROYAL LONDON SOCIETY FOR THE BLIND, 105 Salusbury Road, London NW6 6RH. Tel: 01 624 8844

ROYAL NATIONAL INSTITUTE FOR THE BLIND (RNIB), 224 Great Portland Street, London W1N 6AA. Tel: 01 388 1266
ROYAL NATIONAL INSTITUTE FOR THE DEAF (RNID), 105 Gower Street, London, WC1E 6AH. Tel: 01 387 8033
ROYAL SOCIETY FOR MENTALLY HANDICAPPED CHILDREN AND ADULTS, Mencap National Centre, 123 Golden Lane, London, EC1Y 0RT. Tel: 01 253 9433

SCOTTISH COUNCIL FOR EDUCATIONAL TECHNOLOGY, Dowanhill, 74 Victoria Crescent Road, Glasgow G12 9JN.
SCOTTISH COUNCIL FOR RESEARCH IN EDUCATION, 15 St. John Street, Edinburgh, EH8 8JR. Tel: 031 557 2944
SCOTTISH COUNCIL FOR SPASTICS, 22 Corstorphine Road, Edinburgh, EH12 6HP. Tel: 031 337 9876
SCOTTISH COUNCIL ON DISABILITY, Princes House, 5 Shandwick Place, Edinburgh EH2 4RG. Tel: 031 229 8632
SCOTTISH SOCIETY FOR THE MENTALLY HANDICAPPED, 13 Elmbank Street, Glasgow, G2 4QA. Tel: 041 2264541
SENNAC (Special Educational Needs National Advisory Council), Hillside, 271 Woolton Road, Liverpool L16 8NB. Tel: 051 722 3819
SENSE, (National Association for Deaf/Blind and Rubella handicapped), 311 Grays Inn Road, London, WC1X 8PT. Tel: 01 278 1005
SHAFTESBURY SOCIETY, Shaftesbury House, 2a Amity Grove, Raynes Park, London SW20 0LJ. Tel: 01 834 2656
SOCIETY FOR MUCOPOLYSACCHARIDE DISEASES, 30 Westwood Drive, Little Chalfont, Buckinghamshire HP6 6RJ. Tel: 02404 2789
SPASTICS SOCIETY, 12 Park Crescent, London, W1N 4EQ. Tel: 01 636 5020
SPASTICS SOCIETY EDUCATION DIVISION, 840 Brighton Road, Purley, Surrey CR2 2BH. Tel: 01 660 8552
SPECIAL EDUCATION MICROELECTRONICS RESOURCE CENTRES (SEMERCs):
Bristol Polytechnic, Redland Hill, Bristol B56 6UZ. Tel: 0272 733141
Manchester Polytechnic, Hathersage Road, Manchester M13 0JA. Tel: 061 225 9054
Newcastle Polytechnic, Coach Lane Campus, Newcastle upon Tyne NE7 7XA. Tel: 091 266 5057
(Redbridge SEMERC), Dane Centre, Melbourne Road, Ilford, Essex. Tel: 01 478 6363
SPINAL INJURIES ASSOCIATION, 76 St. James, London, N10 3DF. Tel: 01 444 2121
SPORTS COUNCIL CO-ORDINATING COMMITTEE ON SWIMMING FOR THE DISABLED, Sports Council, 16 Upper Woburn Place, London WC1H 0QP. Tel: 01 388 1277
SPORTSMAN'S FUND FOR HANDICAPPED CHILDREN, 262 The Broadway, London, SW19. Tel: 01 534 5979

STUDENT TAPE LIBRARY, Braille House, 338–346 Goswell Road, London, EC1V 7JE. Tel: 01 837 9921

THOMAS CORAM FOUNDATION FOR CHILDREN, 40, Brunswick Square, London, WC1N 1AZ. Tel: 01 278 2424

TRUST FUND FOR THE TRAINING OF HANDICAPPED CHILDREN IN ARTS AND CRAFTS, 94 Claremount Road, Wallasey, Merseyside, L45 6UE. Tel: 051 638 1422

TUBEROUS SCLEROSIS ASSOCIATION OF GREAT BRITAIN, Little Barnsley Farm Catshill, Bromsgrove, Worcs. B61 0NQ. Tel: 0527 71898

U.K. SPORTS ASSOCIATION FOR PEOPLE WITH MENTAL HANDICAP, Hayward House, Barnard Crescent, Aylesbury, Bucks. Tel: 0296 436484

ULVERSCROFT LARGE PRINT BOOKS LTD., The Green, Bradgate Road, Anstey, Leicester, LE7 7FU. Tel: 0533 364325

UNESCO Special Education Programme, 7 Place de Fontenoy, 75700, Paris, France

VACCINE DAMAGED PAYMENTS UNIT, DHSS, North Fylde Central Offices, Norcross, Blackpool, FY5 3TA.

VOLUNTARY COUNCIL FOR HANDICAPPED CHILDREN, 8 Wakley Street, Islington, London, EC1V 7QE. Tel: 01 278 9441

WALES COUNCIL FOR THE BLIND, Oak House Office, 12 The Bulwark, Brecon, Powys LD3 7AD. Tel: 0874 4576

WALES COUNCIL FOR THE DEAF, Caerbragdy, Industrial Estate, Bedwas Rd., Caerphilly, Mid Glamorgan, CF8 3SL. Tel: 0222 887575/887702

WALES PRE-SCHOOL PLAYGROUPS ASSOCIATION CYMRU, 2a Chester Street, Wrexham LL13 8BD. Tel: 0978 358195

Appendix B

List of some useful reference books

Clegg, J., (1980) *Dictionary of Social Services*, London, Bedford Square Press.

Collins, K., Downes, L., Griffiths, S. and Shaw, K., (1973) *Keywords in Education*, London, Longman.

Davies, Meredith J. B., (1982) *The Disabled Child and Adult*.

Department of Education and Science, (1978) *Special Educational Needs*, London, Her Majesty's Stationery Office. (Warnock Report).

Drever, J., (1984 reprint) *Penguin Dictionary of Psychology*, Harmondsworth, Penguin.

Good, C. V. and Carter, V., (1973) *Dictionary of Education*, U.S.A. McGraw-Hill Book Company.

Gordon, P. and Lawton, D., (1982) *A guide to English Educational Terms*, London, Batsford Academic and Educational Ltd.

Harre, R. and Lamb, R., (Eds.) (1983) *The Encyclopaedic Dictionary of Psychology*, Oxford, Blackwell.

Harris, T.L. and Hodges, R.E., (1982) *Dictionary of Reading*, Delaware, International Reading Association.

Kelly, L.J. and Vergason, G.R., (1978) *Dictionary of Special Education and Rehabilitation*, Colorado, Love Publishing Company.

Levy, P. and Goldstein, H., (1984) *Tests in Education*, London, Academic Press.

Page, G.T. and Thomas J.B., (1979) *International Dictionary of Education,* London, Kogan Page.

Pates, A., Good, M. and Thomson, A., (1983) *The Education Fact Book,* London, MacMillan.

Rowntree, D., (1981) *A Dictionary of Education,* London, Harper and Row.

Stone, J. and Taylor, F., (1977) *A Handbook for Parents with a Handicapped Child,* London, Arrow Books.

Urdang, L., (Ed.) (1983) *Mosby's Medical and Nursing Dictionary,* St. Louis, C. V. Mosby Company.